11/09

This is home now

Kentucky Remembered
An Oral History Series

James C. Klotter
Terry L. Birdwhistell
and
Doug Boyd,
General Editors

Barry Bingham
Barry Bingham

Bert Combs the Politician
George W. Robinson

Conversations with Kentucky Writers
edited by L. Elisabeth Beattie

Conversations with Kentucky Writers II
edited by L. Elisabeth Beattie

Tobacco Culture: Farming Kentucky's Burley Belt
John van Willigen and Susan C. Eastwood

Food and Everyday Life on Kentucky Family Farms, 1920–1950
John van Willigen and Anne van Willigen

This Is Home Now: Kentucky's Holocaust Survivors Speak
Arwen Donahue and Rebecca Gayle Howell

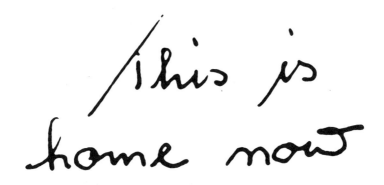

Kentucky's Holocaust Survivors Speak

ARWEN DONAHUE

PHOTOGRAPHS BY
REBECCA GAYLE HOWELL

THE UNIVERSITY PRESS OF KENTUCKY

The author gratefully acknowledges permission from the United States
Holocaust Memorial Museum to reprint excerpts from "The Holocaust
Survivors in Kentucky Interview Project" (RG-50.549.05).

Scholarly publisher for the Commonwealth,
serving Bellarmine University, Berea College, Centre College of Kentucky,
Eastern Kentucky University, The Filson Historical Society, Georgetown
College, Kentucky Historical Society, Kentucky State University,
Morehead State University, Murray State University, Northern Kentucky
University, Transylvania University, University of Kentucky, University of
Louisville, and Western Kentucky University.
All rights reserved.

Editorial and Sales Offices: The University Press of Kentucky
663 South Limestone Street, Lexington, Kentucky 40508-4008
www.kentuckypress.com

13 12 11 10 09   5 4 3 2 1

Library of Congress Cataloging-in-Publication Data

This is home now : Kentucky's Holocaust survivors speak / [compiled and
edited by] Arwen Donahue ; photographs by Rebecca Gayle Howell.
      p. cm. — (Kentucky remembered, an oral history series)
      Includes bibliographical references and index.
      ISBN 978-0-8131-2547-3 (hardcover : acid-free paper)
      1. Jews—Kentucky—Interviews. 2. Holocaust survivors—Kentucky—
Interviews. 3. Kentucky—Ethnic relations. I. Donahue, Arwen, 1969-
II. Howell, Rebecca Gayle.
      F460.J5T55 2009
      940.53'180922769—dc22
      [B]   2009010818

 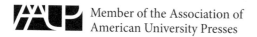 Member of the Association of
American University Presses

CONTENTS

Photographs follow page 112

PHOTOGRAPHS

SERIES FOREWORD

In the field of oral history, Kentucky is a national leader. Over the past several decades, thousands of its citizens have been interviewed. The Kentucky Remembered series brings into print the most important of those collections, with each volume focusing on a particular subject.

Oral history is, of course, only one type of source material. Yet by the very personal nature of recollection, hidden aspects of history are often disclosed. Oral sources provide a vital thread in the rich fabric that is Kentucky history.

This volume, the seventh in the series and the first to focus on the topic of immigrants' experiences in Kentucky, presents the narrated journeys of European Jews who survived the Holocaust and, following World War II, came to the United States—and eventually to Kentucky. Diasporic studies often focus on individual and group memories as they relate to the homeland and identity left behind. Arwen Donahue and Rebecca Gayle Howell have woven together the memories, images, and identities of these survivors with their experiences as members of various Kentucky communities.

Throughout Kentucky, oral history efforts have increasingly focused on the immigrant experience. *This Is Home Now* effectively reveals the powerful stories of Kentucky's Holocaust survivors, their journeys to Kentucky, and their postwar lives as Kentuckians. Oral history gives voice to those not always heard. This book reminds the reader that hearing the immigrant voice is critical to remembering and understanding Kentucky's past.

James C. Klotter
Terry L. Birdwhistell
Doug Boyd

FOREWORD

After World War II, European Jews faced the daunting challenge of rebuilding their lives. In rare cases, entire families were lucky enough to survive the Holocaust, but in no cases did communities survive. The question of where to make a home—and indeed whether the word "home" had any meaning in the aftermath of such annihilation—was faced by all survivors.

The majority of Holocaust survivors immigrated to Israel or the United States. Of the approximately 140,000 survivors who came to America, about two-thirds made their homes in the New York metropolitan area. Most of the remaining one-third settled in mid- or large-sized cities that offered the support of Jewish communities, other survivors, and resources for émigrés. In these larger cities, particularly in New York, it was possible for Holocaust survivors to form communities of their own.

Yet Holocaust survivors also made their homes in places around the world where these support systems did not exist, from small towns in the southern United States to cities in Europe whose Jewish communities had been decimated by the Holocaust. Many of these survivors have been interviewed by oral history projects in the United States and abroad. However, these interviews tend to focus primarily on the survivors' Holocaust-related experiences, rather than exploring the experiences and choices that have defined their lives in the sixty-plus years since the war's end: their work, their friendships, and their reflections on the places in which they live.

In fact, Arwen Donahue's collection of interviews with Holocaust survivors who settled in the state of Kentucky is, to my knowledge, the only oral history project that takes as its focus the postwar lives of a group of Holocaust survivors within a particular geographic region of the United States.

Arwen Donahue was particularly well-situated to take on this project. In 1995, when the Oral History Department of the United States Holocaust Memorial Museum began to interview survivors about their lives after the Holocaust, Donahue (then the department's program coordinator, when I was director) helped to train interviewers, write interview guidelines, and review the interviews once they were completed.

The Holocaust Museum had established the Post-Holocaust Interview Project after conducting hundreds of interviews over many years that focused on survivors' Holocaust-era experiences, and we in the Oral History Department believed that a good portion of peoples' lives were—understandably, given our historical focus—ignored in these interviews. Understandably ignored, but perhaps not justifiably so. As oral historians, our subject, ultimately, was not only the Holocaust: it was as much, if not more, about the Holocaust survivors themselves. Yet the Holocaust Museum was far from alone among archives nationally and internationally in conducting interviews with Holocaust survivors that focused almost exclusively on their wartime experiences. In fact, the Holocaust Museum's Post-Holocaust Interview Project may be unique in its focus on survivors' postwar lives. This collection, which now consists of more than 120 interviews, is among the Oral History Department's most important projects. These interviews were conducted on audiotape with survivors whom we have previously interviewed on video primarily about their Holocaust experiences.

Arwen Donahue became the coordinator of the Post-Holocaust Project in 1998. By then, she had moved from Washington, D.C., to Kentucky, and she soon began conducting interviews with Holocaust survivors in that state. She also began to co-produce a series profiling five survivors interviewed for the Post-Holocaust Project, which ultimately became the basis for the United States Holocaust Memorial Museum's online exhibit "After the Holocaust." It is an affecting and important presentation that gives a genuine understanding of the differences and difficulties of survivors in putting their lives together following the trauma of the Holocaust.

The interviews Donahue recorded with Kentucky's survivors take the work of the Post-Holocaust Project in an intriguing and valuable new direction. By focusing on a particular geographic region, the interviews explore the interaction of these survivors with their communities on an intimate scale, a scale that could not easily be approached through the national scope of the Holocaust Museum's post-Holocaust interviews. For example, the museum's interviewers asked survivors about various aspects of their experiences in America: their arrival in this country; their adjustment to American life; the process of becoming citizens and reflections on their citizenship. These are important inquiries, to be sure, and they often yielded intimate responses—yet they focus on survivors' experiences on a national level, rather than on a local one. The interviews were conducted in various cities around the United States by interviewers who had little contact with one another. The Kentucky interviews, by contrast, demonstrate that survivors who settled outside metropolitan areas with support systems faced entirely different challenges in terms of creating community, even in creating their own identities.

It is particularly satisfying to see the ways in which the post-Holocaust interviews have been enlarged and illuminated by Arwen Donahue and Rebecca Howell in this book. Their simple but extraordinary exhibition about Kentucky's Holocaust survivors at the Lexington History Museum in 2005 was strikingly moving. The text and the accompanying photos wonderfully complemented each other and created a significant contribution to our understanding of these survivors and the lives they lived. This book expands that accomplishment by bringing the details and nuances of the survivors' experiences—in their own words—to the page.

I believe that Donahue and Howell's work makes the lives of survivors closer in some ways than we have known before. There are relatively few books about the postwar lives of Holocaust survivors in America. Most of those that have been written focus—understandably, given the dearth of literature on the subject—on the experiences of the majority: that is, those who have settled in major urban centers. This book tells a very different story. In fact, it tells a few very different stories. Jewish communities in rural America have not received a great deal of attention in the nation's literature, to say the least. And of course Holocaust survivors in rural America have received even less attention. This book brings to light for the first time a sense of the challenges—and rewards—American Holocaust survivors faced when they chose to live outside of the mainstream.

This Is Home Now gives voice to people with fascinating stories to tell, people who have never been heard from before and who deserve a wider audience.

Joan Ringelheim
Former Director, Department of Oral History
United States Holocaust Memorial Museum

ACKNOWLEDGMENTS

We would like to thank some of the key people who have guided this project since its inception in 1998 as a series of oral history interviews, since each step of that process ultimately made the creation of this book possible. During the interviewing phase of the project, Joan Ringelheim, then of the United States Holocaust Memorial Museum, offered dependably excellent advice and mentorship, and oversaw the interviews' placement in the museum's archives. The people at the Lexington Jewish Federation and the Louisville Jewish Community Center provided valuable resources and helpful guidance. Kim Lady Smith and Doug Boyd—both then of the Kentucky Historical Society's Oral History Commission—provided enthusiastic and invaluable support, from the interviewing phase through the mounting of the exhibit, and generously agreed to host a symposium on Kentucky's Holocaust survivors in 2005; more recently, Doug, as oral history series editor for the University Press of Kentucky, offered much-appreciated encouragement and advice in the development of the manuscript.

Sarah Wylie Ammerman, with her perfectly tuned eye and mind, has been heroic in her contributions to the aesthetic dimensions of *This Is Home Now*, from assisting the photographer to designing and installing the exhibit. Alex Brooks also generously contributed his elegant and thoughtful work as an exhibit graphic designer. James Baker Hall and

Mary Ann Taylor-Hall provided many hours of support to both the photographer and the author during the installation of the exhibit, as well as access to Jim's studio and equipment, which brought the large-scale photographs into reach. Rob Magrish has our thanks for providing the space and support of the Lexington History Museum for the exhibit. Rebecca Howell would also like to thank Harriet Logan for her early, instructive advice regarding the documentary process.

In the creation of the manuscript, Terry Birdwhistell helped guide the project through its various incarnations, and his advice was always spot-on. Shana Penn and David Wagoner read drafts of the manuscript and offered excellent feedback. David also deserves enduring gratitude for supporting Arwen Donahue—materially and otherwise—during the hundreds of volunteer hours spent on this project. Arwen would also like to acknowledge Rebecca Howell's crucial contributions to the manuscript: this book would not exist without her, not only because of her stunning photography, but because of her sharp insights and clear vision as a reader and editor. To the team at the University Press of Kentucky—Steve Wrinn, Candace Chaney, and Derik Shelor key among them—we owe our heartfelt thanks for their unwavering support of this book.

The following organizations provided essential support of various phases of this project: the Taube Foundation for Jewish Life and Culture; the Zantker Foundation; the Kentucky Arts Council; the Kentucky Humanities Council; the Kentucky Historical Society; the Lexington Arts and Cultural Council (Lexarts); the Lexington History Museum; and the United States Holocaust Memorial Museum.

Finally, our deepest thanks go to Sylvia Green, Oscar Haber, Robert Holczer, Abe Jakubowicz, Ann Klein, Justine Lerner, Alexander Rosenberg, John Rosenberg, Paul Schlisser, and the other Holocaust survivors who gave so generously of their time for this project. These people opened their homes, hearts and minds to us—we will be forever grateful. This book is dedicated to them.

LISTENING TO KENTUCKY'S HOLOCAUST SURVIVORS

On a hot May night in 2005, hundreds of people crowded into the former Fayette County courtroom in Lexington, Kentucky, to hear six people speak. The Lexington History Museum, which now occupies the former courthouse, had never before hosted a crowd of this size. The air conditioner was defunct, and the room's two fans did little to ease the heat of the windless night. The old courtroom did not contain enough seats for everyone, so people sat on the open windowsills and spilled out into the hall. The crowd had come from as far as four counties over, a few from neighboring states. Some city officials had caught early flights back from out-of-town trips to attend the event.

The six speakers were not famous; some had never before spoken in public. They were Holocaust survivors, who had come to the museum from around the state—Louisville, Lexington, Winchester, Paris, Prestonsburg—for the opening of the exhibit "This Is Home Now." Although some of the speakers had attended public Holocaust-related forums together before, this was the first statewide gathering of survivors, and most were meeting each other for the first time.

Earlier in the evening, Robert Holczer and Ann Klein, both Hungarian survivors, sat together in the Lexington History Museum's conference room, eating sandwiches brought in from a Louisville kosher deli, talking about the 1944 siege of Budapest. In another room, Alexander Rosenberg and John Rosenberg learned that they had many things in common, apart from their last name. Both men were chemistry majors at Duke University in the early 1950s, when Duke still maintained a quota on Jewish students. Both men were born in Germany, Alexander in 1927 and John four years later, and both of their families moved from Germany to Holland once anti-Jewish hostilities escalated. Yet while John's family escaped Europe in 1940, Alexander's family spent the war in concentration camps.

After Oscar Haber arrived—at ninety-five, Mr. Haber was the oldest survivor in attendance—he was soon found deep in conversation with Robert Holczer, one of the youngest. The two sat in a quiet corner, holding hands and leaning in close to each other, despite the fact that they had met only minutes before.

Downstairs, in the exhibit hall, people moved quietly through the show: Rebecca Howell's larger-than-life black and white portraits of the survivors; text panels of excerpts from my own oral history interviews; and the survivors' enlarged signatures, which had been stenciled in white on the deep gray walls. In one of the exhibit's two rooms sat a red table and chair, where visitors could pick up a telephone-style handset and listen to the survivors tell their own stories.

Rebecca and I saw the crowd through sleep-deprived, exhilarated eyes. We had dreamed up the idea of this exhibit a year and a half before it opened, and had been working on it day and night, with the help of a few devoted friends, for many intense weeks. The Lexington History Museum generously gave us the space on short notice, and set us free to do as we pleased. The past eighteen months had passed in a flurry of fund-raising, writing, photographing, editing, designing, and publicizing.

Many people who visited the exhibit were familiar with Holocaust history, but had never before seen it as a significant part of their own communities. A number of the survivors' own family members and friends also saw their loved ones' experiences in a new light after visiting the show. "I've heard these stories growing up," said Michael Rosenberg, whose father, John Rosenberg, is a civil rights lawyer and human rights activist. "To me, John is not a Holocaust survivor, or civil rights crusader—he's just 'Dad.' But to see his story and his life placed in such a powerful context . . . the exhibit honors these, as well as those gone before. I am proud, stunned, sad, and amazed."[1]

Rebecca Howell (left) and Arwen Donahue install "This Is Home Now" at the Lexington History Museum in May 2005. (Courtesy of David Stephenson, *Lexington Herald-Leader*)

The exhibit continued to be received with great enthusiasm throughout its run. It was given front-page coverage in the *Lexington Herald-Leader*, and prime-time coverage on television and radio news programs. Teachers at the elementary, high school, and college levels brought their students to the exhibit, some of whom were being introduced to the subject of the Holocaust for the first time. Visitors repeatedly commented on the impact of encountering such a history within the context of their own communities.

Of course, "This Is Home Now" was far from being the first Holocaust-related program in the state, and where such programs exist, they have generally been greeted with great enthusiasm. Annual Holocaust remembrance ceremonies in Louisville and Lexington often attract standing-room-only crowds. A Holocaust history course at the University of Kentucky draws more students than it can accommodate. The list goes on: teachers and citizens across the commonwealth have made tremendous efforts—often grassroots, with little institutional support—to promote Holocaust education. And, to all appearances, 2008 was a watershed year for Holocaust education in the state: that year, Kentucky signed into law the Ernie Marx Resolution. Named after a Louisville Holocaust survivor and educator who died in 2007, the resolution mandates the creation of Holocaust-related curricula for use in public schools.

The presence of survivors in Kentucky has played a decisive role in many of these Holocaust-related programs. If not for Ernie Marx, for example, there may not have been a Holocaust education bill at all. His numerous classroom visits to the St. Francis of Assisi School left a deep impression on its students, one of whom was first to imagine lobbying for state-mandated Holocaust education.

Mr. Marx, a German-born survivor of the concentration camps Dachau and Gurs, accompanied hundreds of Kentucky teachers and students in the later years of his life on nearly eighty trips to the United States Holocaust Memorial Museum. There, he served as a guide and counselor, and emphasized the need for tolerance and the value of diversity in the classroom. His efforts have inspired numerous worthy causes that bear his name: in addition to the Ernie Marx Resolution, we have the Ernie Marx Holocaust Education Fund, administered by the Jewish Community Federation of Louisville, and the Ernie Marx Peace Prize, awarded by Louisville's St. Francis of Assisi School to a graduating eighth grader. (Marx himself, whose education was disrupted by the Holocaust, is an honorary eighth grade graduate of the school.)[2]

Marx was just one survivor among perhaps a dozen in Kentucky who devoted a substantial portion of his life to promoting Holocaust awareness. In this regard, the impact of survivors within their communities is often undervalued, not only in Kentucky but across the nation; credit is usually given to representations of the Holocaust in movies and other media, or to the work of scholars. Yet Holocaust awareness and education in the state would unquestionably be at an entirely different level were it not for the efforts of the resident Holocaust survivors who have spoken out in public about their experiences.

A MINORITY WITHIN A MINORITY

Despite the progressive efforts in Holocaust education mentioned above, misinformation and even outright denial of the Holocaust have played a crucial role in the public face of Holocaust education in Kentucky. The University of Kentucky, for example, was forced, beginning in 2007, to struggle with an Internet hoax of international proportions, which claimed that the Holocaust had been removed from its curriculum—a hoax that has been attributed, in part, to stereotypes of Kentuckians as educationally backward.[3] (In fact, the University of Kentucky was among the first ten to twenty schools in the nation to offer a course on the Holocaust: Professor Jeremy Popkin began teaching such a course in 1979.) Yet over twenty years before this false message began to circulate, Holocaust denial *was* being promoted in a Lexington classroom. When this fact came to light, it mobilized key endeavors to increase Holocaust awareness in central Kentucky—and changed the lives of some of the area's Holocaust survivors.

In 1981, a history teacher at Tates Creek High School in Lexington taught his students that the Holocaust had possibly never happened. The story was reported in the *Lexington Herald,* and within several days the teacher, Anthony McCord, was ordered to "stick to the textbook" when teaching the Holocaust.[4] It was a problematic order, however, since no "textbook" lesson on the Holocaust had been mandated in any American high school in 1981. Indeed, the Holocaust had only recently begun to receive widespread public attention in the United States. Thus it was up to Mr. McCord to interpret just what sticking to the textbook meant. Former Tates Creek principal Warren Featherston said that he heard no further complaints about McCord after the order, which led him to believe that he had changed his lesson (however, Featherston did not recall there being any formal review of McCord's lessons following the incident). Former Tates Creek teacher Loris Points, a contemporary of McCord's at the school, emphasized her belief that her colleague's revisionist teachings went on until his retirement.[5]

Ms. Points, who is not Jewish, described the incident as "a colossal cover-up" and "one of the most amoral experiences in our community." She remembers the *Herald*'s report revealing a Lexington divided over the issue: "Students and their parents would laugh at this stuff. They'd say, 'History isn't important.'" Meanwhile, the school's few Jewish children were stoic about the revisionist lessons, according to Marilyn Moosnick, who had a son in McCord's class at Tates Creek. "I don't think the kids thought of [McCord's lessons] as a big deal," she said. "They were used to shrugging off anti-Semitism." In the aftermath of the report, Principal Featherston said he had received several calls from Jewish people concerned about McCord, but had also received calls in support of the teacher. "McCord was a negative person about a lot of things," Featherston told me, "but some parents and students really liked him."

Yet Ms. Moosnick and other members of the Jewish community were deeply alarmed, and felt that something must be done. Plans were soon hatched to produce a Holocaust-related documentary on Kentucky Educational Television, with Moosnick and David Wekstein—another prominent member of Lexington's Jewish community—acting as its chief producers. Ultimately, Moosnick approached her friend Sylvia Green, a survivor of Auschwitz and Bergen-Belsen, and told her that she must speak out to a public audience about her experiences to set the historical record straight for Kentuckians.

For Sylvia Green, McCord's revisionist teaching was an unwelcome wake-up call. She had spent thirty years in small-town Winchester carefully concealing her past. Although she did what she believed was her duty, and told her story on-camera, it did not come easily: before the documentary aired, and throughout its taping, she was terrified she would break down in tears. The truth was, she had not even told her own grown children that she was a Holocaust survivor, although by then they had figured it out for themselves. The first time they heard their mother talk about her own past was when they saw it on television.[6]

The burden of Mrs. Green's memories was made heavier by her geographic location in Winchester, a central-Kentucky town of less than twenty thousand. "I did not talk about it to anybody," she says. "It was like I was ashamed of it, like some of it was my fault. I knew it wasn't, but somehow I just couldn't talk about it. And then it was a small town with not many Jewish people. I already had one monkey on my head, to be a Jew in a small town." She felt compelled to keep silent not only to protect herself, but her children as well: "I never talked to them about [the Holocaust]. They were Jews in the little town. Grades were important [to] get out of here, and they both did. Now when I complain, Sandy will say, 'Mommy, you pushed us out.'"

Although speaking about her experiences was (and continued to be) a harrowing experience for Mrs. Green, her relationship with her community changed after her neighbors learned that she was a Holocaust survivor. "I think they accepted me more somehow. I really think maybe they felt sorry for me. . . . I'm part of Winchester, all in a sudden. The first twenty-five years, I did not feel like I was part of it."

Sylvia Green's story speaks to the complexity that Holocaust survivors faced in making their homes in the Bluegrass State. While most of the fourteen people interviewed for this project felt welcome in Kentucky, they were often keenly aware, as Jewish Holocaust survivors, of being a minority within a minority. As Jews, they sometimes felt inadequately understood by Christians, and as Holocaust survivors, they sometimes felt isolated from American-born Jews. As of 1984, Kentucky's Jewish population as a whole was about thirteen thousand, close to three-quarters of which was concentrated in Louisville. Perhaps about thirty Holocaust survivors lived in the state.[7] By contrast, the Jewish population in the New York metropolitan area at the time was 1,742,500, of whom possibly as many as 90,000 were Holocaust survivors.[8] Whereas survivors in New York could easily disappear into the crowd, Kentucky's survivors were often thrust by their "outsider" status into roles as spokespeople for Holocaust awareness: if they didn't speak about what had happened during the Holocaust, who would?[9]

HOLOCAUST DENIAL AND KENTUCKY'S SURVIVORS

More than one survivor in Lexington was motivated by the Tates Creek High debacle to educate Kentuckians about Holocaust history. Like her friend Sylvia Green, the Hungarian-born Auschwitz survivor Emilie Szekely began speaking about her experiences during the Holocaust only after moving to Lexington in 1986. Mrs. Szekely remembered being told by her beautician, whose daughter was a student at Tates Creek High, that McCord (by now a substitute teacher) was still teaching that the Holocaust had not happened. "I didn't speak [about the Holocaust], even in New York, never," Mrs. Szekely told me. "[In] New York, I didn't have to, because there were so many [survivors], I never heard denial. And here I started only because I heard denial."[10]

Speaking out against those who deny the existence of the Holocaust was a key motivation for many survivors who settled in Kentucky. Most survivors, however, did not consider Holocaust denial to be a problem particular to the commonwealth—they implied, rather, that it is an international problem. Paul Schlisser and Alexander Rosenberg, for example, do not wear the "Holocaust survivor" label on their sleeves, and both prefer not to speak to anyone about their Holocaust experiences. (Mr. Schlisser was born in Hungary and imprisoned in the concentration camps Ravensbrück and Bergen-Belsen. Mr. Rosenberg was also interned in Bergen-Belsen, after being imprisoned in the Dutch transit camp Westerbork.) Both agreed to speak with me *only* because they were alarmed at the prospect of Holocaust denial. As Mr. Rosenberg said, "I think there needs to be as much evidence as possible to show that it really did happen. And that those many of us who survived are perfectly normal people."

Objectively speaking, however, there is no need for more evidence to prove that the Holocaust happened. The extermination of Jews and other groups deemed "inferior" by the Nazis and their collaborators between 1933 and 1945 was one of the most thoroughly documented events in history. Holocaust deniers have no voice in any legitimate historical discourse. In addition, the memories of Holocaust survivors, recounted sixty years after the end of the war, are often problematic as sources of pure fact. However, this is not because the survivors are untrustworthy, but because it is the nature of memory to change over time. One might ask, then: if we do not need the testimonies of Kentucky's survivors as further evidence that the Holocaust did indeed happen, why do we need to listen to these stories?

It seems to me that what we gain is not only more evidence of personal experience in this historical tragedy, but something of profound human value: a deeper knowledge of our neighbors and the time and place in which we live. Our present lives are shaped by the people who make up our communities, as evidenced by Sylvia Green's experiences following the Tates Creek debacle. Her community required her participation, which necessitated a change in the way she lived her daily life, the way she communicated with her neighbors and with her own family. In turn, Mrs. Green affected her community. The same can be said for Emilie Szekely. Their willingness to talk openly about their experiences let their contemporaries know that Holocaust history is not only about *others,* it is also about *us.* It is not only about *then,* it is also about *now.*

Holocaust survivors have settled in communities throughout the United States, and while it is impossible to gauge the impact their presence has had upon their communities, it is clear that they have had a significant effect on the way Americans think about Holocaust history. Most of the Kentucky survivors interviewed for this project—nine of the fourteen—had spoken in public forums within their communities on several occasions about their Holocaust experiences. In their interviews, they often discussed these encounters in terms that suggested the events' charged intensity, both for the speakers and for the listeners.

The Burdens and Benefits of Speaking Out

Although Mrs. Green found talking about the Holocaust harrowing, she acknowledged that listening to her might be helpful for other people. From this, it is tempting to believe that all survivors feel that they are doing a service to us in recounting their traumatic history. Of course, this is not always the case.

One survivor, in our first interview session, initially echoed the sentiments of other survivors in his motivations to speak out, saying that he believed people could learn compassion through witnessing the suffering of others. However, his confidence in the power of compassion was not absolute: although he had not encountered any particular problems as a Jew living in Kentucky, he told me that he believed another Holocaust against the Jews would eventually occur. Still, he did not seem hesitant to schedule another interview session, and after over five hours of taping, my interview with this man—who I'll call Mr. Perlman—was one of the longer interviews I conducted for this project.

But when I visited Mr. Perlman again, one day a few years after the taped interviews, his perspective had changed. He was sorry he had ever done the interview, he said; it had taken him over a month to recover after it was done. When I told him that I was preparing to mount an exhibit in Lexington about Holocaust survivors who live in Kentucky, he asked why I would want to do such a thing. People, he said, would come in and say, "Look at these monkeys, why didn't Hitler kill all of them?" He now believed the majority of Kentuckians were anti-Semitic, and he had come to think that any efforts related to Holocaust education were a waste. It soon became clear that my further objections would only cause offense.

"I always carry a gun," Mr. Perlman said. "I always have and I always will. So when they come to take me away, I will kill them first." With that, he stood and held out his hand, saying he'd be happy to be of assistance to me in any way, so long as it did not involve the subject of the Holocaust.

Mr. Perlman's vehemence was surprising and troubling. He was a capable professional, who ran his own business, read widely, and had a sharp memory. Although I utterly disagreed with him, I could not write off his perspective as the rantings of an unstable man. His point of view was extreme, and certainly not representative of most Holocaust survivors. Yet Mr. Perlman is far from alone among survivors in voicing the terrible pain they live through when speaking about their experiences. Mr. Perlman's passionate rejection of the notion that any good could come of this pain has often reminded me of the burden that survivors bear in choosing to speak, and the responsibility that those of us who listen have to understand the price at which we hear their words.

For some survivors, however, speaking openly about the Holocaust with other Kentuckians has also brought a sense of fulfillment, especially speaking to young people. Melvin Goldfarb, a Louisville resident and Polish-born survivor of Auschwitz, Birkenau, and Ebensee, didn't speak about his experiences until he had been in the United States for fifty years. His first public speaking experience was in the mid-1990s, at the Trimble County High School. Located in the rural town of Bedford, Kentucky, about fifty miles east of Louisville, the school serves all of the high school students in the county.

"They didn't know what a Jew looks like!" Mr. Goldfarb said of the students. "He's got horns, maybe. They had never seen a Jew, and they never seen a Holocaust survivor. They received a message such a wonderful way, because they actually cried there, and they actually went out with me to the car, because they didn't have enough of me. It made me feel good. Because you could see, you could hear, you could tell, you could *smell* the attention. You could feel it in the room. . . . They will never forget this, this is a lifetime experience for me and for them. I've never experienced anything like it."[11]

Still, by the time of our interview in 2000, Mr. Goldfarb did not speak to school groups any longer: he had had a stroke that he believed had been caused by the difficulty of giving such talks.

Emilie Szekely, who never spoke about her experiences before moving to Kentucky from New York in 1986, had spoken publicly on over 150 occasions by the time of our interview in 2000. "If I cannot do it," she said, "I will be the most unhappiest person in the world, because I feel the commitment that I have to do it. . . . I cannot explain it, when I talk, I am very enthusiastic and I live it through again. I have to take a tranquilizer before I go."

Robert Holczer, who survived the war in Budapest and lived for over ten years on a horse farm in Paris, Kentucky, was also passionate about speaking to school groups. "I do this with great pleasure, because I know that in this area there are very few people who experienced the Holocaust, and even know what it is. . . . So, I consider it a mission."

Some of these survivors said that they found the young, non-Jewish Kentuckians to generally be far more interested in listening to their experiences, far more receptive to their stories, than were their own Jewish contemporaries. Joseph Gavi, who as a boy escaped the Minsk ghetto and joined a partisan group, described speaking at a school in a primarily African American neighborhood in Louisville; he was invited not only to teach the students about the Holocaust, he said, but to introduce them to the notion that a Jew can be something other than a crook. All fifty of the students had questions after his talk, Gavi said, and twenty-eight of them wrote him thank-you letters, of which he was extremely proud. He had also talked about his Holocaust experiences at a Louisville synagogue, but found the congregation to be not nearly as interested in his speech. "Maybe for the rest of the population this [the subject of the Holocaust] is new; for them [the Jewish community], they know very well," Gavi told me. "I am just one of them, not less, not more. And I understand this."[12]

CHALLENGING COMMUNITIES

The first interviews I conducted for this project were with Robert Holczer and Sylvia Green, in 1996. These first interview sessions with Mr. Holczer and Mrs. Green took place when I still lived in Washington, D.C., and worked full-time in the Oral History Department at the United States Holocaust Memorial Museum. Because one of the department's projects focused on the lives of survivors in America after the war, I knew that Holczer and Green, as Holocaust survivors who had settled in rural America, were geographic anomalies. I did not know, however, whether their experiences differed in other key ways from those of the majority of American Holocaust survivors. I was aware of various regional oral history projects that recorded the stories of Holocaust survivors who had settled outside of major American urban centers, but these projects tended to focus on recording the survivors' Holocaust-era experiences. What of the challenging communities in which they lived now? Did Jewish identity remain important to those survivors who chose to live in communities in which few, if any, Holocaust survivors resided? If so, was their Jewishness an integral part of their relationships to their communities—in their work, their friendships? Was community-building important to them, or did most lead more private lives? I also did not know how many other survivors had made their homes in the Bluegrass State, although I guessed there must be some. How and why did they come, I wondered, and what kept them here?

Soon after I moved to Kentucky in late 1997—my husband, David Wagoner, and I had bought a farm near David's ancestral homeplace—I began to research Kentucky's survivors in earnest. The project began, in part, as a way of getting to know my new home, but it was sustained by a genuine interest in the stories that emerged.

I learned that most of the state's survivors live in the Louisville area, which at a population of over 250,000 supports a Jewish community of about 8,700, including seven Jewish congregations and a Jewish Community Center.[13] A few survivors live in Lexington, and even fewer have settled in small towns and rural areas. Some came to the state for work; others for family. Some came immediately following the war; others have settled here only in the last few years.

Life in Louisville is, of course, very different from life in Winchester, or Prestonsburg. I expected to find that the lives of those survivors who had settled in Louisville would resemble in some key ways the lives of survivors in major metropolitan areas, such as New York: they would count other survivors among their closest friends; they would socialize mostly within the Jewish community. Literature on the postwar lives of Holocaust survivors in America tends to emphasize that survivors by and large need not only the support of Jewish communities, but of other survivors as well. "They frequently functioned as a separate community within American Jewish life, they perceived themselves as such, and they were seen in this way by outsiders," as William Helmreich puts it in *Against All Odds: Holocaust Survivors and the Successful Lives They Made in America.*[14] Yet even in Louisville, this was usually not the case among the survivors I interviewed. (Of the ten Louisville-based survivors I identified who spent the war years in Nazi-occupied Europe or other Axis countries, I interviewed seven. It is to these "full-term" survivors that Helmreich refers.)

Abe Jakubowicz, who was born in Poland and survived the Warsaw ghetto as well as Auschwitz and other camps, came to Louisville in the mid-1950s. Mr. Jakubowicz had been close with other survivors during his early years in Louisville, but he found that these relationships could not be sustained: "We formed a world within ourselves. But you cannot live in this world, because there [are] no walls." He even felt it necessary to distance himself from the Jewish community as a whole: "Sometimes it crossed my mind, why don't you go move near the Jewish Community Center? But then I thought, you know what, sometimes it is better when you stay away. They created their own ghetto."

As a Jew who had remained in Germany after the war and married a non-Jewish German woman, Jakubowicz had long since ceased looking for the support and approval of his Jewish friends and acquaintances. Yet he was one of the few Louisville residents I interviewed who described having friendships with other survivors. Others, such as Melvin Goldfarb (whose wife, Esther, also a Holocaust survivor, declined to be interviewed for this project), may have liked to befriend other Holocaust survivors in the area, but he told me he was too busy working and raising a family to have much time for friendships. Ann Klein, a Hungarian-born survivor of Auschwitz, mingled with other survivors at the Jewish Community Center's annual Holocaust remembrance event, but did not count any survivors among her friends—friends who came from both within and outside of the Jewish community. Justine Lerner, a survivor of Auschwitz from Poland, craved contact with other survivors, having moved to Louisville from New York in 1997, but found it hard, at her age, to make new friends.

When asked if he had friendships with other survivors in the area, Joseph Gavi answered, "No, I don't have time." He did not understand, he said, how survivors could believe that only other survivors could understand them: "Everybody understands that this was terrible, to kill people just because they are Armenian, or Jews, or Gypsies, or blacks or something. Everybody knows what is terrible, like I know what is terrible. . . . I don't feel [that] you have to be a Holocaust survivor to understand what happened. Everybody can understand what happened, if you've got heart."

Paul Schlisser, of the Louisville group, was the most vehement in his response to the question of whether he had contact with the Jewish community in Louisville. His words contain an implicit criticism of the Jewish community that, to my ear, strikes a puzzling note of pride in the distance he feels between himself and other Jews:

"Most of my friends are from the Army and none of them are Jewish. And with my views and my way of thinking, I probably wouldn't fit very well in with the Jewish community, to be perfectly honest with you. There is no connection between me and my view of things and most of the Jewish Community Center. They're mostly Americans, who were born here and raised here. So, we have really nothing in common. I've never been in business, never plan on being in business. I couldn't sell you a glass of water if you were dying of thirst. I'd give you a glass of water, but I wouldn't sell it to you. I'm just a different type of person."

Elsewhere in the state, too, survivors tended to have little contact with other survivors, apart from, in a few cases, their own spouses.[15]

"The survivors, especially those who were [religiously] observant, conversed in Yiddish and clung to the old and familiar, becoming only as American as seemed necessary," writes William Helmreich in *Against All Odds*. "As is true of virtually all immigrant groups, the bridge to the New World was crossed by their children."[16] That certainly does not describe any of the fourteen survivors that I interviewed in Kentucky, most of whom said that many of their closest friends were not Jewish.[17]

FAITH AND ASSIMILATION

In fact, six out of the fourteen survivors married outside of the faith—a surprising statistic, given the assertions in key published sources on survivors' feelings about interfaith marriage. "On a personal level, probably no other subject is as troubling to survivors as that of interfaith marriage," writes Helmreich, citing the families that were torn apart when survivors' children married outside of the faith. The subject of interfaith marriage between the Holocaust survivors themselves and non-Jews is so eccentric in Helmreich's study as to scarcely merit mention.

Similarly, in *The Aftermath: Living with the Holocaust*, Aaron Hass writes: "[T]wo of the most disconcerted survivors I interviewed attributed their ongoing upsetness to the fact that their children had either married outside of the faith or were involved with a Gentile partner. For survivors, this catastrophe implies not only a further victory for Hitler, but also their inability to undo previous losses and provide future reclamation."[18]

"Only a few survivors married outside of the Jewish faith," Hass notes. "Some of these men and women located to American cities with small or nonexistent Jewish populations." Curiously, however, five of the six Kentucky survivors who married outside of the faith were married before they moved to Kentucky, and most were married when they lived within communities that supported significant Jewish communities.[19]

For his book *Holocaust Voices: An Attitudinal Survey of Survivors*, Alexander J. Groth surveyed survivors about their perceptions of the Holocaust and its aftermath. This survey revealed that at least 75 percent of Holocaust survivors' children married within the Jewish faith. (Again, interfaith marriage between the survivors themselves and non-Jews was presumably deemed by the author as insignificant; no question on the subject was included in the questionnaire.) Groth, himself a Holocaust survivor, interprets these statistics as pointing to an "achievement" among survivors: "[O]ur evidence suggests that the Holocaust at its worst . . . increased the sense of Jewish identity and the commitment of the survivors to a Jewish life and a sense of solidarity with fellow Jews. From this perspective, . . . the Holocaust may be seen as a singular Nazi failure."[20]

The experiences of the Kentucky-based survivors who married outside of the faith, or whose children did, raise a challenge to such commonly held perceptions of what it means to carry on a Jewish tradition. These survivors do not view themselves as lacking solidarity with their fellow Jews, and they certainly do not see themselves as doing anything that might contribute to the long-term success of the Nazi program. All of the six survivors who married outside of the faith still vehemently identify themselves as Jewish. Their sense of what "being Jewish" means certainly varies from person to person; for many, Judaism evokes more of an ethical code and a cultural inheritance than it does a religion. And according to at least one study, these survivors would be considered by their suburban American counterparts as "good Jews": by all appearances, they lead ethical and moral lives; they accept being Jewish and do not try to hide it; they support humanitarian causes; and they promote civic betterment and improvement in the community, among other attributes.[21]

Consider Oscar Haber. Mr. Haber is one of the eight survivors I interviewed who married within the faith. He is, in many senses, a deeply traditional Jew; he was raised in an Orthodox Polish household and now attends a Conservative synagogue, whose modernizations—such as the ordainment of women rabbis—he tolerates rather than embraces. He observes the Sabbath and prays in Hebrew. Yet when Mr. Haber needs a friend, he does not turn to anyone within Lexington's Jewish community—most of his closest friends are Polish Catholic expatriates. His son, who considers himself a "Jew for Jesus," is married to a Christian woman. I asked Mr. Haber if his son's departure from the traditions of Jewish faith hurt him. "On the contrary," he replied. "I am happy, because he is happy."

THE STATE OF HOLOCAUST EDUCATION

The Ernie Marx Resolution, which will make Holocaust-related curricula available to public school teachers, makes Kentucky one of the twenty or so states in the nation that have similar Holocaust-education laws. The bill's near-unanimous approval in both the House and Senate also suggests that Kentucky is becoming increasingly progressive on the subject.

Yet Fred Whitaker, a teacher at the Catholic St. Francis of Assisi School in Louisville, fought on behalf of the bill from the time it was introduced in 2004 until it was signed into law in 2008, and saw it repeatedly watered down. Contrary to popular belief, the bill does not mandate Holocaust education. According to Whitaker, Kentucky teachers have never been required to so much as mention the Holocaust in their classes, and the bill merely stipulates that Holocaust-related curricula will be developed and made available for optional use by the state's educators by March of

2009. Whitaker had originally pushed for a mandate, yet after seeing it die in the legislature, he and the bill's other advocates settled for an optional-curriculum bill.[22]

Even passing such a "symbolic" bill, however, proved "unbelievably controversial," Whitaker said. Although it passed 94 to 1 in the House, the resolution was killed on the Senate floor. Whitaker could not understand why until one senator told him, off the record, that it had to do with two words: the bill contained a clause about the Nazis' persecution of groups considered to be undesirable based upon, among other factors, their *sexual orientation*. After the bill's sponsors removed the offending clause, the Kentucky Senate passed the resolution unanimously.

"I've had a baptism by fire in terms of the undercurrent of anti-Semitism and homophobia in Kentucky," Whitaker told me. One senator told him that a Holocaust bill would not pass in Kentucky because "this is a Christian state"—and the Holocaust is pigeonholed as a Jewish event. Some senators supported the bill, Whitaker said, "because they thought we were doing Jews a favor."

Still, Whitaker stressed that many Holocaust educators across the state are doing exemplary work. "What's happening in the state is so eclectic," he said. "Kentucky is not backwards as far as Holocaust education is concerned, but we are behind the times. We have a generation that's exposed to genocide and mass killings on a daily basis. The question that we all should have is, what are we going to do about this?"

This is what Whitaker is doing about it now: working with his eighth-grade students to create a book about Kentucky's Holocaust survivors—something his students can use to learn about the Holocaust after its survivors are no longer with us.

According to Lexington-based Holocaust educator Rachel Belin, the kids she teaches in Kentucky—who are primarily Jewish, since government funding for the general-populace workshops she once conducted has dried up—report that "they got nothing, or very little" Holocaust education in their school classrooms. "Unlike in other parts of the country, Jewish kids are truly a minority here," she said. She had recently gone to a baby's baptism, and heard a sermon about how the Jews killed Jesus. "This is what these kids are up against," she said, "so in history classes, they have to know their stuff."

"This is America"

On the fourth night of Hanukkah in 2007, I arrived at Oscar Haber's apartment in an assisted-living facility in Lexington. He had accepted an invitation to my mother's home for a Hanukkah party. At ninety-seven years old, he looked sprightly, wearing a green rain slicker and a UK Wildcats ball cap. As we drove toward my mother's house, I warned him that, although this was a Hanukkah party, there wouldn't be many Jews there. After we arrived, Mr. Haber sang the prayer for the lighting of the menorah, blessed our meal in Hebrew, English, and French (*"bon appetit"*), taught my daughter how to spin a dreydl, and ate a latke or two.

"Who *were* those people?" Mr. Haber asked after he had settled in the car later that night for the drive back to his apartment. When I told him who those people were—among them a couple who jointly pastor at a Christian church in Henry County, a Muslim family, and my Jewish mother, who clearly takes an ecumenical approach to religion—he shrugged his shoulders and said, "This is America."

Kentucky's Holocaust survivors are a remarkably diverse group. While Paul Schlisser was fighting the war in Vietnam, Robert Holczer was marching against the war in San Francisco. While Sylvia Green could not bring herself to have anything to do with Germans after the war, Abe Jakubowicz has been married to a German woman for over fifty years. Some of the survivors are atheists, while some are deeply faithful. If these survivors share a common trait, it may be their resourcefulness and adaptability, their readiness to call a place where little was familiar *home.*

A NOTE ON METHODOLOGY

When I began to search in 1998 for Holocaust survivors in Kentucky, I relied on several sources, primary among them the Benjamin and Vladka Meed Registry of Jewish Holocaust Survivors at the United States Holocaust Memorial Museum. Through the registry, the Louisville Jewish Community Center, and word of mouth, I identified seventy potential interviewees; of these, I was able to make contact with forty-three survivors.

The term "Holocaust survivor" itself is a tricky one; some believe that a Holocaust survivor is a Jewish person who lived through a Nazi concentration camp during World War II, and draw the line there. My definition is more inclusive. Twenty of the forty-three potential interviewees I identified left Nazi-controlled Europe early in the war or before the war began. While I would have welcomed the opportunity to include accounts from non-Jewish survivors, I was not able to locate any in Kentucky at the time these interviews were conducted. This book should thus not be considered a comprehensive representation of Kentucky's Holocaust survivors.

Eventually, I chose fourteen survivors to interview for this project. In choosing whom to interview, I had two main priorities:

1. *Survivors who spent the war in Nazi-controlled Europe.* All but one of the interviews (John Rosenberg is the exception) were conducted with people who had lived through the full arc of the war, whether in camps, in

hiding, or living under false identities. My intention was not to minimize the experiences of those who left Europe before the war's end, many of whom lived for years under Nazi-controlled regimes. The focus on survivors who lived through all the years of the Holocaust is, however, shared by most published accounts of the postwar lives of survivors, which gave me a better basis for understanding the Kentucky interviews within a national context.

Before I began conducting interviews for this project, I was able to identify twenty-three Holocaust survivors throughout the state who were in the European theater for the entire duration of the war. Of those, I was able to interview thirteen. Of the ten I did not interview, six refused, saying that they did not wish to speak about their experiences during the Holocaust. Of the remaining four, one spoke only Russian, two were unreachable, and one (Ernie Marx) I chose not to interview because he had been interviewed previously by two prominent institutions: the United States Holocaust Memorial Museum and the USC Shoah Foundation Institute for Visual History and Education.

2. *Geographic diversity.* I wished to interview survivors in various locations around the state, which made survivors who had settled in rural areas a priority. Ultimately, half of those interviewed—seven of the fourteen—lived in Louisville, a mid-sized city with a significant Jewish population. Three of the remaining seven were from Lexington, Kentucky's second-largest city; the remaining four lived in either small towns or rural areas in which there are no synagogues, temples, or Jewish Community Centers.

The interviews varied in length, from under two hours to over twelve hours. Some interviews lasted only one session, others consisted of many sessions, and stretched over a span of several years. In general, I decided to re-interview people who were eager to speak about their experiences, had chosen to settle in rural or small-town areas, or had complex postwar stories that had not been recorded previously.

Of the fourteen survivors originally interviewed for this project, five are not represented in this book. Of those five, two passed away before Rebecca Howell was able to photograph them, one was too ill to have her picture taken, another we were unable to track down, and one (the pseudonymous "Mr. Perlman") refused to be involved in the project any further.

My aim in editing was to preserve the flow and character of the interview while making it more concise and readable. Occasionally the interviewer's questions were re-structured to reflect things that were said off-tape, in order to make the interviewee's answers more clear. (This was made necessary by on-tape references to other interviews that had been conducted with the survivors by other individuals and organizations, interviews which I used to inform my questions, but which would have been confusing to include in this text.) I did not correct the interviewee's grammar, although some phrases were edited to be more concise. Where words other than those spoken by the interviewee were inserted for clarity, I placed them in brackets.

The complete, unedited transcripts of the interviews contained in this book are available through the Kentucky Historical Society's website at www.history.ky.gov. (Search the Digital Collections for Oral History, then go to the Holocaust Survivors in Kentucky Oral History Project.) Interviews can also be accessed through the United States Holocaust Memorial Museum (www.ushmm.gov).

CHAPTER 1

Sylvia Färber Green

Sylvia Green (née Sylvia Färber) was born in Karlsruhe am Rhein, Germany, in 1924. Sylvia, as she pointed out to me, never had a teenage life, the years of the war having coincided almost exactly with her adolescence. When I met her in 1996, she had recently passed some of the milestones that are significant for many American teens—in her sixties, she had become a Bat Mitzvah and had earned her driver's license. And she had undertaken a trip to Israel alone, one of the high points of her life.

When I interviewed Sylvia again in 1999, her husband, Jake, had passed away, and she deeply mourned his absence. Her work at the Clark Regional Medical Center, where she had volunteered for over twenty years, was some consolation. But Jake's support had been crucial in dealing with her painful memories, and she had decided that she would no longer speak about her wartime experiences.

In that interview session, we focused on Sylvia's postwar life. But near the beginning of our first interview, she remembered her first impressions of the man who was to be responsible for the near-destruction of European Jewry.

AD: Was your family afraid when Hitler came to power?
SG: Well, I saw Hitler many times. I was a nosy child, and whenever he came, I would not go down to see him in my neighborhood, because everybody knew I was a Jew. I would go blocks and blocks out of my way,

where they didn't know me. And I was just fascinated by him. It was like he hypnotized people. I was there in the front row with everybody else, and everybody yelling, "Heil Hitler!" He always came in a convertible and he would hold his hand on the belt. I can close my eyes and see him. "Heil Hitler, Heil Hitler!"—And people just went crazy screaming, you know. And they all were running, and I was right there with them.

In October of 1938, over fifteen thousand Polish-born Jews were forced to leave Germany and return to Poland. Sylvia's father was among them. The following month brought the anti-Jewish rampage that came to be known as Kristall-nacht ("Crystal Night" in English), or the Night of Broken Glass.

SG: Crystal Night, it was wild. They banged at the door and my mother yelled, "We don't have any men here in the house. You deported my husband." My brother hid, I think, in a closet. We didn't open the door. And we screamed and they screamed, and then they went away. Several times they came that night, then later on we found out they burned the synagogues, they burned the Torahs, they took the rabbi and set his beard on fire. We were too scared to go out. We lived on Main Street and there was so much yelling going on. I stood behind a curtain just to see something and then they broke all the glass in the Jewish stores—and there were quite a few Jewish stores on Main Street. They went berserk.

Sometime after Crystal Night, they called a meeting to all the wives of Polish citizens. We were told that there is going to be a meeting at the police station and if we [were] not going to be there, then they were going to arrest us. My mother was sick and she sent me. When they called her name, I stood up and apologized that my mother couldn't be here, but I will give her the message, whatever the meeting is about. He yelled at me to come forward, he yelled so hard, and I was a child, you know, I was fifteen years old. I was shaking from head to toe. He gave me a pencil to sign my mother's name, that we had to leave Germany by August '39, or we were going to be arrested. Well, I couldn't hold the pencil, my hand was just shaking, so he took his gun out and put it to my temple. And I really don't remember whether I signed the name or I put the X mark—he was satisfied, so maybe I signed the name.

That took a long time to overcome. Because after I became a U.S. citizen, I remember when I needed a Social Security number, it took me three hours to get enough nerve to go in there. And the first time I voted, you have to sign your name, and it was going pretty shaky. It took years. Doesn't bother me anymore now.

Meanwhile, Sylvia's mother was given the opportunity to send one of her children to a foster home in England. Thinking that the danger was greater for boys, she sent Sylvia's brother, Bernard.

AD: How long did it take until you actually had to leave Germany?
SG: I think they gave you a few months to get ready. So, [by the] beginning of August, you just had to leave. My brother went to England the same night my mother and I caught a train to Poland, but we stopped off in Berlin. My mother wanted me to talk to the American Consulate, that maybe we could get out and come to America. I didn't even get to see the Consulate in Berlin. I just talked to the secretary or somebody at the front desk. Maybe some other people had the same idea, too.

After we crossed the border, we went to Kraków, because my aunt lived in Kraków. My dad was there also. And it was great, I just thought, well now, everything is going to go get back to normal, but we were wrong, we really were wrong. Beginning of September, the Second World War started. That's when [Germany] invaded Poland.

In just a few months, we had to sweep the streets, we had to wear armbands [identifying us as Jews]. We had to clean barracks, we scrubbed the barracks on our knees, we carried railroad tracks. And my trouble was, I was very tall, I was five-eight, and they would line us up, the tallest in the middle and then the shorter ones and shorter ones, and I really got the heavy load. And they were not very kind to us when we cleaned the barracks, I mean they would yell and scream, or kick, or scare us they were going to shoot us, but in the evening, after we went back, my mother always had a hot meal for us and I can hear my mama say, "It's not going to get any worse, it's not going to get any worse." And all during the war, I can hear her say, "It's not going to get any worse," but it did.

And then [in] '41 [a Jewish] ghetto [was established in Kraków]. We were notified we had to leave [for the ghetto]. So we grabbed a bedsheet again, we dumped everything in there, and a suitcase, and you walked. And that was no picnic—five, six people in a little apartment, where you barely had room even to sleep on the floor. Well, we did the same thing there, we would march to work outside the ghetto. We shoveled snow, we washed the streets, and the same yelling. There were different faces watching us, but it seemed like they were all the same.

AD: So you were doing the same—

SG: The same thing until '42, my aunt and I got the job and we marched from the ghetto to Kabelwerk every morning. It was a cable factory, and there were different departments there. I had to cover cables. I was in charge of ten machines, and there was another person [in charge of] another ten machines, and then in the back of you there were ten machines, and they had to be in operation at all times. For a while, I just worked daytimes, but then you worked one week twelve hours daytime and the following week twelve hours nighttime. And they did this on purpose, because you never could sleep. I mean, there was no way to get adjusted from one to another.

I always ate kosher, and when I started working in Kabelwerk, they served us meals and it was the same meal the Gentile workers got, so that wasn't that bad because it had a lot of vegetables in there. And I wouldn't eat, I came home and my dad said, "What's the matter?" We were still in the ghetto at that time. I said, "Dad, I can't eat it, they serving *trayf*" [food that is not kosher]. And he said, "You have to eat. You have to have strength to survive this. You have to eat." So the next day, I ate and I couldn't keep it down, I was throwing it all up, I came home and I told my dad, "I can't keep it down." He said, "You have to eat. You have to force yourself." And the third day, I was glad to get it. So I started eating trayf and was lucky enough to get it, you know, at that time.

Then, I think it was towards end of '42, we were concentrated in Płaszów, the concentration camp, and we went to Kabelwerk from Płaszów. I was promised that if I would work in Kabelwerk, my parents would be safe in the [Kraków] ghetto. But naturally, it was broken promises. The liquidation of the ghetto was March the 13th, 1943.[1] And my father got killed in the hospital. My cousin was in the clean-up crew, and he saw him laying there on the sidewalk, and there were pictures of my mother and of me and my brother around him. I don't know what happened to my mother. I thought my mother might have ended up in one of the concentration camps, but she might have been shot in the ghetto, because they were just shooting left and right.

AD: Do you remember the last time you saw your parents, before the ghetto was liquidated?

SG: The last time, it might have been maybe a month before. I went first and saw my mother, and she told me my dad was in the hospital.

What happened was, every so often in the ghetto, they were round-
ing up people to send them to concentration camps. They rounded him
up, and he jumped out the window—he was going to run away and hide
somewheres in the ghetto—and he fell, he broke his leg. This was a make-
shift hospital, and they had some Jewish doctors who practiced. So I went
to the hospital and I only had a very short time, maybe a whole hour or
a half an hour. And my dad said he was so happy to see me, he was just
smiling and he had his leg in traction. So he said, "I want you to meet my
doctor, he is such a nice man." I said, "Dad, I have to go, I have to go. They
just gave me so much time." We hugged, I kissed him, and I was walking
out and the doctor just walked in. And my dad said, "This is my daughter
I have told you about." I was Dad's little girl always.

After the liquidation of the ghetto, then they built barracks in Kabelwerk and we were not walking to Płaszów any more. We were concentrated where the factory was. And that wasn't that bad, the only upsetting
thing is, they were supposed to have a Red Cross representative come from
Switzerland. We had to clean the barracks and we all got a care package,
which we had to open but not touch. So the representative looked around,
the barracks were clean and we all talked to him on the side how bad it is,
you know. And he was not very sympathetic. He said, "The barracks are
clean. Look at the nice care package. What are you complaining? People
are getting killed, there is a war going on, you got it good here." So we told
him, "We will have to return those. The order was to open it up, but not to
touch it." And they took those care packages away, but it was so upsetting
to us that he didn't believe us, the representative from the Red Cross.

We were sent back to Płaszów in September '43. And when I got there,
we had to work in the concentration camp. We had to open graves, pull
out gold teeth. The people who were in charge of this place were German
prisoners and they were completely out of control. They were in prison
because they were murderers from way before the war and they let them
out to oversee us. I saw [Płaszów camp commander Amon] Goeth many
times, and as soon as we heard he was walking in the camp, I was running
away because we knew he was target shooting, he wanted to see how close
he could shoot or how far he could shoot.

It was always cold in Płaszów. And there was no mirror, but I looked
at my aunt and I knew what I looked like: a skeleton. We wore prison garb
and it was in the wintertime, and Poland is cold. And then you had to
stand *appell* [roll call], they would count you and count you, they wanted

to make sure that a half a person wasn't missing or something, sometimes it was for hours just of meanness, till they got bored with it. The barracks had bunks with wooden slats—you couldn't call it a bed.

AD: Did you ever get beaten by the Germans?

SG: I got beaten one time in Płaszów. There was a bad odor in that neighborhood where I was on the double decker wooden thing where we were laying. And somebody had their period and they put something over where I was sleeping and she said it was mine. It didn't happen to be mine, [but] I got twenty-five paddles. But I think that was the only time. My aunt always told me, "Don't walk erect, make yourself shorter," that you wouldn't stand out, and wherever I went, I just walked like that. Some girls got raped and I was pretty fortunate, but I wasn't much to look at because all those years already took its toll at a very young age.

AD: What kept you going?

SG: Well, this is [an] interesting question. I don't know what kept me going. The only thing, my aunt and I talked all the time. Somebody had to survive to tell the world. We did not know that the world knew about it. People say, "You must have been very healthy." I wasn't any healthier than the ones who died next to me. The only thing I can think of is, my time was not up. Somebody still had some purpose. Also, maybe it was a strong will to live, to tell the world. But my world crumbled pretty quick after I came to the United States, when I found out the world did know and didn't do a thing about it. And maybe it was lucky I didn't know, because I am pretty sure I would have given up, my aunt would have given up.

But in January '44, we had to line up, we had to be counted, and they were telling us we were going to a wonderful place. "There's going to be clean beds and plenty food, you're going to work hard, but you're going to have it good." And my aunt said, "Wow, it sounds like paradise." And then we were crammed into [a] cattle wagon.

Auschwitz is not that far from Kraków, but it took such a long time because the train stopped every few feet because the planes were bombing. The Germans jumped out of the trains, and they were hiding in ditches, and we really were laughing. There was a little window up in top of those cattle wagons, and we would get on each others' shoulders to lift them up to see so we could get a good laugh because they were so scared. And we yelled, "Bomb us, bomb us, come on." You know, we didn't care, we really didn't care as long as [the Germans] would have gotten killed.

And then we went a little bit longer, to me it seemed like we went the whole week, but we didn't. But you see, time didn't seem important at all. It was just running into day or night till the cattle wagon stopped. They opened the doors and they were yelling, "Out, out, out, out, out!" Kicking, and dogs, and we were running. And then we looked and we knew where we were, because we saw the chimneys burning.

AD: You had heard about Auschwitz?

SG: Oh, yeah. Everybody heard about Auschwitz. And you could smell the smell of human flesh.

You know how they kept the records so neat, they had to have orders. We arrived without orders, they didn't know what to do with us. And we just sat. It was cold, it was January. Finally, there still were no orders, but I guess they were afraid to send us to the ovens, if the orders came that we should not [have] been killed, they couldn't bring us back after they gassed us, you know. So then they told us to go in to showers and we took the shower, and then we walked out in the nude, in January in Poland, shivering. And then we got prison garbs and they gave me wooden shoes. I couldn't walk in the shoes. It seemed like those shoes had a mind of their own.

In the evening you got watery soup, and we had to carry heavy kettles. It was my turn to go, and some other girls also went, and coming back—and we were almost to our barrack—and those stupid wooden shoes wouldn't stay on my feet and I dropped the kettle and our whole supper was there. And really I was scared that the people are going to kill me, the hungry people, but they didn't. We just all lay down and we licked the floor, whatever fell there.

After about twelve or fourteen days in Auschwitz, we were shipped back in the cattle wagon to Bergen-Belsen. I think it was still January of '44, because we were pretty much one of the first ones there. When we came to Bergen-Belsen, it was very quiet. My aunt said, "You know, Sylvia, in comparison to Auschwitz, this is a vacation." We didn't know that it was no gas chambers, but it was a starvation camp. They just starved you to death.

[The camp's administrators] were looking for somebody who spoke a lot of languages, so I applied for it. I spoke German fluently, by that time already I spoke Polish fluently, because when you're young you pick up languages. So I got the job, not very long, but enough that I had a foot in the kitchen. And so I could steal food so my aunt wouldn't be hungry.

My Aunt Mina was just like my mother, really. I lost my mother while I was still a child, and I was with my Aunt Mina, I worshiped the ground she walked on, to a point that I modeled myself after her. We were just constantly together. By yourself you could not survive, you had to have somebody to care for. The ration of bread we got, she wanted to share her portion with me. "I'm really not very hungry, Sylvia, why don't you take this? I just couldn't eat it." I said, "Mina, I don't want it. You just want me to have it because you know I am so hungry." "No, no, no, honest, I just can't eat another bite. I'm just not hungry." That was my aunt. God bless her.

We were liberated April the 14th of '45. It was really strange, by that time I wasn't working in the kitchen anymore, nobody was working anywhere because there was no food, and [we] already knew that [the Germans] were in bad shape because the guards were disappearing and they came back, there was no place for them to go. We didn't know that they were surrounded by the Russians, by the British, and by the Americans, and there was no place to run around, so they were digging ditches. And oh, they were angry, I'm telling you, you couldn't even set a foot out. If not, you got shot.

AD: Before liberation, did you have the sense that the end of the war was coming, and that you were going to survive?

SG: No. That would be too much thinking. I didn't have the energy. You did what you were supposed to do, and hour went into hour into day and night . . . there was no difference. Sometimes we would sit around and be miserable and then somebody would say, "You know, on Shabbat, Friday night? Boy, my mother set a table fit for a king." "What did she cook?" "Well, there was fish and chicken soup and chicken and roast beef and vegetables and dessert." And somebody would pop up, "That's enough food, I can't eat another bite." You know, really, I'm not kidding, we could taste that food.

AD: Did you have other fantasies?

SG: No. Just blank, just a zombie. And I don't think I was the only one, I think everybody was that way. I was so conditioned from the time I was nine years old until the end of the war, that only thing many times you ask yourself, "Why, why, why?" When my time comes, I'm going to have a list that long and when I get upstairs, I'm going to ask Him maybe, "Why this, why that," you know.

We stayed pretty much indoors, and everybody was sick—no energy, no water, no food—and then I got dysentery problems again. I went out one night to relieve myself and I felt something cold I was sitting on and I looked—it was a body. I just moved over. Evidently, you got conditioned to that. And I crawled back in.

So, early in the morning between April 14th and 15th, we heard a lot of tanks rolling and rolling and rolling, we didn't know what was the matter. The British were driving the tanks, and somebody said, "We liberated, we liberated!" And I remember I crawled out, I did not walk out. I crawled on all fours. And somehow, I had the energy, I don't know where it came from, I stood up, and I sang the British anthem, "God Save the King." I learned that in school.

So, they were wonderful. This camp was just completely diseased. It was typhus and lice and any kind of disease you want was found in there. And so many piled up, all the ones that died. So I think the first thing they did, they took us to delousing, and they gave us clean clothes. Then they gave us a box of food, like a ration. And I remember I ate everything in sight. I did not know what instant coffee was, and powdered milk, and sardines, cigarettes and chocolate. That whole thing was consumed in the few minutes.

I already was sick, I already had dysentery. I had diarrhea, everybody did. It is amazing that it somehow blew over, because so many died, with all that rich food, and your stomach conditioned to nothing, emptiness. They meant well, but I think that the world learned from that, whenever prisoners come back, they kind of condition them slowly with food.

The British burned this diseased camp we were in, and they gave us the German barracks. We were moved right away, this was the first thing.

My brother was in the American Army, and I wrote a letter, but there was no mail going between Germany and America at that time. I gave it to a British soldier which I got acquainted with. I had about two years of English and I didn't do too well. And he sent the letter to England, and his mother sent it to [the] Urbachs in Lexington, Kentucky. I didn't remember the street, but I remembered the name, because my mother drilled it into us. Whoever survives, get in touch with Leon Urbach. And at that time, Lexington, Kentucky, was small, there were about sixty-five thousand people, so everybody knew each other. So it got there, just "Leon Urbach, Lexington, Kentucky, USA."

AD: Had your brother lived with Leon Urbach?

SG: Yes. Urbach sent him an affidavit from England to come to the United States in 1940, and he was drafted in '41. So he was still serving in the American Army, he was with Intelligence, he spoke seven languages fluently. The Urbachs got in touch with him, and he came to Bergen-Belsen.

They came running in, telling me that my brother was out there. And I run out and all in a sudden I just stopped. I thought my dad was there, because they look so much alike. It was scary, I couldn't talk, I just stood there, like paralyzed. [He] even had a mustache like my dad at that time. And then I was very happy.

He went through his own hell, because he went in my place to England, and all during the war that was on his mind. He told me, "I'm so happy that you are alive, I don't know how I would have managed to live, to know that you got killed and I'm alive." After we survived, Mina and I talked a lot about that, how lucky, because he never could have survived it, he was a scholar. He wasn't strong. He couldn't have made it in any of the camps.

When he came to the camp, he brought oranges, food, and ah, we just had a party. My brother said, "I just brought it for you and Aunt Mina." I said, "I can't eat that by myself, not sharing it, what you talking about?" He didn't understand. You know, you're hungry together, you party together! So it was good food, it really was.

He spent a few days and then he had to go back. My brother was stationed in Munich. He sent an American ambulance after us, and a registered nurse, because he didn't know how we were going to travel, and he was worried about that. [Mina and I] left Bergen-Belsen in October '45.

And my brother rented an apartment for us in Munich, and he just told the Germans to get out. They were crying, "That's our apartment." He was not very sympathetic. We got the apartment, and they came ringing the doorbell, "We want to move back, this is our apartment." So I was angry, I said, "What are you talking about? I'd like to see my parents, too, what did you do to them?"

AD: And they just left?

SG: Yeah, they left. Looking back now, I mean, it was theirs, but look what they did to us. I was angry, it was just all bundled up, and all in a sudden it just had to explode. But Munich was great, it really was. We went to museums and we went to concerts, we went to the opera.

Oh, I was having fun. And I'm not the only one, I mean everybody had fun. I used to be a kind of golden-blonde as a child. And somebody said, "Oh, you got brown eyes. Blonde hair and brown eyes is unusual, how about bleaching?" So they used peroxide. And I came to the United

States as a blonde. And then there was a museum, it was kind of a meeting place of the survivors, and once in a while you can meet some which you knew. And we grabbed and we hugged and we were wild.

AD: During this time, did you reflect much on what had happened to you?

SG: No, not too much. I had a lot of living to do, because I didn't live before. Everybody felt that way. We ate too much, we drank too much, we just felt like a bird coming out [of] the cage. It's very overpowering, all that freedom. You were not told what to do, you could walk, you could go to bed when you wanted, you had nice beds and sheets. I mean, things you take for granted.

I didn't even think where I was, I was free, I was wild, and just go, go, go, go. People say, "Hadn't you thought about going back to school?" I said, "No, I wanted to live." That's the only thing. I mean twelve years out of your life, I didn't have a teenage life.

AD: Did you think much about the future, about what you would do?

SG: Well, I knew that we were coming to the United States. And finally, the day came when we left Germany. We came over on the ship *Marine Perch,* from Bremerhaven. And I think we were on water about eleven days because they had to stop, there were some mines, and they didn't tell us they had mines in the water until they deactivated it. But I would say there were about eight hundred passengers, maybe with the crew also, it was a very small ship. And it was not a luxury liner. From the eight hundred people, there might have been about forty, fifty who didn't get seasick. My aunt was seasick. I went down every day to see her and I want[ed] to bring her some food and she said, "Get out of here. I can't look at that food!"

It was just amazing to us, when we got to New York, all in a sudden those people start pouring out the ship, you know, you haven't seen them, "How did you get on? I didn't see you." But so many were sick. Then we had to wait, [because] relatives or somebody had to pick you up at the pier. They wouldn't just let you go loose. And [my cousin] came and he looked like a Färber, he looked like my dad, he looked like my brother, and we just start hugging and kissing.

I really loved New York, I wanted to stay there, but my brother wouldn't let us. He said, "Listen, we're going to make a home in Lexington, Kentucky. It's a beautiful little town. And that way we can be together, we don't have parents." And I listened to him and I stayed in Lexington. Do you know where he ended up? New Jersey.

AD: How did you get to Lexington from New York?

SG: By train. I remember it very well. Because there were no seats on the train, people stood up. People sat on their suitcases. It was just right after the war. Soldiers coming back. We couldn't even get near a window, would have to climb over people. And the ladies' restroom, they had a couch there. We had the nerve, Mina and I, we lay down on the couch. It was for somebody who got sick. But we were so exhausted, we fell asleep on the couch, and nobody woke us up till the night was over with.

We both were scared, Mina and I, we talked about that. Well, you come to a strange country, you're scared. All right, the Urbachs were related to my aunt, but they were no relations to me. I wasn't feeling numb then. I was angry, I was full of hatred.

But [the Urbachs] picked us up at the train station, and they really were great people. I mean, you don't know how you're going to be treated. But I just was a very lucky girl. Because they took me in right away. And Dolly, their daughter, said, "It's unfair, I have a curfew on a date. Sylvia can go and she can stay out." She was jealous of me, you know. But then, she didn't realize I was older. But they were wonderful to the day they died. I loved them dearly. And I always told them, "My God, you took such a chance, taking a stranger in."

But we didn't stay very long. My brother came in September and we rented an apartment and we lived on my brother's Army pay, ninety dollars a month, forty-five dollars rent. Water bill was cheap, two dollars, electric bill, and we made it, can you imagine? And we only had hamburger on Sundays. We wanted to be independent. Urbachs didn't want us to leave, but we wanted to get started.

AD: Tell me what you thought of Lexington.

SG: I loved Lexington. It was a small town. People were very friendly. In '46, it had sixty-five thousand people, and now it's bulging out in the seams, isn't it? I had to go to work in December, and I applied in factories, but they wouldn't take me, because I didn't speak English. I got a job at Wolf Wile's department store, downtown Lexington, wrapping packages. They were Jewish people. And I think they gave me a job because they felt sorry for me, and then I was a novelty. And I wasn't very happy, because I felt like it was demeaning. I said to myself, "You're not that stupid. You can do better than that." So I always sneaked out, and tried to wait on customers. By April I was on the floor, waiting on customers. The first year, I had the most sales for the year, and the second year the most sales. People were curious, so they waited for me.

AD: They knew something about your background?

SG: Well, it was in the paper. Refugees, survivors, you know. We were the only ones in Lexington. [*Mrs. Green retrieves the article.*] This was 9/27/46, and it was the *Lexington Leader*: "Polish Refugee, Ex-Prisoners Now at Henry Clay High School."[2] We just sat through English classes, American government classes. And then some of the students gave up their study hour to help us learn how to read. I thought it was very nice of them.

AD: Did people come in to Wolf Wile's and ask about what had happened to you?

SG: No, not really. They just wanted to see me, like I was a novelty. I would not have been ready to talk [about] what happened to me. It took years and years before I was able to talk. I didn't talk about it until '83.

In fact, people must have talked about this—a Holocaust survivor— and the buyer for another department store, Martin, came up to me and she said, "I really would like for you to work for Martin's. How much money do you get at Wolf Wile's?" And I said, "Eighteen dollars a week." She said, "We can do better than that, we can pay you twenty-five dollars." So, I said, "Let me think about it." So I went to Joe Wile, I thought that was the right thing to do because he gave me the chance. He said, "Well, if Martin's can pay you twenty-five, I can give you twenty-five." I did feel guilty because the people I worked with, some been working there ten, twenty years and didn't make more than twenty-five or twenty-seven dollars, but I told him, "You know, we need the money." He said, "I know." So people in Lexington were very nice, very decent.

My Aunt Mina got acquainted with people who had a photo shop, sold cameras and tripods and bulbs and everything. And she developed pictures. She was very good at it. My Aunt Mina was sick with cancer for four years off and on. And even if she didn't work, he paid her to the end, till she died.

AD: When did you meet your husband?

SG: I met Jake in September '47. The first night we went out, he took me dancing, we had a marvelous time. I always said, "How could you understand me?" We spoke some German, and then English. He said he understood me very well. So, we married January the 16th, '49.

My brother said, "It won't last." I said, "Why?" He had nothing against Jake, he just said, "Nobody could live with you any longer [than] ten days to three weeks." He meant well, but he was so strict with me. When I had a date, even before Jake, they had to come inside the house, he had to look them over—whether they were good enough for his sister. But I wasn't a child, I already was twenty-two, twenty-three years old, but he just took it on himself like he was my father.

But then, after we got engaged and everything was all right, he said, "Oh well, it's not so bad. I'm not losing a sister, I gained a bathroom." I had a problem after the war, I took an awful lot of baths—three, four times a day. We didn't have a shower. I just felt dirty. You know, you had lice in the camps and you were itching and it was terrible, you were dirty all the time. But everything turned out all right.

AD: Had Jake's family been in the Winchester area for a long time?

SG: Jake was born here in Winchester. They had the business downtown. When he was born, Pop, his father, already was in business. It was a small Mom and Pop store, with everything in there. The Hub Store, on Main Street. And he was raised on top of tobacco cotton [row covers for tobacco seedlings]. They had those bales, you know, rolled up. It's a miracle he didn't fall off.

He graduated from University of Kentucky in '36, and he couldn't get a job. So he just fell in there at the Hub Store, and then he was too lazy to get out. He always said, "We never going to be rich. You're going to have a roof over your head, you're going to have food on the table." And that's what we had.

AD: Did you talk to him about your experiences during the war?

SG: I don't think that we talked about it when we dated. But after we were married, we wanted children pretty soon, because he was thirty-four, I was twenty-four, and when I got pregnant with Jerry, that was when the nightmares started. He would come with dry, clean pajamas and a towel, and he sponged me off with a washcloth. He changed the sheets, it just went through.

The nightmare was the Germans came to take my baby away and kill it, because I saw many babies killed, and they just threw them against the wall, because they couldn't waste bullets. So, that's when we talked. He got me all dried off and everything, we would sit on the couch in the living room, and many nights we never went back to sleep. And all the time I lived with that man, he never complained. His ear was always there. One time I told him, "I don't know whether you're listening, but your ear is there." He was a good soul, he really was. I was fortunate.

AD: Did you have faith at the time?

SG: I didn't have much religion all during the war—and after the war, oh God, I was bitter. I blamed God, what happened and why. And I've still got a lot of whys. Thank God I got over the bitterness. The bitterness eats you up alive and it doesn't harm the people you hate. I couldn't even talk German after the war—a complete blank. I blocked it out. And my brother told me, "Sylvia, the German language is beautiful." I said, "The German language? I connect it with Hitler, it's not beautiful, it's terrible." And then to meet people who had anything to do with Germany or German descent, I had to run away.

And this kind man helped. He was so kind, because I just wanted to shut the door and that's it, not think about it. When I got married, and even after, I was an atheist, I didn't believe in anything. So after I got married, I still did not talk about it to anybody. It was like I was ashamed of it, like some of it was my fault. I knew it wasn't, but somehow I just couldn't talk about it. And then it was a small town with not many Jewish people. I already had one monkey on my head, to be a Jew in a small town, but the door would not stay shut when I got pregnant.

AD: Did having the baby change your experience with nightmares?

SG: Yeah, it got better. I mean, the nightmares were only once in awhile, and then later on, with Sandy, it got less and less. My son Jerry Walden Green was born June 1950, and Sandy—Sandra Ann Green, now Zuckerman—was born December '54.

AD: Did you continue working after you married?

SG: No. We had an agreement, Jake and I, that I wouldn't work. I was the good *hausfrau*. It was all right with me. I needed peace and quiet anyway. And then Jake was from the old school. Listen, we go way back. It was before your time.

AD: When did you become a United States citizen?

SG: 1952. That was a very important event, because I never was a citizen of any country. I was born and raised in Germany, but my father was a Polish citizen, and your nationality was what your father's nationality was. So, in Germany, I was a Polack. Then, after we lived in Poland, I was a German. So I never had a country to call my own, and this was a very happy moment. And I did good, I passed, I had no problems. At that time, I still had a good memory. I felt like an American, but I was very upset with the judge. They called you up there and you sat in front, facing the people, and all in a sudden he said, "I notice here you were incarcerated.

What were you incarcerated for?" And that's all it took. I start crying and screaming. Jake said you could hear me in the back row. "The only crime I ever committed was I was born to Jewish parents." That's what I told him.

AD: What did he say in response?

SG: "I'm sorry." Nobody heard him. I did.

AD: And did you feel at home in Kentucky?

SG: Well, that was the only state I knew. I would go to New York or New Jersey, to visit, but I only lived in Kentucky.

AD: When you would visit New York, did you meet people who had stereotypes about Kentucky?

SG: No, no. The funny part was, I had a silk blouse, that was the style, and *Sylvia* handwritten all over it. I wore that blouse, and a guy passed by and he looked, "Hi Sylvia, how are you?" I says, "Do I know you? I never met you." "Oh, yes, you know me." Then he start kind of laughing, then I look down, and I saw it. And so I laughed, I said, "Oh, you tricked me, I forgot I wore the blouse with my name on there." He said, "You're not a New Yorker." I said, "No, I'm from Kentucky." And he said, "I noticed the different accent." Oh, that is funny, isn't it?

AD: You didn't encounter people who thought Kentucky is just a place for hillbillies?

SG: Oh, about that, listen. I had a cousin, he's gone now, Cousin Harry, and that's the one I stayed with when I first came to the United States, and spent one week in New York. About a couple months after we were settled, he came to visit. He came because he was worried. He heard that in Kentucky people don't wear shoes, and they don't have many Jews, and he wanted to see it with his own eyes, and to take me back to New York. I thought it was very thoughtful, and very sweet, just the cousin who I met, you know. So, he fell in love with Kentucky, but he wouldn't move to Kentucky, but he thought it was such a quiet life.

AD: Did you encounter any anti-Semitism after you arrived in Kentucky?

SG: I found it more in Winchester than I did in Lexington. And they didn't even know about my past, because I had problems enough. I really don't know whether it was so much anti-Semitism as it was ignorance. Also, they didn't like strangers. They wanted Winchester to stay a little town. I have talked to people who were not Jews who came, and they had the same feeling, that they were not treated right. And I said, "I always thought they were anti-Semitic."

[My experiences during the war were not] made public until '83, when I made a documentary with [former University of Kentucky president] Dr. Otis Singletary—he was the moderator—and three survivors and two liberators. It was shown all over Kentucky. The reason for it was that in '81, there was a history teacher at Tates Creek High School who said the Holocaust never happened.

At that time I walked two miles every day, and people stopped me. There was a man one time, "Oh, I feel so sorry for you." And I said, "Please don't feel sorry for me. I'm proud what I've done with my life, and that's the past. I don't want anybody to feel sorry for me." He apologized, he said, "That's not what I meant. I meant what you had to go through as a child."

AD: Did it change how people related to you in general? Did they start to ask you questions?

SG: Yeah, [after the documentary and other local publicity] I think they accepted me more somehow. I think maybe they felt sorry for me. Right now, I'm part of Winchester, all in a sudden. The first twenty-five years, I did not feel like I was part of it. And really, after Jake retired in '83, I wanted to get out of here. And he didn't, he loved it here, he was born here, he was raised here.

AD: Did you talk to your kids about your experiences during the Holocaust?

SG: No. Sandy says it came out a little bit. She said, "We knew more than you think." My children were different. They were Jews in the little town. So I didn't want to load that on them, being a survivor, also. Sandy was the only Jewish child in the school system, the only Jewish child in high school. She had a stupid teacher, who said one morning before Christmas, "I was driving up and down Boone Avenue, all the houses were decorated for Christmas beautifully, except Sandy's house. Let's take up a collection." How do you think she felt? She came home and she cried.

AD: How did you convey a sense of Jewish heritage and history to your children?

SG: They are not observant like I am. We took them to the synagogue, we took them to Sunday school, we took them to Hebrew school, and that was about the best we could do. And I kept kosher. Friday night the candles were lit. Every holiday was a holiday. Passover, we always had college students. So what else could I have done? I mean, you come to a point that they have to do it themselves.

AD: When did you start to have a religious practice again?

SG: We joined the synagogue as soon as we were married, Ohavay Zion [in Lexington]. Jake's father was one of the founders of that synagogue. So, as soon as we got married, there was no question about it. We have been members for fifty years.

AD: Did you start to recover a sense of faith, or were you still an atheist, just going to synagogue?

SG: I don't know how it happened, it was so gradual, but it happened a lot more since I can participate. I always say I'm a reborn Jew. I was Bat Mitzvah eleven years ago, because women couldn't participate when I was a child. And when I was Bat Mitzvah, there were two other young girls. I'm the only old woman who was Bat Mitzvah, and I don't know whether I did it as much out of religion, as I think I was jealous of my brother as a child. All that attention and all the gifts. I knew his speech by heart, as well as he did. And they made such a big deal over him. So, in my speech eleven years ago, I said, "You probably are asking why I'm doing this now. I raised my children in a kosher home, in the Jewish religion, to the best I could. I don't know whether that has anything to do with the religion, I am Bat Mitzvah, or it was jealousy. I had to prove to myself I could do it." That was my speech. And I said, "I doed it."

But it was a lucky thing, because it helped me a lot after Jake died on January the 9th, '97. The people are wonderful. I'm almost the oldest one there. After Jake died, they came for a whole week here, just saying prayers. Sometimes we had up to thirty here, because they wanted to come. And if I don't go on a Saturday, I miss it. I feel like this is my family. And in fact, last Saturday, they were wishing me a happy birthday and clapping, you know. They called me up to say a special prayer, and I cried, I couldn't help it. I just looked around, there were people there, but I was alone. So one said, "What's the matter, Sylvia?" I said, "I feel so alone." And he said, "What are you talking about? We are your family." That was sweet. And it helped.

AD: Has it gotten any easier for you to speak about your experiences, over time?

SG: It still upsets me. Sometimes I wish it'd just go away. But the only way it's going to go away, when I go away. People should know, but . . . maybe I'm selfish, it just still gets me upset, and I don't like to be upset. I would like to live my life out in peace.

I feel like I've lived more than two lives. Looking back, if Jake would have lived, we would have been married fifty years in January. Everybody goes through some kind of hell in life. You're not promised a rose garden, and I always felt like, well, you've gone through your hell at a very young age, and everything was smooth, everything was fine. We had no problems here, the marriage was good, the children were wonderful, and then when Jake passed away, it hit me again. I just thought maybe I will have smooth sailing the rest of my life, but there's no guarantee.

I first visited Oscar and Fryda Haber in their Lexington home in May of 2000. On that day, I interviewed each of them, beginning with Fryda, who spoke carefully and graciously, yet somewhat reluctantly. Oscar, by contrast, was impulsive and eager to speak. Two weeks later, he and I continued our interview, and after five hours of taping, we had still barely begun to scratch the surface of his memories.[1] Oscar learned the English language relatively late in life, and sometimes his phrasing is difficult to understand. Listening to him speak is, nonetheless, a riveting experience.

Oscar Haber was born in Brzeźnica, Poland, in 1910. He was one of ten children (including a half-sister), raised in a family of devoutly Orthodox Jews. His family owned the biggest farm in the village; they kept cattle and horses, and grew everything they needed to survive.

AD: What language did you speak at home?
OH: Well, the first language we spoke, that was Yiddish. My father was very religious and he want us to know the Yiddish. But we had Polish Gentile servants, so we have to speak Polish, too. And [we were] surrounded by peasants who are speaking Polish and you have to know the language. In the school was Polish of course. When I went to school there was German, too. So I had German, Polish, and Yiddish, and of course, Hebrew, which was the liturgical language, to pray. At the age of three we

started already to learn Hebrew, and we knew to pray, and most of the prayings until today, I know by heart. And the first when you opened eyes at the religious house, the first [thing to do] is to wash your hands. And to make a blessing about the washing the hands and you make a blessing for the food and you have to thank God that you got up in the morning.

AD: You had the opportunity to attend a public high school, a big step for a Jew from a shtetl. Did you go to high school because your father wanted you to have special opportunities?

OH: Further studies wasn't the main purpose of my father. My father would have very much liked me to go on and study Jewish, maybe [even] rabbinical studies. But I was very stubborn. A cousin of mine was a dentist. And I liked the way he was living. My older brother remained Orthodox. I was enjoying more the free life. This religious life didn't match my character. I was always looking on the broad world, and life was, for me, more interesting outside the religious life.

AD: You mentioned that you were a Polish patriot.

OH: Yes. Deep in my soul I was Jewish, but we are living in a Polish country, this is Poland and this is our homeland and we owe to be loyal to our country. By [age] twenty-one everyone has to [serve in the] Polish Army, except somebody unable to fulfill the demand, sick and so forth. And a lot of my colleagues and a lot of Jewish people started to do everything to avoid to go into the Polish Army. I didn't try it even. I did it full-hearted, and I think it was my obligation to do it. I understand that it is a common responsibility when you are a citizen of a country, you live there, you have to do what belongs. I loved Poland. I loved the country. It gave us opportunity and then that's it.

AD: When you were in the Army then, in 1935 and '36, were you discriminated against at all for being Jewish?

OH: It's difficult to say, because you have so many things to do that you don't have the time to play these games. But the Polish officers generally, *generally,* were anti-Semites. Of course, they didn't want to show up as anti-Semites. But you could feel it, you could feel it. It was difficult to advance, to be a Jew and to be a high officer in the Polish Army.

AD: When war broke out in 1939, you wanted to fight for your country, and you went away to the Russian front. By that time you were engaged to your wife, Fryda. You were caught underneath the Russian occupation in the East for several months, and then you made your way back to your home village of Brzeźnica, where Fryda and your family were waiting. You and Fryda married in 1940. And then you were working in Pustków, a concentration camp. Were you interned there as a prisoner?

OH: No, never. That was one of the miracles of this war maybe. There were not many Jews who are allowed to go in the camp and to leave the camp. When I came to this camp, I volunteered. That was a working camp and therefore I was put into this camp as a dentist. At the end of 1940, I organized this little dental clinic there. And what could I do? If somebody has toothache, I could help, or to make an extraction, to pull out a tooth. And so in beginning, that was about a year, I had an SS ID, that I could come to the camp and I left. After a year approximately, there was an order to take the SS ID's from all the Jews. But, I think because I was there [as] a volunteer, there was an order of the commandant of this camp. He said, "The Jewish dentist can come to the camp whenever he wants. And every time when he comes, they will give him a post [an SS escort] who [will] bring him in the camp and when he is finished, he will come to pick him up and take him out from the camp." That was unbelievable.

AD: Did you know him personally?

OH: No. I knew the head of the working office. He was an officer in the Polish Army with a German name. Only when the Germans came in, he became a German. And he was very good to me. I was very good to him. I gave him all kind of bribes. And when I came to this post, I said, "I am the Jewish dentist. I need to go to the camp, please give me company." And they give me an SS man, who brought me to the camp. By the entrance to the camp there was another SS man, he gave me over to him. He opened the gate and let me in. And when I was ready, I went to the office and I said, "I want to go out." Well, it is miracle that I am alive and that I am here. But that was something which was really extraordinary. I didn't hear [of] a similar case in all my experience of camps and Jewish labor.

AD: Were you treating Jewish patients only or were there other prisoners there who you were treating?

OH: My treating [within the camp itself] was only Jews. But the SS commandant took my treatment—and other SS people came—in my private practice [at] home. Because in the house where I live I make also a little clinic what gives me my income. A barter business, people brought me food and I treated them. The SS were not allowed to go to a Jewish dentist, not to a Polish even, nor to a [non-SS] German. They had to go to an SS. But they knew that they will have a special treatment at the Jewish dentist, so some of them came. And that was a very difficult task, because I didn't have this modern equipment, which the German have. And there was a lot of cases which I couldn't treat them at all. But they were insisting, they were insisting. And so some of these SS people came in and they brought me also some tea, some coffee, because it was not on the market, even black market was not to get it. But the SS had everything.

In May of 1941, when Jews in the area began to be deported to ghettos, the Habers were told by the German authorities that they had a half hour to leave their farm. But because of their good relations with their Polish neighbors, they had been warned about the evacuation orders the day before, and so had time to transfer their belongings to a neighbor's house. Meanwhile, Oscar went to the regional governor and asked to be allowed to stay, since he was working in the camp as a dentist. Due to a miscommunication between the authorities, Oscar's family was allowed to stay as well—but they had to give up their home to Polish villagers who had been evacuated from their own homes when the Pustków camp was built. A Polish woman, Mrs. Soltys, who had two rooms in her house, took Oscar's entire family in.

The following May, when the area was supposed to be "cleansed of Jews," Oscar was told that he could no longer work in Pustków. One of Oscar's patients—a priest—offered to help by providing the Habers with false papers that would enable them to live clandestinely as non-Jewish Poles. However, these papers were only offered to Oscar and Fryda, who did not look Jewish, and who spoke perfect Polish, unlike other members of Oscar's family. Making the decision to accept the papers and leave his family was "the most tragic decision of my life," Oscar said. Only three of his brothers survived the Holocaust.

Oscar and Fryda were sent by the priest to a dairy farm, where they passed, with the help of their false papers, as non-Jewish Poles. Oscar posed as a Polish officer in hiding from the German Army. As such, he was soon asked to fight with the Armia Krajowa, the Polish underground Home Army, also known as the AK.

OH: Where I was there on this farm, there the Armia Krajowa started to organize. And I went there [posing as] a refugee from the German-occupied territory. I said I am from Poznan, and I am hiding away because I was a Polish officer and I am hiding from the German Army. I organized a sanitary station. When some of them were wounded they brought them to me and I gave them some bandages or some treatments.

AD: The AK has a reputation for being very anti-Semitic. Did you have any trouble or close calls with that? With anybody finding out you were Jewish?

OH: From person to person, I didn't. They didn't know that I am Jewish. We never spoke about it.

AD: Were you afraid at all during that time?

OH: Well that is difficult to say, afraid. But you are always watching what you are saying, what you are doing, not to be different. You have to drink alcohol, the moonshine like they are, and to do everything like they are doing when they come together. And if they are cursing, you have to curse, if it is damn, or another. Scared? Of course, you are always scared.

AD: Was your Polish good enough that you could pass well as a Pole without worrying about language problems?

OH: Our Polish was exceptional, very good. Otherwise the priest wouldn't give us papers.[2] Appearance and language, that was the things which was the most important. And there was no blemish in my language, and so till today the Polish people who come here and we are friends, they say our Polish is immaculate.

AD: Did you have any challenges with being in church and having to adopt this persona, where everything had to be just right?

OH: Not at all. First of all, I adopted it very easy because living in a village, you are involved in the peasant's life. And so I knew about the habits and about everything how the Poles live. And even being Orthodox, my father was very, very accepted in the peasant community. They respected him very well and they came and they lived together. And he spoke immaculate Polish and so did all my family. And interesting enough, the children all were speaking Polish [at] home, only when father wasn't there. Because we had a farm, in the summertime father was always in the field. When my father came, approaching the house, immediately we have to speak only Yiddish.

AD: Your family was unusual, then. I mean, it was common for Polish Jewish families to be segregated and to just associate with other Jews. But your family was much more integrated.

OH: Our closest Jew was living a mile from us. A mile in Poland is like hundred miles here. Distances are different. And the other Jews were coming to us to study religious things by the teacher which we have in our house. And they were really poor Jews, poor Jews.

AD: Did the people who were sheltering you know that you were—

OH: Oh no. They knew that I am AK, and that I am officer, but no, they are not suspicious that I am Jewish. Because the son, which is studying for priest, said, "If I will catch a Jew, I will cut in pieces and they should put salt on it." He was a very, very bad anti-Semite. At this time they were still teaching that the Jews killed Jesus and so forth. So, this young priest, no wonder that he hated Jews. That was indoctrinated.

On the dairy farm, Oscar became friendly with another farm worker: Franciszek Musiał, a non-Jewish Pole who was to be instrumental in Oscar and Fryda's survival. Eventually, Oscar drew Musiał into working for the AK.

OH: And this Musiał was a very nice man, very nice man. And he was not like the common peasant. He was already more civilized because he was working in France as a miner, several years. And we exchanged different opinions about the political situation. About the Germans, about the Russians, so forth. He was inviting me in his home. We are drinking and eating there. And he invite the neighbor. And I have also some news from my fellow man. So they accepted all the news from me as an intelligent Polish officer and Polish patriot, of course. And that was always with the alcohol, with moonshine. I drank moonshine in my life, maybe I could make a bath in it and swim.

AD: Was that hard to get used to? Drinking that much without letting something slip when you were drunk?

OH: I never allowed [myself] to be drunk. I always want to have my clear mind, because that was the most dangerous thing, to lose your mind. To be drunk. So when I felt, I run it out somewhere, I make like I am drinking another one, another one, but I didn't drink it. But still it was quite a bit. I am happy that I could tolerate it as much as I could.

In May of 1943, someone in the village who knew that Oscar and Fryda were Jewish denounced them to the authorities, and the Gestapo came to arrest them. They escaped, however, to the forest, where they made contact with a peasant who, at their request, contacted Musiał. Musiał then risked his life, and the lives of his family, by arranging for the Habers to live with his sister. They lived there and with the sister's son, passing as Polish Catholics, until the time of liberation.

AD: What happened towards the end of the war? Did you have information about the position of the Russian front through your involvement with the AK?

OH: Well, you could hear. First of all, there was a situation, more than four months. The Russians stopped on the river, they didn't cross the river Vistula to help the Polish resistance, the Uprising in Poland, for political reasons. They want the Poles to be annihilated by the Germans and then will go and kill the Germans. And we have all the news about the uprisings. In the bunker where our commandant was sitting, they had a radio, which they are listening to BBC, they have all the news and the movements of the Russian Army. And we are waiting, and then you didn't need the knowledge, you heard the bombardment with the Russians started on the river there, from a distance to bombard artillery. And then they started to move. And that was it. And so we became so-called liberated.

It was the greatest shock and the most difficult moment in our lives. That was the liberation. You don't have where to go. You couldn't find nobody you know, or anybody of your people. You cannot stay in the place where you were. We were in a village. They were not sympathetic to Jewish survivors. I survived not a Jew, but suddenly I felt that I am back a Jew. But I couldn't officially declare it. I had to stay on my Aryan papers. And how to go and where to go? Because to go to my other village where I was born, I wasn't sure that I will be accepted. And I wasn't sure to go to Kraków, for example, because I didn't have where to go. Even not where to sleep at night. And you don't have money. And you don't have nothing, because you have already sold out whatever you had. So, that was the most terrible time in all this events which we had, the so-called liberation. But when I came to Kraków, I started to settle, I start to organize my life.

AD: Did you feel in any way as if you were free?

OH: It was a very, very mixed feeling. On one side you felt the Russians are coming, you will not be more in danger as a Pole, but as a Jew, you continue to be in danger. And then came the reality. You find out what happened. Because until now, you heard only, they killed here, they killed here, they killed here. But the disaster so big, you realized only slowly when you were liberated. When you came to the big city, Kraków, which has before the war ninety thousand Jews, and you barely find five or six people which are Jews. That was a trauma. And you were asking yourself, why me? Because there were wiser people than me, speaking Polish better than me or the same like me, having connection with people. Why didn't they survive? And what is the role we have to play by being alive? Try to organize a Jewish life, or forget about it? No Jews, no Jewish life. You are Polish. Go on, be a Pole. And that's what many Jews did. There are until today Jews which are living as Poles. They said, "Forget about it." But we couldn't do it. Our roots are too strong.

We didn't know what to do. We were poor like mices. We had to find something to eat, not to speak about finding a way to organize your life, to start to be a human being. You start to realize you live surrounded in animosity. And you look for some Jews. And I found some. That was already in Kraków. I remember the first night we didn't have where to go. No home. But somehow we met somebody. I think I knew these people or recognize them as Jews. And I did ask him, "Who else is here?" He said, "Come with me." And I went with him. We came in a dark room and there were already several Jewish people, survivors from all kinds of surviving. And we sit there in this dark room and started to sing Yiddish songs, very nostalgical Jewish songs. All the Yiddish songs were sad, all were sad. But in this moment, they were healing. They were like balsam on a wound. Remembrance, for a moment, your heritage. And we passed this night, I don't remember, on songs and somehow sleeping sitting on a broken couch. All together there were maybe six, seven people. And each one with his song, not with story. We didn't talk yet about story.

But we woke up in the morning. We were in the clothes which we had, these poor clothes. We find out from one of them that one of my friends survived. And somehow I met him. He said, "I got back my apartment. There are two bedrooms, a kitchen on the third floor." But he says, "You can go there. And somehow we will find there some way to sleep."

But there were already some people in, which survived Auschwitz. And then came other people. We all were there, but we didn't have a bed to sleep. We slept on the floor.

And so we are being there with all these people around us, other people living there. And Fryda went to the apartment which was their house before the war. And there was the janitor, which was the janitor before the war. A dirty, drunk man. And she gave the address where we are living. And he, "And what will be if I bring you a post from your father?" And she says, "Well, you will get a hug and a kiss." A few days later he came with a card, postcard from Auschwitz. And he said, "Miss Fryda, I get a kiss." And she give him a kiss and a hug. "I got postcard from your father." And he is sick and he asks to come to pick him up.

So I went there with the Russian trucks, I went there with taking ammunition to the front. There was still war, but Auschwitz was already liberated. And he was the one who remained in the hospital there because he couldn't go farther.

AD: This is around January 1945. Did you know what had happened at Auschwitz?

OH: Well, I knew from Polish accounting, but when I came there I found everything. I didn't have the time and the courage to go to look what happens around. And when I saw him, I had all the history. That was a man who was taller than me and he was fifty-six pounds, I guess. I took in a blanket a heap of bones. And Fryda took care of him, and he came to his quite normal.

AD: At that time, were you thinking that you wanted to stay in Poland permanently?

OH: I didn't think so much about Poland. I didn't want to stay with the Russians. I knew the Russians before. Poland I wouldn't mind to stay, because I had my roots there, you know? With all minuses I thought I would be able to organize a good life in Poland, even I thought in my dreams, on our farm. I said, I will keep the farm. I'll keep a clinic there, help the people. And have a nice living on the farm. But when I thought about the Russians and their system, I would not have my freedom, so I start to think to move from Poland somewhere. The nearest approach was to Belgium, where Fryda has a brother of her father.

And we stayed in Belgium for five years. I organize, even illegal, a little clinic, and I treated Jewish patients, refugees who came there. But slowly I make a living off it and I had a possibility to make a decent living. In the meantime, as we have been there for close to two years, Israel was established. So I said, "I want to go to Israel." Well, Fryda's father didn't want to go. He preferred to stay in Antwerp. Well, he knew the languages and he had his brother there and he had the support from [his] two brothers, so he decided he will not go with us. In the meantime, our son was born. He was already two years old.

My uncle from the United States sent us a visa and he even want us to come to the United States. But I found that, after all we survived and surpassed, my place is Israel. This is the only place for a Jewish person to live. That was my conviction.

AD: What happened after the war that made you come to that conclusion?

OH: In Antwerp, where there was quite a number of Jews, when you were looking for an apartment for rent, it was in the windows written, "Not for foreigners." And that meant not for Jews. In some of the apartments was written exactly what I said, "No Jews." We came, and the administrator showed us the apartment and the conditions where it was not expensive. It was nice and the place was nice. And when it came to write the lease, he says, "Yes, but you are not strangers?" And we said, "Yes, we are strangers. We are from Poland." And he said, "But you are not Jews?" I said, "Yes, we are Jews." So, "I am sorry, I have instructions from the owner, no Jews. I am sorry, no Jews." And that gave me a lot to think about. So that means there is no place to live here for the Jews.

And therefore I decided to go home. Nineteen forty-eight, when Israel was declared [an] independent state, I was doing everything possible to go to Israel. I want to go home, because after all I am Jewish. There we have a state. I don't want anymore to be a stranger. I said, "That's the one place where nobody would tell me as a Jew you have to live. You have all the rights." And that was the reason.

It was a very hard time there in Israel, too. And when I decide we are going, we organize. We brought everything, because in Israel we knew there is nothing, refrigerators and the stove, furniture, hardware, what we need for the kitchen for a living. We took everything.

In April of '51 we left for Israel. And we rented an apartment, which was a living room and a bedroom, a hall, a kitchen and a bathroom. That was all. It was in Givat Haim, a suburb of Tel Aviv. I organized in these three rooms, the hall was the waiting room, the bedroom was the clinic. And there was a bed which was, in the day, closed like a cabinet. In the day I could accept patients. And the living room was the bedroom for us. We were sleeping there in the bedroom. And the child was there. There was a terrace. It was nice. After working there about two years, I made one bigger apartment and a separate clinic. And life became more comfortable.

AD: You spent some time studying in Germany as well. Did that happen after you had gone to Israel?

OH: Yes. I became vice president of the organization of the dental association in Israel. A big part of Jewish dentists in Israel, their origin was countries where they spoke German. And there was not world literature in Hebrew in this profession. So we needed German-speaking [lecturers]. So we started [to] organize at the universities in Germany some courses for professional progress. And I went to Bonn, where I stayed for three months. And I make my graduation doctor there in Bonn and then Marburg.

AD: How did it feel, as a Jew, to be doing these studies in Germany?

OH: In general, the staff of each of these universities were very forthcoming and very gentle and very willing to help us. Even we knew that some of them were with a Nazi past. The more Nazi they were before the war or during the war, the more forthcoming they were after the war. They didn't know, they said, about anything what happened before.

You come there, you have to accept the reality. Of course, you knew exactly that you are stepping on the burning ground. You know this is not the place where you should be. But it is not only there. This is the reality of life and this is the future of life. There is no place for you on this world. Israel has relations with Germany, with France. However, we know there are still a lot of anti-Semites. And they are everywhere. There are anti-blacks, there are anti-yellows, there are anti-Asians, there are all kinds of antis. This is the reality of the world now. You know, it sometimes is for me difficult to accept the general view of the Jewish world about the Polish anti-Semites, about Poland. I born in Poland. I got my education in Poland. I lived there. And I was a Polish patriot. And so were many, the majority. And to say that the Poles were all anti-Semites, I will not put them in this category. People are behaving very often, very different in different situations. There is in every human being, there is an *anti*. But you have to come to some point that you are living in this world, which is very differentiated, and if you will not accept this, there is no place for you. Because every day brings surprises. We are not done with wars. We are not done with discriminations. It was, it is, and it will be forever, forever.

AD: When you first moved to Israel, did you feel a sense of relief, or a sense of being at home, as you had hoped to feel?

OH: Well, this is a very sensitive question. When you came to Israel— how difficult it is to say—there was a gap between these born Israelis, long living in Israel, and newcomers. Like everywhere, a stranger gets feeling of a stranger. But in the beginning, a lot of people who were the elite in Israel came from Poland, Russia, maybe Czechoslovakia. Some came from Germany, too. Zionists. They felt [they were] the elite, and you felt [that they regarded you] when you came in with a feeling, "How could you survive? You must have done something which is not right, that you could survive the Holocaust. Because my parents, my uncle, my grandparents, my brother, my sister, they were killed. Everybody. Nobody is here. And you survive. You must be guilt of something. You have to feel this guilt."

AD: Did people actually say that to you?

OH: I heard it. It wasn't meant maybe special straight to me, but I heard it. I heard it in a quite clear voice. "These people who survive, they were collaborating with the Germans." And that gave you a very, very bad feeling.

AD: Will you say a little bit more about how you dealt with that? I mean, you had such high hopes of finding a place where you would really be at home.

OH: I was maybe more fortunate than the majority of newcomers. First of all, because I was involved in the Zionist organization, and secondly, because I knew the language. And that gave me a very great advantage not to be singled out. That was worse with people who couldn't communicate. And they had to communicate in other language, which was in Yiddish or in German, and the Israeli-born children didn't speak Yiddish. They didn't want to speak Yiddish. I think they're quite chauvinistic. And the same thing can be said about the long living in Israel. "We came here and we built this country. We fought for this country and we gave us a country." You know, that was also a very strange feeling. But with the time you got used to all kind of treatment in your society.

But the problem of Israel is not solved and will never be solved in my opinion. That's war . . . my son, for example, was in two big wars, in the Six-Day War and the Yom Kippur War. And that was one of the main reasons that he left Israel. He said he had enough of wars, when he came to the United States for studying his business, so he found that he would be better here. And he stayed here. And therefore we are here. We came after him, otherwise we wouldn't be here in the United States. I would be in Israel until today. And I'm not sorry that I did it, because I'm not sorry of one step in my life. I don't look backwards. I take the reality. I am here happy. I live happy. And so is my son. I have two grandchildren. My granddaughter graduated now from the university here in Kentucky. But she lives also to Austin, Texas, where my son lives. And our grandson is in Virginia Beach. So now we are without children and without grandchildren, but we have here very good friends. And we are happy here, making our life here.

AD: When your son was growing up in Israel, did he ask you about your past and about the Holocaust years?

OH: The first years, I myself couldn't talk about it, neither could my wife. And she is until today not so outspoken. And then concerning our son. In the first grade, he asked about whether we could help him with something in his homework. And mother told him, "I'm sorry, but go to Father because I don't know." So he ask a very simple question, "Mom, did you ever go in your life to school?" So it is difficult to say that we spoke with him about the Holocaust because it was a painful thing to go on to put it on your children. But of course when he growed up, when he went to high school and later on to military, he realized what happened and he asked some questions. But not too many, not too many, not too many. And I think until we came here, to the United States, he learned more about all of this than all his staying in Israel.

AD: I would have guessed that in the schools your son would have been taught about the Holocaust because he's living in Israel. But from what you're saying, it sounds as if there was not very much talk about the Holocaust.

OH: You are right. In the first maybe ten years there was no talk about the Holocaust. Later on, bit by bit it came out and they start to exchange knowledge of the world with all other countries in Europe and the United States. And the Jews from the United States used to come, family members looking, searching for family, and some of them finding. Here they found a sister, here they found a brother, after not knowing that they survived. So when they start to come somehow together it was more exposed in the reality of course, and this opened the door to more knowledge about the Holocaust.

AD: When did you first go back to visit Poland?

OH: I went to Poland about after fifty years. We decide to go when the parents of our good friends, which live here in Kentucky, came to visit here. It was a very old Kraków family which knew the business of Fryda's parents and he by himself helped one Jew to survive. And they are very, very nice people. We met them and became friendly. They really embraced us and they asked us to come to Poland, to be their guests there. And to see, "You will see it is not so bad." That was one thing. The other thing was we wanted to see our savior, Musiał, and his family. We wanted to see him because he was older than we are and we wanted to see him alive still. We supported him from Israel. We were sending parcels and money from time to time. And we supported him and he was very thankful. They were not rich people, very poor peasants. And he also wrote us that he will be happy to see us. So we decided we will go, we will see how it is. We had a very good time there. We went to these villages where we used to be in hiding. And we went there and met the people. There was a very exciting experience. And we really enjoyed to see everything from [this] perspective, it gives us some good feeling that we could do it.

AD: When you left Poland, there were people who didn't know at the time that you were Jewish, but you were friendly with them, such as the people who hid you. Did you have any encounters with people like that?

OH: No, I didn't meet more people. I will tell you, I didn't want these people to have different feelings, that I was Jewish and they couldn't know and could even help me, maybe they will be sorry that they did it. I don't want to put them in this conflict. You can never know human thinkings, human spirits, human soul. You never know. I don't want to hurt people.

AD: Do you consider yourself an American now?

OH: Yes, I'm an American, a loyal citizen, and I know about what happened in the United States, politically and socially, and I am very involved. I mean spiritually, because physically I can't more. But I am a Republican. I cannot say I don't like Democrats because they are democratic. But I don't like Democrats because they are more socialistic. And whatever smells of socialism or communism is for me a red flag.

AD: When did you come to the United States?

OH: In 1980. Because my son was living in Kentucky, I came to Kentucky.

AD: Are you a member of a synagogue here in Lexington?

OH: Yes, I am a member of the Conservative movement. I accept it. Many things which they change in the meantime [since I entered] the synagogue. There were no women called to the Torah. There were no women rabbis. Now there is. But if they ask my opinion, I will not be an exception. I am for the majority. You decided that you want it this way, I will agree. But not that I am fond of it, not that I like it. And that is my opinion.

AD: Do you have friends here in Lexington who are Jewish or non-Jewish? What kind of community do you have here?

OH: Well, I can say really friends are non-Jewish. This is the majority. These are really the Polish people, which are helping me in need, when I had to go to an emergency, I call to the Polish people. They come even in the middle of the night and they bring me to [the] emergency [room]. I don't have to go in ambulance. And other things also, they are really good friends. So, I really don't differentiate it. But they are my friends not because they are Polish, [or] because they are Catholics or they are Christians.

AD: Was it ever important to you to talk with other people about your experiences during the Holocaust? Did you get to a point where you felt like, "I really have to tell people that's what I experienced and to be around people who understand?"

OH: I was talking several times in school, whoever invite me to give them, I give them my own experience. But there was a Remembrance Day in the St. Luke Church where there are members, two or three Christians, which are my friends. And they are always counting on me that I will be the speaker. And I for nine years will be making the Remembrance. And they make it such a honorable day that was really a pleasure to talk to these people and to explain to them.

I must tell you, to my disappointment . . . I don't know, maybe not disappointment, but take the reality like it is. I didn't have occasion to say my opinion or even something about the Holocaust to Jewish people [in Lexington]. If they invited me to the temple when there was Remembrance Day, they were asking me to light a candle. That was all. And they were making some prayers. The same was here in our synagogue. And such a small number of people [come] that it is really not worth it even to open your mouth to talk to them. But I wasn't asked to talk about the Holocaust. I wasn't asked. They talk, they make some prayers, and that's all. And that was very miserable, miserable. I was ashamed that I was a part of this Remembrance Day. Jews are not interested in it. Maybe they have it enough in books.

AD: Do you feel that the people who were born here and who are from here have been less receptive to you personally than have the newcomers?

OH: Well, I feel it maybe personally, but I don't blame them. Maybe they were expecting more involvement from my side in their community life, which I couldn't do, first [because] of my age, secondly my language is not good enough. To speak with my accent, to talk about my experience and to be active in their community, it wasn't easy. The other thing is, one influential person told me that they feel humiliated in my company. That I am too special for them, so therefore they are hesitating approach me. I am a stranger for them and I will remain always to them a stranger. However, they are friendly. If I approach them they answer my questions, but that's all, that's all. What can you do? That's the reality.

I did not interview Oscar again until December of 2007. His wife had passed away two years before, and he now lived alone in an assisted-living facility. He answered the door in a black kimono, brightly patterned with cherry blossoms and figures of Japanese women, which he wore over pajamas. He apologized for his informality, saying he had been at a party until two in the morning and had forgotten our appointment. I marveled at how dapper he managed to look despite my knock having woken him up, and at the fact that at age ninety-seven he was still partying into the morning hours.

AD: When you were a young man in Poland, you had a strong Jewish identity, you had a strong religious sensibility in your home, and yet you were surrounded by Polish Catholics and you felt very comfortable with Polish Catholics. And now towards the end of your life, your closest friends are not Jewish, but many of them here in Lexington are Polish Catholics.

OH: [*Laughing*] That's right! That's the reality. I have here more Polish friends than Jewish, which are really my good friends and supporters in all kinds of ways of life. And they are Catholics and going to the Catholic church, and I am going to the Jewish synagogue. And they know that I am Jew, and I am invited to their parties, and they all know me as a Jew, and they are all welcoming me, and they are all hugging me and kissing me and happy to have me.

I am living the life now, American Jewish Polish. And that's what I am. I am American the same way that I was Polish. I never thought I would live here, because I thought Israel is my home. But I decide to live in the United States. I am a member of the Republican Party, and I love my life here. That's it. I have my grave already paid, and my bones will lie here, close to my wife where she lies. Unfortunately she passed away two years ago. And I am continuing. Sixty-five years together, in bad and in worse. What can you do? That's the will of my Lord. He gave me life, he keeps me, and I hope he will keep me as long as he wants. I am ready every day to meet him, when the time comes.

AD: Did your childhood in Poland prepare you for your life now?

OH: That's very difficult to say. I am not the same I was fifty years ago. I still think about my past and I remember everything, exactly everything. Nights and days and even hours. I remember, I remember, I remember the first people I met when I open my eyes. Who, what, where. God gave me the ability to remember. I don't know if it's good or bad. But that is his will, I cannot change. I am looking on the world, on my life, with open eyes, with a strong belief in reality. And in destiny. Whatever happens to me, that is destiny. You have to be prepared for everything, but this is my theory: a human being is the victim of his own destiny. There is no two ways you could go. You make plans, but you will go where the Lord will bring you, and there you will be.

Robert Holczer was born in Budapest, Hungary, in 1929. Soon after the German invasion of Hungary in March of 1944, the country's Jews began to be deported to Nazi camps. Robert and his mother ultimately managed to avoid deportation by moving into an apartment building that served, during siege of Budapest, as a clinic for wounded Hungarian Arrow Cross soldiers, who were Nazi allies. Meanwhile, with the secret help of an Arrow Cross officer, the clinic saved the lives of the four hundred Jews who lived in the building.

In the years following the war, Robert lived in Israel and Hungary before immigrating to the United States; once in this country, he lived and worked in Missouri, Colorado, Alaska, and California, and then Germany, before settling on a horse farm in Paris, Kentucky. By the time I began interviewing Robert in 1996, he had been living on the horse farm for three years. Our interview sessions continued occasionally over the next ten years.

AD: You have lived in so many places. Where is home?

RH: I was always a free spirit. I have always dreamt about freely roaming the world. And in Hungary my first favorite magazine was the *National Geographic*. I said, if I grow up, and if I can go and see all those places, I will never rest. So actually my intention was always, see as many places as you can, experience as much as you can. And I'm glad to say, looking back on my life, I have done my best. But I don't feel in any way disloyal to any place where I have been. I don't feel any bitterness—I left a place because I wanted to see something that was on the road, the next station.

AD: You don't have any bitter feelings for Hungary?

RH: That's the only exception. I never had really a childhood, I never really felt belonging to a country. Patriotism or anything like that was a totally unknown concept to me. Because I was not treated like a human being. The humiliation and the constant fear of being killed or tortured just took away all my feelings.

AD: Did you have particular interests as a child, or special things that you liked to do?

RH: I loved to bicycle. There was a so-called rose garden in the center of Pest,[1] and that's where I met with my friends every afternoon. And we were comparing our bicycles. So I was heartbroken when, in 1944, one of the first things we had to take in when the Germans occupied Hungary was the bicycle and the radio. I also belonged to an underground Boy Scout group. The reason I say underground [is] because we couldn't be legal Boy Scouts. The Boy Scout movement, which was based on brotherhood and equality of all, declared that Jews are not equal and therefore all Jewish Boy Scout organizations were disbanded.

There's one incident that I felt had very, very important consequences for the rest of my life. I really didn't pay much attention to being Jewish or not Jewish until this incident happened. In fifth grade, the idea of art was for the teacher to draw on the blackboard and then for the rest of the class to copy it and color it. The teacher came around and made sure that everybody's following his instructions, and just to emphasize that he means business, he had a big cane in his hand. And for some reason, I missed a couple of the colors and used something different. He became absolutely angry, and started to beat me to the point where I began to bleed through my nose. And I became frantic seeing the blood coming from my nose, so I ran home. The teacher was yelling at me as I was running out of the class, "I hope you go to Palestine to sell oranges. That's where you belong."

I ran into my mother's arms and asked her to clean me up and come [to school], and basically what I wanted is justice. Even at the age of eleven, I couldn't believe that this is going to be the way it is. And after she cleaned me up she said, "Now you must understand, I cannot go in and do anything except apologize for your behavior." So she came back to school with me and instead of demanding some kind of a remedial action for this, apologized to the teacher. Obviously, she was afraid that maybe they will kick me out of school if she does something else. Every Jewish family, of course, wanted to have their son finish middle school. And that incident somehow frustrated me to the point, it created a mental block. I never drew or painted in my life since.

So up until 1944, we had a great deal of anti-Semitism, we had a great deal of persecution of Jews, but we were not in fear of our lives. 1944, March (if I remember it) 19th, is when the Germans marched into Hungary. The yellow star [that identified Jews] had to be worn within a few weeks. And the deportations started. Unfortunately, that was the worst thing, the deportations. They started in the countryside, eventually coming to Budapest. Now, I also have to say that not many of my former Jewish classmates survived, because they were in a labor battalion and they were working outside Budapest on the day when the deportations came to that village.

AD: How did you manage to avoid being deported yourself?

RH: That was just a coincidence, that my aunt said to me, "Please, I just have some very bad feelings, I don't want you to go today out and work. Stay home, stay with me." She took me to her apartment and that was the day when it happened. It was just a miraculous instinct that she had. And that is what saved me.

Now, just to describe the situation in Hungary at that time: we were moved, because you could not stay in your apartment. You had to move first to so-called Jewish houses that had a big star on them, and eventually to the ghetto. So we moved out of our apartment in 1944, summer. My aunt said, "You stay with me," and then my mother came there, too. And this is how we got to this house in Zichy Jenő Street, in the Fifth District of Budapest. And it turned out to be a very fortunate choice because in that house, there was a famous Hungarian [Jewish] psychiatrist. This man had this idea that he is going to save his family and friends by contacting a fascist officer who is willing to play this game of declaring the house a clinic and do everything possible to save the people inside the house. The officer's name was Jerezian Ara George. And Hungarian names are in reverse order, so in English you would say George Ara Jerezian. I remember him, a very handsome man, kind of a man of stature, and a fascist uniform, hand grenades hanging from his belt. I mean, he was intimidating to anyone. With us, he was very kind. There were about three hundred doctors and families in that apartment house—jammed, absolutely jammed. While we could still live upstairs, probably there were at least five to ten people to a room. So this man moved in with a few of his men who apparently were loyal to him and his girlfriend and they set up their headquarters there. The clinic had its official emblem there and the whole operation looked like it was a legal operation to save anybody who is injured.[2]

Even in the last week, we were in danger of being taken to the Danube. That was the most common way of getting rid of Jews who were discovered outside the ghetto: [they were] marched down and shot into the river. It was a cold, bitter, snowy winter and the Danube was red and full of corpses. But I remember that even the last week, somebody from the neighborhood reported us to the fascist authorities and they came and tried to disarm Jerezian Ara George's own people in the house, the bodyguards. And he almost seemed helpless. We were already lined up and then he again arrived there, amazingly, he did this more than once, with some paper from a very special higher authority that said, "Clear out of here. This is a protected territory and we do our job for the government and leave us alone."

It was a very strange period for a fifteen-year-old boy. My job was basically to take legs and arms up that were cut off, operated on in the so-called operating room, which was a dark part of the basement, and kind of arrange them in the courtyard. And when, [after Budapest was liberated] on January 18th, we went upstairs, everybody was horrified. There were huge piles of limbs just piled up on the courtyard. The doctors operated without any anesthesis, anything. There was nothing, and of course the survival ratio probably was minimal, you know.

We did not play any games, because the day went by with constantly watching out to survive. We watched the streets, we listened to the radio. My uncle reminded me that my constant question to him was, practically hourly, "How long will this last? How long will this last?" We knew that the street fighting between the Germans and the Russians cannot be more than a couple of city blocks away. We saw German soldiers, injured, moving down the street and we heard the gunfire as if it were next to us. There was just no mood for playing. We were not children. None of us were children. All our conversations with the kids of my age down there, everything was always revolving around survival.

AD: Do you remember when the siege began?

RH: Yes. It was December 20th or something, very close to Christmas. Really, all of a sudden we were shot at from every direction. We knew that Budapest was totally surrounded. The airplanes were just coming day and night. They were called Ratas, these small Soviet airplanes machine-gunning anything on the street that moved. And it was a lot of noise, a lot of injuries, the stench of gunpowder and corpses came closer, you know? War has a certain smell, a very, very unpleasant smell that you can really honestly feel.

The entire Budapest lived in basements. I would say we were a few hundred people in that basement. It was a good-size apartment house floor, okay, just picture it. And everybody brought the mattresses down, and there were people very closely situated. In a way, it was kind of a warm place.

AD: So the medical treatments continued, then?

RH: Yes, yes, yes. Up until practically the last minute. And then the liberation, January 18, we heard a knock, and by law, there was an emergency entrance to every one of these basements between two houses that consisted only of one layer of bricks. We heard that a pick was working, breaking through. Must have been about five o'clock in the morning, and all of a sudden the furred hat of a young Soviet soldier came through, and then the whole body. This was first time, I think, that he got a hug from people, and he was absolutely bewildered because, of course, the Soviet soldiers were not welcomed with great enthusiasm anywhere since most Hungarians were hoping for a German victory. And we, we were just hugging and kissing him.

What did I do after that? Well, I did what probably is a natural thing to do. I went with the Russian soldiers and whenever they broke into a store—and they broke into every store that still had anything—I put back my yellow star and I went with them. After they were through and took what they wanted to take, I took what I wanted to take. I was full of hate, I was full of frustration, and I thought this was the way to get even, probably. I enjoyed the fact that nobody, nobody can really give me any orders. And my mother could not control me either, you know? I was now a man, and I was just intoxicated by this. So I had a little store there with all the stolen goods, and my father saw this when he came home and asked me what happened, and I told him. He was absolutely just horrified that I would do something like this, and made me take everything back to the stores where I got it from. And today, of course, I feel very good about this, but not at that time.

AD: You had left the house on Zichy Jenő Street.

RH: Yeah, I left it practically the day after we were liberated and went back to see what happened to our apartment. I think it must have been April or May [1945] when my father finally appeared.

In 1942, my father [had been] taken away. He was in a copper mine in Bor, which is Serbia today. And when he came home, I remember him coming up on the stairs with a rucksack. The rucksack was full of sausage and potatoes. He knew that we were starving, and so that was it.

I was very naive at the age of fifteen. For some reason, I thought that a better world is coming. And I was deeply disappointed when I heard that people survived Auschwitz, came home, and [were] killed in a pogrom in Hungary and in some other Eastern European countries. That made me very bitter, and my idealism and my naivete really evaporated.

Then a year went by and I joined the Zionists. There were a lot of things that appealed to me: the fact that finally I am going to have a homeland, there was adventure. And I became a youth leader in the movement and I loved to be with young people. Many survivors in Hungary, young people of my age, just chose this as a lifestyle. We received a lot of instructions in agriculture, in Hebrew language, in Jewish history, to prepare us when we go to Israel.

That was just a marvelous high of my youth. The Zionists did a fantastic job in catching the spirit of young people and really giving us what we wanted to have. We had a relatively free life, we had a picture of a heroic future for us, whether we are going to be serving in the army in Israel or just working in a kibbutz as farmers, almost everything about it had a kind of a super-human touch, that I'm going to be better than all these people around here who are running around like ants on the [streets] of Budapest, I'm going to lead a very healthy life. Also, until 1946 or so, most of the picture that we saw of Jewish people is like sheep going into Auschwitz. And all of a sudden these people come from Israel, they are beautiful-looking people. Not only that, they had courage, the way they carried themselves. The whole image of the Jew has changed in our mind and we said, "God, it's beautiful."

So it took me only a year or two to realize my real emotions: that I'm not a Hungarian, I never had a Hungarian passport, you know? I never had any Hungarian identity. I was always denied of being a Hungarian even though my parents were born in Hungary and practically everybody back generations [was] born in Hungary. And in 1948, the communists completely took over the government. They called it the Year of Turn. And all other organizations except for communist youth organizations were banned. So again now I was in the underground Zionist organization.

By early 1949, the situation almost was intolerable and the Zionist movement wanted to get as many people out as possible, fearing that if Czechoslovakia is going to turn also completely communist, that there will be no way from Hungary to go anywhere. By that time we could only go illegally across the border. At the age of eighteen, just a few weeks before finishing high school, my Zionist organization [gave] me signals that it was time to go to Israel because they couldn't guarantee that we would have more time. The communist police and the border guards were really closing everything very tightly. And I think it was in February 1948 that we took off for the border. And eventually, we ended up in Israel.

AD: What did you do when you arrived in Israel?

RH: Basically, I spent most of my time living in a kibbutz. I learned to work with the tractors at that time, and then, with a hundred other Hungarian youth, we received land near the Jordanian border by a town called Afula and started our own settlement. So, I was really working as a farmer on a kibbutz.

It was a very dangerous place. The first day we went out there was really hair-raising, because the tractor drivers had to go down and plow, and the weed in Israel is much higher than a human being and also we didn't know if there were any mines. And even though the army supported us, and they did give us generous support there, the tractor drivers had to go down and practically open up the area. And so we were very respected in the kibbutz for that reason. Above us was an Arab town, Tul Karem, which today is under Israeli occupation and still a very hot spot for riots. Of course, I had a lot of adventures because of living on the border.

One day I was plowing, and I had to have always a guard on my tractor with a submachine gun who was constantly watching because I was so close to the border. And all of a sudden we saw an Arab Legion patrol right by the barbed wire and they were motioning to us to come down and we said no. And so they went away. Next day they came and again they were motioning, they said, "Peace, peace." So finally they went back about fifty yards and they put their guns into a pile and then came back, showing that they had no weapons, and they told us, "Sit down on that side of the border. What can we do [to you]?" We said, "Okay, let's go down. What do they want?"

They just wanted to talk to us, and from there on, every day they would come down at a certain time. The Arabs have watermelon all over, so it was like a party, they would yell at one of these poor fellows who was working there, and this is all I learned in Arabic: "Hey, bring me a watermelon." And this went on for weeks and weeks. It was a very simple conversation because we had a language problem, it was mainly sign language, and these people were talking about their children, they showed pictures of their families, and the word peace, *Salaam*, or *Shalom* in Hebrew, was constantly mentioned. Eventually we really fooled our countries, because sometimes they came over and ate and laughed that they ate in Israel, and sometimes we jumped over and we said, "Oh, we ate in Jordan."

One day it was our turn, we stopped the tractor, we were already waiting for them on the other side, we put down a little blanket and all the food from our kitchen, and all of a sudden a totally different patrol is there. Apparently somebody saw them and reported them. These guys drew their guns and they are going to shoot us. And you know, that border was no joke, every night somebody was killed there, either an Israeli or an Arab. Very innocent people, they were shooting sometimes for no reason. So that was a very poisonous atmosphere, and the fact that my friend spoke some Arabic mitigated the situation. Finally the sergeant who was leading the patrol said, "You have one luck that I have a son of your age." He said, "If I ever see you even down touching the barbed wire, I am going to just make dust out of you." And of course, we never went back again.

I have a feeling that all of us involved, hopefully they are alive, will always remember this. It was the first time that I realized that an Arab doesn't necessarily have to be my opponent.

AD: Did you find what you were looking for in Israel?

RH: Yes and no. Yes and no. I had some very deep feelings about the country, as such, and then again, I was still a young man, eighteen, and I was also influenced by a great deal of these revolutionary Marxist ideas. At first I was very, very idealistic. Then as the country settled down into so-called peace, the usual symptoms that every nation in the world experiences surfaced, such as crime. And the fact that there were Jewish criminals—that shocked me. I was so naive that I thought that anybody [who] goes to Israel certainly doesn't want to do anything to hurt another human being. But I was still enjoying myself because I love to be outdoors, and we did the physical work and we had a very good self-image.

So when I left Israel, I did not just leave it with nostalgia. I left it because I thought that finally, somehow, in Hungary, I'm going to find that utopistic state that [offers] justice and equality for everyone. And I was just a little bit too stupid to think that way, but I did. It was part homesickness for my parents and part stupidity that I believed that things are the way communist papers describe it in Hungary.

And in 1951, I returned to Hungary. When I arrived, I realized that it was a fatal mistake. It was the grayest, most colorless, most suspicious, paranoid society you can imagine. I was an imperialist agent, as far as they were concerned. Not only that, I was a Zionist imperialist agent. It took me almost six months to get a job to sweep floors and clean oil off the concrete in a state-owned garage.

Through a series of fortunate incidents, Robert was eventually admitted to a university. He graduated with a degree in geography, after which he became a teacher.

RH: And I was running the geography group. I took them to hike and I taught them orientation in nature and everything that was romantic in the Boy Scouts. And from this, I organized a group of very enthusiastic kids who eventually would follow me anywhere, and so then people saw this and they hired me to run big camps. I still corresponded with many of my kids who were in my group as adults. And when I went back ten or fifteen years later, some of these kids were running the same kind of camps and organizations, and they said, "You know, if you had told us that in the middle of the night we have to leave our homes and assemble in a place, we would have been up there. And we would have been following you all the way out to the border."

Then I taught in a junior high school in a working-class suburb of Budapest until 1956, when the [anti-Stalinist Hungarian] Revolution broke out. And I had very ambivalent feelings about the Revolution. I was not a Party member, they knew that I was not also an anti-Party member either because, as a Jew in Hungary, as long as the Communist Party was in power, there would be no pogroms and your life is safe. I understood the anger of the people and I sympathized with the desire to have a free country, but I didn't trust some of the groups that participated in it. And what really precipitated my departure is that I saw some groups with Arrow Cross [Hungarian fascist party] armbands, and that did it. All my desire to ever do anything or to stay there just went away. Right in that moment. I realized that this is now when I have to leave. There will be absolutely no peace for somebody who has a Jewish background or favors a peaceful lifestyle. Hungarians, with the Austrians and Poles, [are] probably the three most anti-Semitic countries in Europe. I felt much less anti-Semitism, frankly, in my nineteen years that I recently spent in Germany than in Hungary or in Austria. And I told my parents, "In two weeks, I'm leaving."

In November of 1956, Robert and a cousin escaped Hungary, illegally crossing the border into Austria. Robert never intended to come to the United States.

RH: I wanted to stay in Europe. But my cousin got away from me, and left a note for me to come and follow him. And I promised his mother that I would take care of him, so I followed him. The Red Cross sent me to St. Louis, Missouri, to be reunited with him.

My cousin stayed with me for about two months, not even that much. Well, I [realized] that I was in a trap. Once you were placed in a country, you couldn't really do much about it any more. So I knew I had to make the best of my stay here.

Since I came from a communist country, and before that a fascist country, the U.S. was never painted as a country that is desirable to live in. All I heard about it was negative. However, my father was a very enlightened man, and he raised me on the truth, so I knew that this is the country of the free. The thing that bothered me a great deal about coming here . . . I was never that much in favor of modern times and fast times, and a landscape with skyscrapers, that was not my vision of my future life. I was a typical European, who felt a lot more comfortable on a narrow street with half-timbered houses, and a lot of people on the street, and sidewalk cafés, and little restaurants. I had no qualms about the United States politically, but I was worried about how can I adjust to a place that doesn't have much tradition.

I became an American citizen in 1961. Unfortunately, in the twentieth century, the fact that you are a human being, with two eyes and a nose and everything else on you, is not sufficient proof for you to travel around the world and be protected by international law. Considering all this, I felt much safer now that I have a country behind me and I am protected in case I am in trouble somewhere. I do not have nationalistic feelings, as most people would have. The flag or a national anthem doesn't really mean much to me. I don't consider that patriotism. But I like a lot of things here, especially the Constitution, and I appreciate the fact that I can live a free life, and for them I am very grateful. My patriotism manifests itself this way, and not by waving the flag. I'm not a person who really believes much in national identity. I feel that causes more problems, that and religion, than anything else.

[In St. Louis,] I was within weeks working for a wholesale jewelry company. I was just a stock boy. Very simple work. It was a German company basically, and you cannot name a group or a race around the world about whom they were not talking during the day, always in very derogatory terms. And luckily, when I became very, very upset about this, my black fellow workers invited me on weekends to go around with them, because they said one cannot just sit at home. And they introduced me to the St. Louis that most people who were born there, probably, wouldn't know. I went to just about every nightclub, I heard just about every jazz band that came to St. Louis. And many times, in a huge dance hall, I was the only white face. Of course, sometimes, I ran into almost trouble too, because of that.

AD: So you came with some ideas about this being the Land of the Free. Did it surprise you to see what a division there was in this country, the problems with equality?

RH: Yes, yes, that surprised me very, very much. In one of these weekend excursions, I was introduced to a very charming college student, she was black, and we started to date. Eventually, she explained to me that we cannot see each other any more, because her life was in danger, and my life was in danger. She said, "You don't understand this now, but twenty years from now you will understand. And as much as it hurts me, we have to stop seeing each other." That was my first great introduction to prejudice, really, on a personal basis. I came from a society that was tremendously prejudiced, and I thought I am coming to a society that is much more positive about these things. It really surprised me that there was so much dislike and hatred, that I knew could not be erased very soon.

And then eventually, I met a professor of Hungarian ancestry and origin at Washington University in St. Louis who had in Aspen, Colorado, a house, and he and his family spent every summer there because he was a member of the music festival. When they heard that I was very unhappy, they took me to Aspen, and they said, "You can always work here for a dollar an hour, too."

I loved it. I stayed there for almost three years. And most of my friends and connections and everything in my American life practically comes from that period. So, I was very lucky again to end up there. Of course, those days Aspen was not what it is today, you know. What appealed to me is, number one, up [at an altitude of] eight thousand feet, you need each other. The winters are pretty harsh, and the summers were filled with tourists coming to the music festival. You needed other people's help and you had to help others, too. There was just a camaraderie there, a very open attitude that appealed to me a great deal. I felt so free. There was so much color in the place. All kinds of people coming and going.

As Aspen became more and more fashionable, everything became more expensive. Besides, I had no interest in opening a business. I always thought of myself as an educator. I wanted to go back to school, and luckily, I got together with some adventuresome kids, and they told me about Alaska. They said that in Alaska you can make a lot of money and it's fascinating and beautiful. I loved to travel, so it was just a spur of a moment when I decided that at the end of the season, around April, I would go and follow them. I went up to Alaska and worked for the Forest Service and then, that fall, I was going back to school in Fresno [California]. Why Fresno? Because I had trouble getting my records together from Hungary. And so, a college had to accept me on my word, and apparently [many colleges] were afraid to do that. But Fresno said okay, you can come, spend a semester, we'll find out how you function here. And I stayed in Fresno for two years, when I got my teaching credentials and my master's degree in history. And then I ended up in the [San Francisco] Bay Area, where I wanted to be.

When I arrived at the Bay Area, for me that was just incredible. I practically pinched myself every morning when I woke up and I saw the sun and looked around. It's almost like Europe in the United States, when I walked the streets of San Francisco. I lived in Tiburon, which at that time was affordable for a bachelor schoolteacher like myself. Today, of course, it would be impossible. And I had a nice little apartment in a duplex, overlooking what they call Raccoon Straight. The sailboats were going back and forth all day. And those days, I just was a restless spirit. I had a tendency to walk down at night, and see the lights of San Francisco, and feel that there is something going on in the city that I'm not part of, and I just have to hop into my car and go there. And I did that, and it was then twenty minutes, I was in the city. I was walking around and I was happy. And then I looked back and I saw the lights of Belvedere or Tiburon or Sausalito, and I felt that something must be going on and I'm not part of it, so I hopped in my car and went back. So I was just restlessly looking for that unknown beauty which really was around me, all over.

It was very difficult to get a job for a teacher in the early sixties, and the only job available, finally, was teaching special ed classes. And I said, children are children, I don't care. I thought of the old Hungarian proverb that said for something that you like, you would even let people chop wood on your back, and I strongly believe in this. And this is where I met my wife. She was also teaching special ed classes.

But I was thirty-six and a bachelor, and I just was not going to get married without giving it some thought. So, I signed up for one year to go and teach for the Army in Germany. And I arrived there, and I spent a year in Germany, and that year convinced me that yes, she would be the right person for me, so I came home. And we got married on the top of Mount Tamalpais, the mountain I loved to hike around, and the mountain we both saw every day, coming and going to school. I married my wife with three children in 1967. They were tiny, their father abandoned them, he was alcoholic. And so my wife and I raised them.

AD: Did you talk with your wife, in the early times of your getting to know each other, about your experiences during the Holocaust?

RH: Yes. She really wanted to know everything and I told her everything. And she read a great deal. As a matter of fact, she is my police woman, because she doesn't allow me to watch anything concerning the Holocaust on television, because she says I have such nightmares that she doesn't want to wake me up. But I was amazed after we got married, how much time and effort she spent in reading books on Jewish history [Jan is not Jewish], and then, of course, her favorite theme, cookbooks. So today, when somebody ask me about some Jewish custom or holiday or something, I always refer them to her, because she knows a lot more about it than I do.

AD: During that time, were you aware of how Americans in general thought about the Holocaust and Holocaust survivors, and some of the stereotypes that were attached to them? And did you think of yourself as a Holocaust survivor?

RH: Now that is a very surprising question, because I never really thought about it, but as you were asking me, I realize I didn't really think much about myself any more as a Holocaust survivor. I just thought much as a member of the scene, so to speak. I was more involved in what is happening in America, and thought more about it day by day, than to give too much thought about the past. So, in this respect, it was good, because one should not constantly be visited by ghosts. And you know, I was part of the whole story then—an American fighting to end the [Vietnam] war, and bring justice to people who were oppressed.

[My parents] came in 1967 to visit. And my mother would have loved to stay here. My father, he was just used to his life in Budapest, and he was very anxious, eventually, to get back. And my father, who has always been around little businesses in his life, did the usual thing that people from Eastern Europe at that time did, traveling to the West: they were constantly counting what certain merchandise would cost in Hungarian money. So, his favorite place was Long's drugstore, which is the equivalent of any big drugstore chain in our area. If the rest of the family did something and he did not want to be part of it, he just said, "Oh, just drop me at Long's drugstore," and he would spend an entire day at Long's, going around, looking [at] everything, figuring out prices. The employees began to get a bit suspicious, what is this man doing here, and he was smiling always, because he couldn't speak a word of English. So, finally, I explained to the people, and said, "This is my father, he doesn't speak any English, and he loves your store. We drop him off here, he's totally harmless. He never killed a fly in his life." And every time we picked him up from Long's drugstore, he learned this sentence to say. First he said it in Hungarian, then I taught him how to say in English, so the children can understand. He says, "This country is invincible."

In 1974, Robert, Jan, and the children moved to Germany. They had both gotten jobs as teachers, working in the Department of Defense School System. They lived in the Frankfurt area for the next nineteen years.

AD: What was it like living in Germany all those years?
RH: Well, it was much more pleasant than I had envisioned, frankly. Naturally, there is an element in Germany that is the scum of earth, but they are very much the minority. So, there is a new Germany. And we befriended Germans who were a lot more even liberal than we are. I mean, you can find all kinds of people. Yes, I heard anti-Semitic remarks, and sometimes, when I felt that it was the proper thing to do, I responded, and sometimes when I looked at the person, and I [realized] it was a primitive old idiot, there was no reason to say anything. I concentrated on talking to people of the middle and the younger generation. And I found that intellectually, at least, they understood what was the Holocaust. They were very ashamed and sorry about it.

I could have gotten German citizenship, but there are so many reasons why I shouldn't have done this, right? Number one is an emotional thing, a rational thing . . . that would be a little bit too much for me to bear. Second is that I have an American family, and my wife was ready to return to the United States. There was no way would she have stayed in

Europe with me. So, I knew that this was temporary, and I enjoyed [it] while it lasted.

When the military was in a drawdown situation where they were pulling out quite a few troops from Germany, my wife reached the point where she just said she wanted to be close to the children. We have four grandchildren. This house [in Paris, Kentucky] was available. My brother and sister-in-law, who own Briarbrook Farm, had called and asked us if we would like to buy a home here. My wife, of course, immediately knew it was going to be our home. I considered maybe just an investment. Because I had no intention to come here. I wanted to be near a big city and I loved California. [But] my wife said, "Look, I stayed in Europe for nineteen years with you, now I would like you to stay where I would like to be, and it is so nice to be so close to family."

We used to visit here almost every summer while we were in Europe. I was always very defiant when it came to this place. I never really opened my eyes as to what is here, rather would sulk. Not in a very obvious way, but call it an inside sulker. That's what I was, sitting on the couch during the day, and occasionally complaining that there is really not much to do here. As I put it to my wife, an area that doesn't even have sidewalks in town, to walk around, what am I going to do there? And also the fences bothered me, that you can't go anywhere, everything is fenced in. And how can you take your mountain bike, and bike somewhere? You run into a fence within minutes. And then, the last time we were visiting here, I think it was in '91, I was walking around, and all of a sudden my past caught up with me, because I spent a great deal of time, as a young kid, out in nature. All of a sudden, I began to smell and look at the very things that were so dear to me when I was little and I was constantly hiking with my friends. And I realized that this is not a bad place, and besides, it was so peaceful. At night there was no noise. And so I came back and the whole family was around because we were celebrating our wedding anniversary. And I said, "I want to say something to you. I just made up my mind, I can live here very well." And that was the end. All my sulking went away, all my reservations went away. I knew that there is not going to be any half-timbered houses, but I thought that I can make the best of it, and that I can live here.

AD: Did you have concerns culturally, what it would be like?

RH: Yes, that was my main concern. I had reservations and I still have reservations. I am still yearning to go to a town where the streets are crowded. I don't want to live on a crowded street all the time, but sometimes. And I want to go to a sidewalk café, and I want to eat some different food that doesn't taste the same, and just converse with people. Violence really kind of poisoned the atmosphere in this country a great deal, and I'm very sensitive to that. So, I would love to just go to a park and sit on a bench sometimes, and just talk to strangers, as I used to when I was younger.

With neighbors, I just don't have that much in common. One neighbor next to our farm is a hog farmer, and I don't know anything about hogs and he doesn't seem to be interested in many other things. However, my association with the so-called Master Gardeners Association in Lexington brought me together with people. I do volunteer work for the arboretum, and these are the people that I am the closest to, because we have a common interest, gardening. But since I came back [to the United States]—and that has also something to do, of course, with my age—I have not found anyone that I can call a friend.

AD: Do you feel that you can live here [in Kentucky] and be at home here for the rest of your life?

RH: Oh, I settled this already with myself. That's it. This is my last station. I am here for good, and naturally, this is not a bad place to be. I could think of some other places where I would rather live, but I am here now, and I make the best of it.

AD: You mentioned that you talk with school groups about your experiences during the Holocaust.

RH: I do this with great pleasure, because I know that in this area, there are very few people who experienced the Holocaust, and even know what it is. And so, one schoolteacher started this program in the local schools, and she always invites me, about two, three times a year. These are usually kids, thirteen, fourteen years old, and I like to talk to them, because that's how old I was when the real disaster hit me. And so I can kind of get down to their level of understanding and explain certain things to them. And I find that they are very receptive, very receptive. So, I consider it a mission.

Just yesterday, I was speaking to a class. And one little girl just stood behind and she was waiting for me. After everybody left, she came up, and she hugged me, and she kissed me, and she said, "This is for all the missed love and kisses that you could not get from your parents during those years." I thought that was just charming. And she just turned around and left.

AD: You mentioned you hadn't experienced anti-Semitism in Kentucky. Have you experienced anybody just expecting you to be Christian?

RH: Yeah, that comes around a little bit more often, when people just cannot comprehend how can anybody who doesn't steal, doesn't cheat, doesn't embezzle, has been married for thirty-three years . . . why am I not a churchgoer? Not only that, when I say I'm a non-believer, of course, I think I'm out of their favors. But I try to make a point there, too, that one does not have to go to church and belong to a religion to lead a decent life.

After my Bar Mitzvah I never probably went to synagogue again, unless it was a tourist attraction, I just wanted to see what is inside. But I never denied my Jewishness. So when my grandchildren especially ask me about religion, I say I am a Jew but I'm not Jewish. And they ask me, "How can that be?" And I said, "Well, it's easy." It's a strange thing that I have never been somebody who believes in the supreme being. And then of course, the war probably wiped out, if I had any doubts.

AD: Do you have any contact with other Holocaust survivors in Kentucky?

RH: No, no, I don't know anybody. I really don't have any connection to any other group.

AD: You live in a rural area of central Kentucky, and I'm interested in hearing your perceptions of how people in the area deal with minority groups, such as migrant workers.

RH: Right now, in the Bluegrass, everybody who can think knows that Mexican workers are fulfilling an important job. They are working here in a job that most other people wouldn't take. So, nobody has great reservations. But my biggest fear is, what is going to happen when this economic boom ends, and here we will be with these people? If they don't work, what will happen to them? I think that we need more education, especially in the schools, to make these people welcome. They are here for a reason, they are human beings, and just like anyone else in America, they came in by the same rights. If there is illegal immigration, that is not for Kentucky to try to stop it, because we can't, it has to be stopped down on the border. But those who are here, they are here. So what are you going to do? But the churches, the schools, any institution, I think should work together to make sure that people know that these are human beings, these are not some alien group that is here only temporarily. They are not here temporarily.

AD: When you think about this issue, do you draw parallels to the experience of Jews in Europe? Do you think that makes you particularly sensitive?

RH: Yeah, in this respect, there is a comparison. They would be made scapegoats, the minute the chips begin to fall. But I don't think that in America we ever have a danger of the death camps or concentration camps any more. I'm more afraid of individual treatment of these people.

AD: In each of the places you've lived, you've had a tendency to sympathize and become friends with people who are entirely different than yourself. To what do you attribute that tendency?

RH: The underdogs. I mean, my father comes from a very poor proletarian family, and so I think he gave me the initial introduction to always stay with the people, don't forget them. My father was a socialist, and I always sympathize with his views. Even today, I consider myself a social democrat, in every sense of the word. And I consider it a mission to explain to my fellow Americans that a socialist has nothing to do with communism. That the socialists were the first ones to be persecuted when the communist regime triumphed in Eastern Europe. So I always feel for the underdog, and I don't know if it's part of being a Jew, or has nothing to do with it, but I taught my children and grandchildren to feel that way. And I am glad to see that every one of them turned out to have the kind of sympathies I feel for people who are persecuted.

AD: The word "peace" has been a recurring theme in our interviews. You left Hungary for Israel in 1949 because you believed there would never be peace in Hungary. You came to believe there was a place in which you belonged, and that it was Israel. You described the exhilaration of the discovery that there was this utopian community you could belong to. When you went to Israel, that evaporated. The Jordanian border patrol you befriended, your common word was *Salaam,* or *Shalom.* When you returned to Hungary, you thought peace was possible there, and of course were disappointed. I am wondering, what happened to that sense of utopian idealism, and is peace still as important to you as it was then?

RH: Well, you can call me a fool, but I believe that one day maybe mankind can live in peace. If I didn't believe in this, I don't think I could get up [the] next morning. What is there to live for, if you don't believe that one day perhaps there can be a universal peace? I don't think it will be in my lifetime, or even in my grandchildren's or great-grandchildren's lifetimes, but it should come, we should reach that point. Yes, I am called by every name by cynics, but I can't help it. That's just my opinion and nature.

Eventually, the feeling of being culturally isolated began to make Robert and Jan feel unhappy in rural Kentucky. In 2007, they moved to Portland, Oregon, where they are near close friends.

CHAPTER 4

Abe Jakubowicz

Abe Jakubowicz lives in a well-kept ranch-style house on the outskirts of Louisville with his wife, Frieda. At the time of this interview, in 1999, Abe still helped to manage his family's five 20/20 Eye Care stores in central Kentucky, although at age seventy-five he had begun to pass the reins to his children.

Abe was born in Piotrków Trybunalski, Poland, on September 24, 1924. When Germany invaded Poland in 1939, Abe and his family—his mother, father, and younger brother—were living in the town of Grodzisk Mazowiecki. There, his father worked as a dealer in leather by-products. In 1941, all the Jews of Grodzisk were forced to move to the Warsaw ghetto, about twenty miles away. A few months later, when food in the ghetto became scarce, his family escaped to Piotrków, where they were again ghettoized.

In the Piotrków ghetto, Abe's father worked as a slave laborer in a glass factory, and Abe worked for a company that made office furniture for the German Army. Then, on October 13th, 1942, the ghetto was encircled, and most of its inhabitants were deported to the extermination camp Treblinka, where they were murdered on arrival. But the two thousand people who worked in the glass factory, including Abe's father, were allowed to stay. While Abe was on the platform awaiting deportation, his mother had the foresight to volunteer him as a carpenter, so that he could stay as well. Abe's mother and brother, however, were taken to Treblinka. A few months later, several hundred more Jews were taken from the ghetto and murdered.

AJ: In fact, there is now a monument where six or seven hundred people got killed. They took all the people in the synagogue, a lot of them kids—they got shot inside. You cannot describe it. After two or three days, the screaming, they took us out and we were supposed to be shot. And when they took me out, there happened to be a gendarme, a German police man, whom I worked with. He says, "Hey, what are you doing here?"—like I volunteered. Kicked me out of it. "You don't belong here."

AD: Do you think he intended to save your life?

AJ: He intended, yeah, because he saw that I had a job. See? Most of them [who were killed], they were hiding out and they had no jobs, and there was a lot of children. But he knew that I worked there. Not because he wanted to save my life. He only knew that I worked for him. I didn't know this guy at all. He was a stiff man, was an older man. In fact, a day or two before, he shot a girl because he thought that she stole a pair of stockings.

You know, this didn't come overnight. You saw it all the time. When they took the people to Treblinka and somebody didn't go fast, they shot him. When an older woman couldn't move, they shot her. You saw literally corpses everywhere. My mother tried to keep me sheltered, but I knew it. We could still not believe it. Why would they take people and put them to death? Always, as long as you live, you have a little bit of hope that the people are lying. But deep inside we knew it.

AD: After this gendarme took you out of the group, the other people who had been gathered were taken away?[1]

AJ: I did not know that they got shot. Rakhov was a little bitty forest and they shot them. I found out when I was back in the ghetto, because they always took other Jews to cover the graves.

AD: After a few days, you were separated from your father, who remained in Piotrków. You were among twenty boys and twenty girls who were sent to Tomaszów Mazowiecki. You were there a few weeks. What were you doing there?

AJ: Same thing what we did in Piotrków. We made shelving, and then they brought everything together and shipped it to Germany. When this was finished, they didn't know what to do with us. Luckily for us, they sent us to Starachowice [a labor camp in Poland].

AD: Where you made ammunition for the German military.

AJ: That is right. That was around June or July of 1943. Starachowice was a big ammunition factory. So, I worked there and it was very hard and very hot. Luckily for me, I met a guy whose brother worked in the kitchen. And by risking his own life, he brought us always food in the evening. Ironically, he didn't survive. Was a very, very good person. He didn't want nothing in return. In life, what I found out everywhere, you need a little bit luck, but other people will help you. You have to be in the right spot. And you can say it's God's will, if you are religious.

AD: Speaking of religion, was that an important part of your life?

AJ: Religion was a very big point until 1939. We went Saturdays to the synagogue. We ate kosher. You know what kosher is? We Jewish people separate the milk, you have to wait when you eat meat six hours after it.[2] I knew what I was. I knew where I belonged. Later on, I suffered because of it, but it was not my main thing.

AD: You mentioned that when the war started, that changed. Did your feelings about religion, about God change?

AJ: No, what had changed is that you couldn't go in the synagogue no more. Because they shot you, or they beat you up if you was lucky. So, we were scared. If you ask me now, I think God is for everybody. There's not a Jewish God, there's not a Catholic God. It's a God, you know.

AD: At the time you were in Starachowice, you were separated from your entire family. You didn't know whether they were alive. Was there even time for that kind of questioning?

AJ: Number one at that time is survival. You ask yourself, "Why me, oh Lord?" But you want to survive, regardless. We become simply like animals.

In Starachowice, when the Russians came too close, there was already a train standing. We did not know where we are going. We thought we all will be liquidated. So we run away. A lot of us got caught, shot by the machine gun. There was [a] very big forest, and being there one night, two nights, you need to eat. And then I came to a hut. I thought, "Okay, I'll try," and I go in. When the guy saw me, he said, "Hey. You're a Jew." [I said,] "Wait a minute, because when the Germans come they will shoot me." But he went on the street and he saw the German police, brought them in. He says, "Okay, where did you run away?" I said I was in this camp. He says, "It's good. I will take you back [there]."

And then I went to Auschwitz. It was maybe a hundred people in a train. They'd say, "Get out, get! Get! Get!" So, you were scared.

AD: I have the impression you were a close-knit family, and your family was all depending on each other. It is really striking that all of a sudden, you are thrust into this independent and solitary—

AJ: Then [something else] takes over. You want to survive to tell it to the other people. That such an atrocity happened. I owed it to my parents. It takes over in your body, the will to survive. And if you have to crawl, you will do it. When you are younger, you got a better chance. Sometimes it's luck, too.

AD: But it was almost as if you became a whole different person.

AJ: A whole, completely different person. But later on, it's a funny thing, when I was liberated, I was the same me, you know.

AD: And you arrived in Auschwitz and were taken to—

AJ: The Gypsy camp.[3] They did not make selections, because they saw all these people worked, and at that time, they needed workers. A lot of Hungarian Jews came in that time, and mostly they put them in D camp. So, since they didn't have any place, they put us for a while in the Gypsy camp. You saw there was whole families living, and here was this family, there was that family, and that was as far as the interaction. Because being there a few days, they liquidated all the Gypsies in that camp. At night you hear the trucks going back and forth, taking them to the crematory.

AD: Had you known at that point that the Nazis were exterminating groups other than the Jews?

AJ: Oh yeah, sure. I knew if you wasn't their way, they exterminate you. But I didn't know before that they took the Gypsies.

AD: First, you worked loading potatoes from a train for five or six weeks. And then you started working with the Kanada commando.[4] How was it that you got that position, because that was somewhat coveted, wasn't it?

AJ: No, nobody wanted it, nobody wanted it. I knew one thing, there was always selection going on. There was selection to go in the crematoria if you didn't look good or if they didn't like you. So, you always watched out. When they called me out, I didn't know where we'll go. You know, nobody wanted to work in two different places. Sonderkommando, where what the people burned them [prisoners were forced to assist in the gassing of other prisoners, and burning their bodies]. And Kanada, where you take the clothes. You told them, "Oh, you will live," and, "It's nothing," whole kind of thing. "Take off, when you come out, you will find it." But this meant a certain death, too. Say, Sonderkommando maybe three months, the other one maybe six months.

AD: I've heard other people say that they would try to get a position, because you would have advantages of clothing and food and so forth.

AJ: Now, you had advantages, but you didn't want to, because you knew that you would be dead, too. And you always have that little hope, you know? They picked you, you didn't pick them. No, I didn't like it. I had a little bit of food, but then I had to watch out. Somebody would see me shoving it down my mouth, they would kill me.

AD: Around September 1944, you were shipped to the concentration camp Oranienburg-Sachsenhausen, where you were in quarantine before being sent to the concentration camp Ohrdruf. In Ohrdruf, there was little to eat, it was winter, and you had to do hard labor in wooden shoes. Someone stole your shoes, and you worked with rags tied around your feet. You mentioned that going there from Auschwitz, you felt you had gone from bad to worse. And then, around February 1945, you set out on a death march towards the camp Buchenwald. It was about a hundred kilometers away, and if you could not walk, you would be shot. And you thought you would die before you arrived there, but some Dutch prisoners helped you, and dragged you into Buchenwald. It's remarkable how there were certain key points where people were there for you.

AJ: If there was something to do, I tried to do it, too. You didn't lose your humanity. When they brought me to Buchenwald, they dumped everybody. No shower, no kind of thing. And they had a small place where girls worked and they needed a few cleaners, because they wanted to keep for the SS some women, you know? It was a brothel. So they put me in there and I was liberated there.

AD: At that time, were you so sick it was hard for you to even get up?

AJ: I couldn't get up. In fact, after the liberation it took about six months until I could learn to walk again. So when the Americans came, I couldn't walk. I couldn't move. That was the 11th of April. I stayed maybe three weeks and then the next little tiny city was Blankenheim. They evacuated schools and they put us in there, in the hospital. I remember a room like this, who knows how many beds. I gained, every week, about five pounds.[5] They had to teach me how to walk.

Then the Russians came in. And I couldn't stay with the Russians. They ask you why you don't go home. I told them everybody got killed. There were a lot of Jewish guys—we went to Berlin, and from Berlin we drove to Frankfurt, to the American zone.

AD: Did you get definite news at that point about your father?

AJ: In fact, when I came to Berlin, and it was all the troops from everywhere, there was a guy, he exactly looked like my father. And I want to believe, and I asked him. I just direct asked him, you know it. I found out later on from people what were with him, that he died [of starvation] in 1945 in [the concentration camp Dora-Nordhausen], not far away from where I was.

It was awful cold and I didn't feel good. I was coughing, and I got X-rayed and they told me, "Abe, you've got TB. You better go to the hospital." [I went to the TB hospital in Rupertstein.] I was in hospital about a few months before I got married. End [of] '46 or the beginning of '47. You felt good, TB doesn't hurt you. You got to lay down and breathe fresh air. It was high in the mountains. They give you decent food, and that was it. Mother Nature in that time had to help.

One of the doctors, Dr. Lucas, was head of the TB hospital. We became really close friends, you know, he always took care. There was a bond because he saw how I was.

AD: And you mentioned earlier that Dr. Lucas was German, a former prisoner-of-war. Some people feel that the German nation as a whole was responsible for what the Nazis did to Jewish people. The fact that you were able to befriend this man, who was a German, non-Jewish man—

AJ: I say the German was responsible, but I didn't say that every German killed or a German hated. I think there's some good and some bad in every nation. And I believe, first, life is too short to hate. Secondly, I believe if I teach my kids to hate, somebody will hate them and it is a vicious cycle. The cycle has to stop. And my mother always told me, "You know, Abe, if somebody throws a rock at you, throw them bread back. Don't hate." So even when I was liberated, I wanted to tell my story, but I didn't hate.

AD: Were you angry?

AJ: I was angry, but I didn't hate. I was angry at the SS. I think they should be punished, what they did, but not hated. In fact, my wife is German, you know. I say you can't make everybody responsible. Then I would be the same thing like Hitler, he said all the Jews are bad.

AD: It strikes me as very unusual that you were able to separate your anger from your hatred and to have meaningful relationships with—

AJ: You have to. Otherwise, you become very bitter. I have a lot of friends who are bitter. If I go around and be mean and mistreat other people, would my mother want me to see this way? No. So I have motive to show that I am different.

AD: Did you have friends who were Jewish, at that time, who couldn't understand why you would want to be friends with Dr. Lucas?

AJ: Oh yeah, especially when I married my wife. They say, you know, "How can you do it?" I say, "Listen, I go to them, they are very nice, they open the door. I'm sick, so money doesn't play any part. I met the most beautiful person and now she is married to me." She was a young girl, good-looking, and at the time, I tell you the truth, I needed somebody. You know, I was not the one what could live alone. And we are fifty-two years married, we had all the kids college graduate. We never had any problem about the religion, about other things.

AD: After the war ended, did you still feel that your main goal was survival?

AJ: When you are sick, you want to get well. And a lot of people, they survived [the war] and they're dying. I was only twenty years old. The will to live is very, very strong.

AD: As you started to recover and to feel healthier, did you start to have other goals? Or did you start to remember, have thoughts about the past? What was going on inside?

AJ: When I got better, you want to live, you want to go to a dance. You're still young. I met my wife and we got married, then you got children. So, maybe I didn't start it from the right side, but sometimes time dictates it. You know, certain people were different. They first want the career. I wasn't smart enough to do all that thinking. I become a child again.

AD: Can you talk more about meeting your wife?

AJ: How I met my wife? We knew a girl, a Jewish girl, and she was sick.

So, [my wife's family] had a house, and rented a room there for her. We always went there to see how she was doing. So, when I came, I say, "My gosh, that's a good looking girl." And at that time girls played hard to get. But my goal was not to stay in Germany having children, [but to] leave, maybe for Israel, maybe for the United States. But since I had TB and I was sick, Israel and the climate would have been very tough. I was supposed to come here [to the United States] in 1952, but my wife talked me out. She says, "Listen, here we got the nice apartment. We got everything to eat. Why do you rush so much?"

AD: Was it difficult for you to live in Germany during those years?

AJ: It was really not, because the Germans are very, very nice. You learn to live with it. And then I thought I needed a trade. So, I went to work for the I. G. Farben. The people I worked with saw that I was not different. I was not what they had told them I am. In fact, when I was supposed to go to the United States, they said, "Listen, we give you a year leave of absence and if you don't like it, you can always come back." And they made an album and everybody wrote something nice in it. I am not a person what carries around hatred.

AD: Did you know, when you started working for I. G. Farben, what their history had been?

AJ: Oh yeah. I knew it, because I saw the Zyklon B. In fact, near Auschwitz there was a . . . called Buna, they made gasoline from coal. And as far as I know it was conducted by I. G. Farben, too.[6] Yes, I knew it, but when you have to live, you have to live. I cannot work physically hard anymore and they paid me good. They were extremely nice. They went out of their way. You cannot forget, but you have to learn to forgive a little bit.

AD: Did they know that you were Jewish?

AJ: Yes, I told them.

AD: You didn't experience any anti-Semitism from them?

AJ: If it was, it was only behind my back. They wouldn't openly show it, no. Germans are different, you know. See, a Russian, if he is, he tells you. And Germans will be very, very nice. The nicer they get, then you know you have to watch out.

AD: Were you afraid, at all?

AJ: Why would I be afraid? No, I wasn't afraid.

AD: You didn't feel that there was a danger of any Holocaust happening again?

AJ: I will say Germany now is different. I was there a few times. Most of them, they're educated, they're adaptable. They know it was wrong. Now, they have a nice country built. When we went to Israel, saw a lot of German tourists. They're interested. And no matter what, if somebody tells me he hates blacks, I know right away he hates everybody, stay away.

AD: How was your relationship with your wife's family?

AJ: Oh, it was good. They live in a little village, they minded their own business. They never knew Jews. We talked a lot about it. They maybe had to play the game, but nobody was in the [Nazi] Party.

AD: You mentioned something earlier about how some of your friends were saying you shouldn't—

AJ: Yes, I was in the hospital with them. They were my age. After we was liberated, they came with me in the same train and we stuck kind of together. If you have nobody, your friends become your relatives. And we could speak openly, you know, that is their opinion. And I value their opinion.

AD: Did they come to your wedding?

AJ: Yes, yes, ironically they came to my wedding, too. It was not very much. We went only to the justice of peace. And he said, "You are man and wife." The style, you would say, was very poor, but it was fine. I got the bride, anyway.

AD: Did you talk beforehand about what you were going to do, as far as religion?

AJ: Well, sure. My wife is not Jewish. And I figured she would not make a good Jew anyway, like I would not make a good Catholic. Doesn't mean that I hate the Catholics, by no means not. But my kids got to choose what they want to. Like Janet, on the holidays, she always goes with me to the synagogue. And my oldest daughter, she lives in Chicago, she does a lot. And what I'm mostly proud is that they're all involved in the Holocaust survivors, the second generation.[7]

They're active. I cannot turn the clock back. But we can let the people know what hatred can do.

AD: So, at that point, religion, which had been important to you before the war, was not as important to you.

AJ: No, I saw people become fanatic. And you start to put religion in front, then you lose your sight. You have to have it in the heart and nothing else. Nobody can force you to be something. If you don't have it, you don't have it.

AD: Why did you want to leave Germany?

AJ: Because I didn't want my kids to be exposed anymore. And truthfully, very truthfully, I didn't want them to get married there and be there, you know? I wanted them really to get away.

AD: So you didn't necessarily feel fully trusting of the German people?

AJ: Yeah, I feel trusting, but if you get wounded, a scar is there. Okay? I had the scar. For me, was too much experience and I didn't want to rub salt in the wounds.

AD: During those years just following the war, was talking [with your wife] about what had happened to you important? And was it a critical part of your relationship?

AJ: It is still very important to me. In order to clear the air, you have to get everything on the table. It brings back bad memories, but you still have to go on, and not forget it. I will not forget it regardless. Life is complicated. You have to learn the Teflon mentality.

AD: When you first tried to systematically tell the story of your experiences, was that powerful for you?

AJ: It was. It was for me and it was for the other people, too. Because it's really nothing to make you happy, and nothing to be proud of—it's part of what you went through. And you have to do it. I told myself in concentration camp, if I survive, I will go out and not tell the people, I will scream to the people. But the real world is different.

I had a few speeches for the [Yom HaShoah, the annual Holocaust remembrance day]. It is not as easy as you think, when you see so many thousands of people. I can speak about everything, I have no problem. But this is hard. And then you don't want to show your emotions. The emotions come, you know it?

AD: What made you want to come to the United States?

AJ: To get away and to be a free person, you know. To be free. The United States, sure there's people like KKK. But most people understand that if somebody is nice to me, what do I care if he's an Arab, or whatever, he's nice to me. People understand different culture. People are more tolerant.

AD: Did your wife have any feeling about where she wanted to be?

AJ: My wife really wanted to stay in Germany. And I told her about the kids and everything. She says, "Okay, then we try, and if I don't like it, you can always go back." The worst thing in life is when people don't try, and you don't know your potential.

AD: Did you have relatives in the United States?

AJ: Yes, I had relatives, but they was very, very far. They lived in Philadelphia. My grandmother was the oldest and she had five sisters. One went to the United States, one went to Israel. One, she went together in the same train with my mother and my grandmother to Treblinka. When you have no family, you look and whatever you can find. And when we came there, they were so nice and they tried to help you.

AD: Did you know very much about the United States before you came here?

AJ: I knew quite a bit, but what you knew as a boy, it's completely different. I read Jack London and had dreams and all kinds of junk, you know it. It's completely different. But later on, I thought I would like to go really to the United States. And we spoke a little bit English already. We knew more than the average. When we needed some oil, we could buy oil and we didn't come home with vinegar.

AD: Did you have an idea of what you would do once you were here?

AJ: I wanted to go in chemistry. But most of them, when I came, they couldn't hire me, because I was not a citizen. I got my first paid job for a person who made glasses for a dollar an hour, and then it worked out and I liked it. Now, we got the 20/20 Eye Care store. We're doing very good. If you feel you like it, you try it. And if you don't succeed, try it again, get stubborn.

AD: What were your first impressions of the United States?

AJ: It was always . . . oh! When I got my first paycheck, and you can buy so many things. And it's a free world. We lived on St. Catherine Street, and you hear the bells from the church ringing. And we lived near a park, and we took the kids to the park. We loved it right away. Even if we didn't have nothing, but we loved it.

AD: But you didn't come straight to Louisville, right?

AJ: I was first in Philadelphia. And in Philadelphia I didn't like it, only because my wife was pregnant. In Germany we had the best hospital, the best everything. And we had a nice home. So it was an adjustment. Like the garbage emptied only one time in a week and was standing around. And we was in a hotel, very old. We was maybe on the 17 or 20th floor, but when you want to see what kind of weather, you have to open the window, everything was dusty. But I had this one friend, and he says, "Abe, if you want to come here, I'm working for Ford Motor Company. I can get you a job." So, I came to Louisville. And here it was different. It's a smaller city, everything was organized. I worked for Ford Motor Company and at that time made about 100 dollars a week. My gosh, I could for ten dollars load up so much groceries I couldn't even carry it.

AD: During this time when you were beginning to rebuild your life, did you take time to mourn what you had lost?

AJ: No. From the beginning, you couldn't even tell nobody. People wouldn't understand it. They thought that you are freaks. They tried to stay away from you. You didn't act like the people here. In fact, it was hard on the kids, too, you know. We didn't speak perfect English. It was hard, but we knew that we would catch up. And then you didn't want to offend nobody. You didn't know how the people would react. No, not from the beginning, but later on, yeah.

AD: Did you become involved with the Jewish community here in Louisville?

AJ: Yeah, I [became] involved. But still, they in that time didn't want to hear it either, until later on when they found out that we are not lying, that such things exist. A lot of people didn't want to believe that such exists, you know. It took a long time.

AD: It seems like that would have made it difficult to form trusting friendships.

AJ: It was not. I'm easy trusting, so I have no problems. But a lot of them [survivors], they couldn't trust, they still cannot trust. And in fact, I cannot blame them. They are different.

AD: Did you start meeting people who were Holocaust survivors in the Louisville area?

AJ: Yeah, that was the first, you start to look for somebody what you got something in common. And Holocaust survivors, we call them the *grine* [a Yiddish term for recent immigrants]. You know, the green people. I try to prove to the other world that I am not really what they think I am, you know? And then you've got a guilt feeling, too. They think, "My gosh he survived, how many people did he kill in order to survive? How come the other ones didn't survive and he survived?"

AD: You felt like people were judging you for surviving?

AJ: I judged myself and other people judged me, too. I must have been very bad, when the other ones didn't survive and I did. So, you got the double whammy.

AD: Was there any kind of formal meeting of Holocaust survivors in Louisville?

AJ: No. They lived here a little bit longer and they tried to share where they shop, and then we bought some records from old country. Yiddish. I still like to listen to them. And we formed a world within ourselves. But you cannot live in this world, because there is no walls. And certain people, they still live with it, they don't speak much English. They don't trust other ones. And in this case I did much, much better than the other ones.

AD: How did you find the other people? Was it through the Jewish community?

AJ: Right, through the Jewish Community Center. And then when one found out, he told the other one, so you knew them right away. Word got very fast out.

AD: Were you aware of other things going on in Louisville at the time that you moved here? Such as the civil rights movement?

AJ: Oh yeah, I read the paper. And I was completely on their side, you know it. Because it's more than fair, those people. In fact, I found out then, the German prisoners of war could go in places where they couldn't, when they were fighting for the United States. To me it didn't make sense. Oh yes, and the one thing about our kids, we do not hate, you know.

AD: Did you see a parallel between the situation of the blacks in the United States and the Jews of Europe? Of course, they're not at all the same. But did you see the issue of racism as being—

AJ: The Jews had the advantage in this case. Because a lot of them don't look like blacks, so they don't judge them. So, if they want to beat up, it was first the black and then the Jew. Yes, if somebody will come to you and tells you, "I hate blacks," you know automatically he will hate you.

AD: Did you experience anti-Semitism in Louisville at all?

AJ: Really, really, no. In business here, I tell them I'm Jewish. They work for us, but we treat them right. You know, we give them health care, and a lot of things. I know what it means to make a very dedicated employee. There is no one-way street. You cannot exploit somebody and tell them, "I'm your friend." It doesn't work.

AD: Did you live in a Jewish neighborhood when you first arrived in Louisville?

AJ: No. I lived on St. Catherine Street, which wasn't a Jewish neighborhood. Sometimes it crossed my mind, why don't you go move near the Jewish Community Center? But then I thought, you know what, sometimes it is better when you stay away. They created their own ghetto.

AD: How do you feel about living in Kentucky?

AJ: It's a very nice state. And you got equal opportunity and it is not like a Southern state, now I know more about states. People are different here. They're much more tolerant. If I go to New York, hustle, bustle, too much running, going to work so long and coming home, you have no time to spend with the family. Here you are right close to everything, you have more time to spend with the family. To bring up children, regardless, Louisville is a nice city.

AD: When did you become a citizen of the United States? And was that a significant occasion for you?

AJ: After being five years here, exactly. We came in '57, [and I became a citizen in] 1962. Me, a poor Jewish guy got it, it's a very big honor, yes. I felt like I am a part of the family. The circle is now getting closed. What's gone, you cannot forget it, but now I'm a part of everything. I'm a citizen. I represent the United States and I know I will make a good citizen. We're involved in a lot of things. We're paying back to society, too. You have to and it's much nicer to pay back than receive, much nicer.

AD: Do you still observe high holidays, and do you go to synagogue at any other time?

AJ: Any other time, no, but the high holidays [Rosh Hashanah and Yom Kippur], I'm going. And the main thing what I'm going to is because that they have a prayer for the [dead], you know it. I know that I can't help them, but at least I can be with them in my mind. You know?

AD: How much of a role in your daily life does that memory play?

AJ: Oh, I have to be thankful always, every day, to my mother, to my father, give me life. They taught me what's right and wrong. And they were good to me, really good to me. Yes, I think of them. In fact, I got their picture hanging where my bed is.

AD: You mentioned that it was maybe ten or fifteen years ago that you really started talking about your experiences. What happened that made you start?

AJ: They came out with the Holocaust survival. They showed movies. People suddenly started realizing, you know. And not only the other people. Jewish people didn't want to listen, too. And you cannot speak when nobody listens.

AD: You mentioned earlier that your children have been interested in Holocaust remembrance. Did you talk to them about your past?

AJ: Oh yeah, surely, my kids have [been] very open minded, you can talk to them. Very little children, you can't, because you break their growing up period and they will have a hard time. When you have formed your opinion, when you are grown up, then it is different. At least I feel about it this way. Not that I'm right in everything. I'm wrong in a lot of things.

AD: You made a journey back to Poland several years ago.

AJ: In 1992, I think. Yeah, we decided we'd take the kids.

AD: Whose idea was it?

AJ: Well, I would say my daughters, Janet and Bluma. My wife got a lot of relatives still in Germany. We flew into Frankfurt, from there we went to Czechoslovakia, because Auschwitz is near the Czech border. We stayed two days in Prague and then we went to Kraków. We went to stay the night at Kraków, then we drove into Auschwitz. We stayed all day long. And then we drove to Warsaw, and made all our journeys from there. First we went to Grodzisk. You felt the hostility from the Poles, but give them a few dollars, it's okay.

AD: How did you feel it?

AJ: First, they are afraid that you come here and you want to take the house away from them and all kinds of things. And then you see a lot of graffiti on the walls. You know, I still speak perfect Polish. But if you win their confidence, at least they are not so hostile. So, this lady, I told her all I wanted was to show my kids where my mother lived, where my father lived, and I give her a few dollars, so she spoke already different. In fact, to be honest with you, before we left the first time, we had candle sticks, some silver. We didn't want to take it in Warsaw ghetto, and they showed me where they buried it. But I saw the Poles [watching, and] I didn't want to risk myself to go take a look. They're probably not [there anymore], but I didn't want to [look]. So, anyway, we went to Grodzisk. Showed them where we lived. Showed them where my grandfather lived, where I went to school. Oh, I made a lot of pictures, too, you know it. And then we went back to Warsaw. Next day we went to Piotrków. And same thing, I showed them where the ghetto [was], and where we were. I couldn't bring myself to go in this room where my parents and my grandparents went out the last time. I told my kids, "I can't go in."

And we went back to Warsaw. Then we went to Treblinka, this is on the other side from Warsaw. You see all the rocks and all the things. It's cold. Here, you know, your mother got killed, but you didn't see it visually. We stayed there, and then we went back to Germany. Went to Buchenwald, where I was liberated. And so we made our way home. At least I showed the kids that we had a house. You know, we were still something. We didn't come out from a rock.

AD: Did you ever consider having your [Auschwitz] tattoo removed?

AJ: Why would I remove it? I will have to die with it. To me, it is now an honor, you know.

CHAPTER 5

Ann Klein

This interview was conducted in Ann Klein's Louisville home in July of 1999. Ann was the youngest of three children, born in Eger, Hungary, in 1921. Her father was a prominent banker in the town, and her mother was the president of a Jewish charity organization. In March of 1944, Germany invaded Hungary. By May, Eger's Jews were forced to live in a ghetto. Weeks later, Ann and the ghetto's other inhabitants were loaded onto cattle cars and deported to Auschwitz, where Ann's parents were both killed.

AK: And you know, I hear stories of people when they arrived and they would see the smoke and they right away would have known what that is. Or maybe if somebody told them, they believed it. Well, I could never have believed anything like that. We did see the smoke, and the people who were there already of course knew exactly what was going on. They were from Poland or Russia and they would tell us. But I assumed that they were kind-of jealous that we were coming just in the last minute of the war. See, they were already suffering for three years and suffered quite a bit, you can imagine. And whoever survived that three years, they were pretty tough and kind of mean. I used to think that they just want to scare us. So, I never thought that since my parents disappeared that first day, they would have been burned.
AD: Do you think it was important for your survival that you didn't believe it?

AK: Well, I hope so. We did not know anything about Auschwitz. And I don't think my parents did. At the same time, my parents were very protective, too. They were the type of people that didn't want to scare you. Even if they would have known a little bit more, they did not discuss that. Like when we're in the train, I never knew where we are going, and I never was afraid that it's going to be Auschwitz. We were going somewhere, and it was miserable, but we didn't know where.

AD: Can you trace in your memory how it happened that you became aware of what Auschwitz meant?

AK: For a long, long time we thought that our parents are somewhere in another camp and taking care of the kids who were also taken away from people. When did we come to the realization? Toward the very end.

In January of 1945, as the Russian front advanced from the east, Ann was force-marched from Auschwitz to the German concentration camp Ravensbrück. Three weeks later, she was transported by train to Malchow [a sub-camp of Ravensbrück], where she stayed for another two weeks before being loaded onto the train again and taken to a camp near Leipzig. There, Ann was forced to work in a factory. As the war drew to a close, the Germans forced their prisoners to march again. Ann was liberated by the American Army in Wurzen, Germany.

AK: And I never remember crying that suddenly now I might not have my parents anymore. Everything was so gradual. I wanted to get back to Hungary. By then, I kind of knew that I'm not going to find my parents there, but I had big hopes that I would find my brothers, because I didn't know what happened to them. Of course, I didn't find them either.

AD: Did you get to any point, even if it was years after the war, when you cried for them? When you felt safe enough to really mourn?

AK: Yeah, well I could even cry now, but during that time that we were in that camp and so many horrible things were going on, I don't remember really ever crying. You know? The shock was so great. And afterwards, when I got back to Hungary, it was such a trauma that it was almost like you were under the influence of some sort of magical thing that everything hit you all at once. And now, for example, I see a program on television about something, a little kid getting hurt . . . I can so easily cry over that, but this big event was just a shock which never left me for ever, ever and ever.

I think that what made me survive, that I must be kind of tough. So, it must be my personality. I was lucky that I didn't get really sick. In those days, being out in January and February, you could have gotten anything and just died, but I didn't. So I'm not sure exactly why I was able to deal with it better than other people, who even now maybe have nightmares about it and they remember all the horrible things. I think about it a lot, but I deal with it, except sometimes it looks to me that wasn't me. That had to be somebody else, because up to this moment, I can't believe and can't understand how in the world somebody can survive it, and then talk about it later in life.

AD: You mentioned that during the war you just didn't cry. But before the war was your personality that way? Did you ever cry then?

AK: No. I wasn't pampered by my parents, although they had the means. But they never, ever shared their worry with me, so therefore I was not exposed to anything bad. It was a close-knit family, but not spoiled.

It was easy to be strong when I had all the comfort. From ghetto time on, it hit us, and we had to face it and I did without any crying, temper, or fighting it. The only upset point I had was when I saw my parents sitting in front of our ghetto home, where it was raining and they had to leave their stuff. I always used to think that they had all the nice things and now you just have to leave it there. So, I always felt more sorry for them than for myself.

AD: What about when the war ended and you started trying to go about your life? Did you feel as if you were a different person than you had been before?

AK: Well, by the time I got back to Budapest, I realized that my parents are gone and my brothers are gone. Everything was still completely like a dream, because I remember that people wanted me to meet friends and get together with them. And I was just like blindfolded. I did what I was told. I didn't have my own personality.

I was in Budapest for a whole year before I came out to this country. I love music and my brother's wife—they got married just before the war—got me some opera tickets, and I went to all that because I was told to, but I didn't have my heart in it. You know? I was so vague.

AD: After your year in Budapest, your sweetheart, Sandy, wrote you a letter asking you to come to the United States and marry him. How did you meet Sandy?

AK: Well, I've known him from the time he was a little boy. He's a year older than I am and we lived just a block away. And at that time, he used to play the violin and I used to play the piano. We belonged to the same music school. We had some pieces that we played together, and then there would be a recital, and then we played tennis together, and his sister was a friend of mine. And then he fell in love with me more. He was only eighteen and I was sixteen and a half, and he left to the United States. Before he left, he said he's going to marry me. He had an uncle in Washington, D.C., who brought him out, and he went to school in Washington. So, for a while, until 1941, he would write very frequently. For my birthday, he would ask his mother and she would send a bouquet of a hundred red roses. She paid for it. I think it wasn't as expensive as it is now. But then the war came in '41 and after that, I never heard from him. First of all, you couldn't get letters. He was in the service, in the Air Force. I mean, Eger is a small town and the Jewish community wasn't really that big.

AD: Were you thinking a lot about Sandy after the war, when you were in Budapest?

AK: See, in concentration camp we only thought about food and never about boys. And after I got back, the first time that he wrote to me, he thought that I could come out and we would get married. If it works, fine. If it doesn't, we could always separate. That was ten years after, and a lot of things happen during ten years. So, when I got that letter, I never had a second thought that that ought not to work out.

AD: You weren't afraid that maybe you'd both changed in that ten years?

AK: I wasn't afraid of it, but it helped me that I didn't have to leave anybody behind, and that's very important. If my parents or my brothers would have been alive, I don't know whether I could that easily leave. Because at that time, you know, America was pretty far. I arrived to New York January the 20th, 1947.

AD: And then you were married on January 29th?

AK: The 29th.

AD: My goodness. And also you mentioned that Sandy was in finals at that time. So he was extremely busy when you arrived. When did you have time to catch up together?

AK: He had an uncle in Washington, so I stayed with them. That was very hard for me, too, because I couldn't speak the language. And they were friendly and nice with me, but everything is so strange when you are at a new place. But I must say that I still, at this moment, compare things to the 1944 situation. I always used to think how much better it is than it was then. If I was able to take that, my God, I should be able to take this. After school he would come over, then we would go out. It wasn't that easy, because ten years went by, but we knew we were getting married. You had to adjust to that, too. Plus, I don't think I talked too much about my experiences then. He loved music, and we talked about music. And then we had a very small wedding. So, I could adjust to things, easier I think than maybe many other people.

AD: Did you talk with Sandy about your experiences during the war?

AK: Oh, I'm sure I did, but I don't recall exactly when. And I didn't talk to other people for a long time about it, till years and years after. When my kids were growing up, I didn't want to make a big emphasis on that I'm Jewish. They knew it, but because you are Jewish, something like this could happen. I didn't want them to grow up like that. My older daughter was, later on in life, objecting to it that I was holding many things back. I did not want them to feel that they would be persecuted just because they are Jewish. So, I didn't tell them stories about it till they got much, much older.

AD: After you arrived here in the United States, did you want to have children? Or did you have any other goals?

AK: My husband wrote me the long letter, when he invited me to come. And since he loves music so much, he even said that he would like to have six children. Like he wanted like a quintet or whatever. And after four, we decided that's plenty. Yes, children we wanted, but I'm not going to tell you that we exactly had it when we planned it. Then it would have taken a long time for us. Because he didn't have much money. When do you feel, now you are ready to have children? That you really can afford it? So, I'm glad just exactly the way it happened.

AD: Did you feel safe in this country?

AK: I did, except I got a job in Washington, D.C., to do alteration at

Garfinkel Department Store. You had to fill out the application and they asked what religion you are. I was very worried about that. I thought to myself, this is a safe country and it's a free country, and why do they want to know? What could be the result of it? So, for a very long time, for years, I worked in that place and I was afraid that they were going to ask me what church I go to. I wouldn't have lied to them. But it concerned me that this should be a topic of conversation and what could be the result if they find out that I'm Jewish.

I thought that in this country, everything is free. When I arrived to New York and we were waiting for a cab to go to the railroad station, my little suitcase was stolen. My uncle in Budapest gave me a lovely black patent leather overnight case with red leather lining. And anything valuable which people gave me was in that. I held onto it in Paris. I took care of all my belongings. When we arrived in New York, an uncle of Sandy and his son waited for me, and by then I felt I don't have to watch that much anymore. And when they were putting the things into the cab, that little black suitcase was missing. Somebody stole it. That disappointed me tremendously, because I thought this country is very safe. Things like that would not happen. Because Sandy always used to write to me that they put 25 cents down near the newspaper and nobody takes that 25 cents and you can just get your paper. So, I thought no crime is happening in this country.

AD: Let me ask you, you had begun to settle down and live more of a "normal," in quotes, life—

AK: Well, not very normal. In Washington, yes, we had couple of apartments and we worked hard to get it. Little apartments. But when we moved to Bloomington, Indiana, we lived in a trailer, in a tiny little place, where I had to bring the water in at night and go to the john and take a shower.

And not many people who were brought up in this country with all the comfort would accept that. And I had a baby by then. My son Andy was born May the 4th, 1948.

AD: How did you manage?

AK: Well, that is where I am tough. I never thought that a baby should not have a bath, so every single day I would go and get the water, put it in that little bitty sink. And you know, I used to think, well, now I'm free and I'm not in Auschwitz. So that was somewhat our own, 25 dollars, all utilities included. You couldn't go any better. Then we moved into another trailer which was a little taller and we didn't bump our heads all the time. And then we got a Hoosier Court apartment, where we had two bedrooms and a kitchen and it was normal, for $42.50. And that's where we lived then all during the time we were in Bloomington.

AD: You talked about how you were kind-of hiding your Jewish identity. You had your Auschwitz tattoo removed from your arm.

AK: Now I can talk to anybody and I don't care. At that time, I worried. We moved to Louisville in 1953. And I was in concentration camp in '45, so that was almost eight years after. We had a neighbor next door, she took me around, showed me the Iroquois Park. It's a pretty city. They had a child my son Andy's age. And she asked me what church I go to. I told her, "I don't go to any church, I'm Jewish." I said it without any worry. But I thought to myself, if she still will speak to me after this, I'm okay. If not. . . . See, and that was eight years after that.

AD: What about your own relationship with Judaism? Did you do anything, go to services?

AK: Not in Bloomington, Indiana. Where was God when all this happened?—That went through my mind a lot. When I came out to this country, we did not belong to anything at all. And I didn't miss it, but when my kids were getting to be Sunday school age—and that was already in Louisville—then we did join a synagogue, because I felt like the kids ought to have some Jewish background. But since we did not observe it, therefore I didn't expect my children to become that religious either.

AD: How did you get from Bloomington to Louisville?

AK: Well, in '51 we moved to Marion, Indiana, and spent one year there. Sandy was having to do his internship in psychology at the VA Hospital. The rents over there were a lot more expensive than in Bloomington. And his pay was a little bit more, but not very much, and I had two kids by then. Many of the wives of the people who were there on internship did some work at night, and I wanted to do some work myself.

There was a glass factory, the Forbes. They manufactured all kinds of bottles, and I got a job there. He came home from the VA at 4:30 and took care of the kids, and I went to work at six o'clock in the evening and came home at midnight. I wanted to do it because I wanted a couple of things that I felt like I can't afford. The best part of my work was when there was something wrong with the assembly line and the machine stopped. Otherwise you just had to constantly pick up the bottles, check them for a minute, like this, and put them in a box. And you could not stop. Then somebody would be coming and relieve you in order to go to the restroom. We went back to Bloomington because he had to get his Ph.D. That was just a year internship. I had two kids and I worked and he worked, so not much was happening.

Sandy got a post-doctoral fellowship at the Child Guidance Clinic in Louisville, which was for one year only. The people at the Clinic practically took us in like a family. They had [a] lot of get-togethers, and we didn't go out otherwise. Because then my daughter Linda was born, in 1954. And our assignment was only for one year. But I couldn't see myself moving in September when she was supposed to [be] born in September. So, the Child Guidance Clinic gave him a part-time job. Then he met two psychiatrists, and they needed somebody who would do some testing for them. He tried it and they offered him a nice salary, and that's how we stayed in Louisville. We stayed in the apartments until 1957, and we were looking for a house and we found this and we have been here ever since.

AD: You mentioned you had taken a walk through Iroquois Park, and it occurred to me that at that time, Iroquois Park was segregated. Did you notice segregation in Louisville?

AK: I tell you, I was terribly disappointed at one time. I met a young Jewish couple, who invited us to their house, and they seemed like they were prejudiced against blacks from their talk. I couldn't believe it. I could not understand it as of today, and I know there are very many Jewish people who are prejudiced towards blacks. I couldn't believe that anybody who is persecuted themselves can be prejudiced towards somebody else.

I remember the civil rights movement in the sixties. It didn't leave any special impression with me. I didn't go anywhere much, you know. I was a very conscientious mother and there was just a lot to do. By then I had three kids and I was very, very busy.

I have a really important story, too, about my oldest son, Andy. He graduated from high school in 1966 and went away to college to Lawrence University in Appleton, Wisconsin. I got him all ready, with clothes and everything else. By then I had my youngest one, Robert, who was six years old.

Well, my big tragedy comes now. Friday before Thanksgiving in November, Sandy went to Atlanta to a psychological meeting. I was just cleaning up all the leaves in the yard, got a call from Appleton that Andy was in an accident. They lived [in] the dorm, and there was a church which was barricaded and people didn't go in there, but sometimes they did—boys will be boys. One of Andy's friends asked him if he wouldn't mind coming up there. And Andy says, "Oh, I've been there last week. I don't want to go." "Oh, come on, I don't want to go by myself." That kid wanted a light bulb. I mean silly thing, it doesn't make any sense. They went up into the place. They were way up high and he stepped on a false ceiling. He was in the front and the boy was behind him and he fell through, thirty-five feet. And I got the phone call.

So, I got into my car, quick went over to that psychiatrist friend of ours, told him quick what happened. He was trying to reach Sandy in Atlanta. He called the hospital. He told them, they do whatever they need to do.

At that time when this happened, I thought to myself, the Holocaust was enough. And I didn't expect to have another something like this to happen. But I handled that pretty well, too. I remember when the telephone calls were done and my friend's wife offered that she'll come with me to Appleton. And I said, "Well, maybe that's not necessary." In the meantime, I had to leave my six-year-old son. Linda was twelve and Elizabeth was sixteen. And Sandy's sister had a daughter who came to stay with us for a whole year, Kathy, who was eighteen. So, I just packed my stuff. I remember the kids all standing next to me. And I thought about cold weather and warm weather and I packed my suitcase.

And I went to the airport. Sandy was on the plane coming back from Atlanta and we flew to Appleton, Wisconsin. It was in the middle of the night. We didn't know what we were going to find. Somebody took us into the hospital and Andy was under all kind of wires. And he was in a coma actually for about three days, completely out of it.

The day we arrived, there was an article in the Appleton paper, and somebody called the hospital and wanted to meet the parents of this young boy. That was a Catholic family, and they came to the hospital and not even knowing me or Sandy, they offered their house. They were wonderful. And now, see, something like that makes me cry. I was there for six weeks and I could walk from the hospital to their home. I could talk to somebody at night about how things are going. And otherwise I spent the whole day in the hospital. Of course, I couldn't sleep well and I got some tranquilizers from this psychiatrist doctor. Which even maybe even two pills couldn't make me relax enough. But I, there again, I don't think I cried. I was under tremendous tension all the time, and not knowing what the outcome will be.

The result of all this was, his spinal cord was injured and he became a paraplegic. But we didn't know that for a long time. When people are this sick, they have movements in their leg, which doesn't mean anything. I have letters and letters and letters people wrote to me, to the hospital. I thought now when Andy died, then maybe I will throw it away. I can not. In fact, just a little while ago, I re-read them.

Finally, with an ambulance, we brought him home to Louisville. And of course, he couldn't sit up or anything like that. I mean, he was paralyzed from [the] waist down. At that time they gave him a final test. And the final test showed that the spinal cord was completely severed. We put him here in Louisville, into a hospital. He was there for six weeks and at the very end, our friend the psychiatrist made arrangements at the Rusk Institute in New York City. That they can transfer him there. Which they did.

The Rusk Institute did marvels. He was there for six weeks. Luckily his mind was completely well. They taught him how to drive. They taught him how to get dressed. They taught him complete independency. Andy used to be a very stubborn kid as a young person. When he wanted to do something, he wanted to do it right then. And that helped him tremendously in his accident. He learned how to do all this. He got a car. It had a hand control. He used to have a girlfriend from Myrtle Beach from before his accident. He says he wants to visit her. And we begged him, "It's too early, yet." He says, "If I would know that I'm going to walk next year, I would wait, but since I know I'm not going to, I want to do it right now." He got in the car, he drove over there.

Then he went back to Lawrence University for a semester. He did very well, but it got very cold there in Wisconsin and the snow was so high that he couldn't even get out of his dormitory to get to the classes. So he was transferred to Houston, Texas. To the university, where the climate is different. And he finished college in three and a half years, instead of four. In summer time, he went to Chapel Hill, North Carolina, and spent summer school there. One summer he went to Boston, to Harvard, just for a semester. So, he made up all his lost time. He finished and then he moved out to California. Then he decided he's going to go to social work school. He met good friends through all those years, who became so close to him. Now just a couple of years ago, he had to have a bladder surgery. And I went to Los Angeles. I stayed with him for three and a half weeks, while he had the surgery. And the people were very, very nice. They gave a big party. And they were singing and they read poetry before he went into the hospital. Then after that they kept on coming all the time.

He recuperated. We went home and he worried that his appetite is not as good as it used to be. I said, "Don't worry, they messed up your stomach. You'll be all right." So, my big job was cooking for him, plus showing him the CD's, which one he wants first. And we played all day long.

Then I came home. And one day, on a Sunday, January 24th, I get a phone call from his roommate. And Chuck says, "I have very sad news for you." I said, "What?" I thought he might have gotten sick again and then I would have gone out to be with him. Well, he died in his sleep.[1]

Sometimes I think of this and I [say], "Is it really true that he's no longer alive?" But then again, I measure certain things. We used to worry, what will happen to Andy when we die, and this group falls apart? My daughter, Linda, she's a nurse and she says, "Don't worry. I'll take care of him." Well, Andy didn't like to be taken care of. He could do everything in the world on his own. Anything. Driving, shopping. We have a friend here who took him on a Sierra weekend, canoe trip. And in the mud, she pushed the wheelchair and he would get into the canoe. I mean, there was nothing that he would not want to do. He was just brave.

AD: Did you ever feel angry after that?

AK: I felt angry when he had his accident, but not really angry. I just could not accept, I thought that there is so much one person should take. And I felt to myself, it's not fair. But in the meantime, this friend of mine, who was very sympathetic, had four kids and one of them was a good friend of Andy. Their older son was coming home from college, not even a year after this happened, and died in a car accident. I told her the same thing I'm telling you, that I thought that I had my share and it's just not fair that now this had to happen. And my friend after that realized nothing is fair. There is no justice. Whatever is assigned for you, it will happen, and you cannot say, just because this happened, nothing else would happen. So, I'm now prepared and I hope nothing else would happen, but after he died, I wasn't angry about that, I was more sad when he had the accident.

If he would have been old in the wheelchair, he would have needed help, you know. Those people were his friends, but they were not the family. If we would have died, we would have wondered. So, I used to think about that, what will happen to him. And he lived on the absolute minimum, you know? In the 1960s, when the civil rights movement was, from Texas, he took a bus to Washington, D.C., when they had the march. And in the bus, his toes got burned, because his foot was close to the heater and he could never feel it. And Sandy was saying, "Do you think you have to go?" He said, "If everybody would feel like that they shouldn't go and use all kinds of excuses, then nobody would be there." Causes were terribly important to him.

AD: Well, I asked about the anger, because it's striking to me that you came out of the war and your whole family had been killed. And that was, of course, a terrible, terrible blow, but my impression is that you were calm throughout. And then you jumped right into marriage and you had kids and you moved and you settled down. And then losing your son to this—

AK: I was thinking then that I would like to have some sort of a memorial service or something for him in Louisville. And we had to get all that put together, so it was February 28, and we played some music, the kind of things that he liked. And it was like a string quartet of Schubert. The name of it is "The Death of a Maiden," and I used to joke with him. I said, "When I die, that's what I want them to play." And he liked it too, so we did that. That I'm not angry . . . I don't know. I'm not that type, I think. I just accept things.

After Andy died, they did that beautiful music, and I have a tape of it, and I go down to my basement and I turn on that cassette when nobody is there. And I re-hear it, and then if I want to shed tears or cry over it, I do. But I'm never the type who does that very much in public.

AD: You mentioned earlier that you've taken trips back to Hungary.

AK: Oh, a lot of times. In 1971, I decided I go back. The first time, a friend wanted to take me to the house where I was living up to the age twelve. So, that person rang the doorbell and I was very reluctant. And somebody came to the door and he says, "Well this young lady lived in this house long time ago." They wanted to know if I wanted to go inside and I said, "No thank you." I really didn't want to go back.

Of course it was really hard. I didn't want to run into anybody who I used to know from olden time, but luckily they died. You know, like I would have never wanted to run into a police official person, who was in charge of making us go to the ghetto. The Germans gave them the orders, but somebody had to carry it through. Well, I never saw anybody.

AD: After you moved to Louisville, did you have any contact with other Holocaust survivors who were living here?

AK: I didn't have really close contacts with people. I had a Hungarian friend who was pretty neurotic and she was supposedly in Auschwitz maybe for a month and then she was taken away. We didn't really talk too much about it. Then I had another Jewish friend, she died too, who survived the Nazism in Budapest. So we once in a while talked about it, but not all the time. And the other people I see once a year, when we have this Shoah [Yom HaShoah, the annual Holocaust remembrance day]. But no, I really don't have any contact with any of the other Holocaust survivors here.

AD: Do you always go to the annual Yom HaShoah event?

AK: That's one way for me to remember my parents and my family. Some people light candles. Some people can go to a grave. In fact, when Andy died, they cremated his body and it came back. And there was a question: how and where? There is a beautiful cemetery here, it's Cave Hill Cemetery. And I didn't know that Jewish people can be buried there. I've heard that Temple Shalom has a lot, and we decided we're going to do that. We went out to the cemetery and we did a private funeral for him. We ordered a marker and that's there. It says, Andrew Allen Klein, above it "Andy," and the date that he was born and the day that he died and there is a little menorah.

AD: You don't have a grave to visit for your parents or for most of the members of your family. Does that make it especially important to you to have that?

AK: That's why I wanted Andy to be here.

AD: And what about for yourself?

AK: I thought about it a lot. So I said to Sandy one day, "You know, I wouldn't mind to get two lots next to Andy's." And he didn't object to it and we did that. So now I feel good, that at least I know what our kids need to do with us.

I'm not the type who would go out every week. But it gives me a comfort to know that he is here and he's close to us. I mean, Sandy will be eighty years old next year. Eventually we will die. We're in fairly good health. At least it makes me feel good, first of all, that we belong to a temple, secondly that our kids can visit our graves. I don't know where my brothers are. I know where my parents are, but we can't visit them, ever.

But slowly we are getting older, and that's why I talk to many schools about this. That's why I'm doing this, too. That I think there ought to be a way of people to know what happened really, after we die. Because there are not that many people left who survived it.

AD: Did there come a point when you felt that you had to talk about your experiences?

AK: Well, it came many years later. The very first time I think I talked about it, that we were going to Cincinnati, to an art gallery, and Mary K. [Tachau] was with me and another friend. It was a two-hour ride and somehow it came up and then I told them. [Also,] I used to walk with neighbors and friends and they have known me forever. So, years and years ago, we would walk for maybe forty-five minutes and one of my friends, not Jewish, asked me if I would talk about it. So, I said, "I'll be glad to," and for many, many weeks that we would walk, we stopped at a certain point and then they wanted to know the rest of it. So, by now it doesn't give me any problems to talk about it. When some of the schools ask me, I did. I couldn't begin to tell you now how many times I did speak in schools. And they might have a Jewish student there or not. And now, I'm completely at ease with myself and I can talk about it. Once in a while I kind of get a lump in my throat, you know, but I can do it.

AD: How do you feel about living in Louisville?

AK: I like Louisville. I do like it and I don't. Wouldn't like to live any other place. I've not been in too many places in the United States, but Louisville is a nice town. And we made a lot of friends. Now that we're getting older we don't see them as much anymore. And luckily one daughter lives here and the two grandchildren, you know. I have, in fact, a little one [who] will have a birthday tomorrow. He'll be seven years old. And I'm invited to go to a cave for the birthday party.

AD: When you first moved to Louisville, how did you integrate into the community here? How did you make friends? And was it with the Jewish community only?

AK: Well for a while, no, not really. When we moved to this house, then we met more and more people and they would invite us. But we're not the type that we congregate only that they have to be Jewish. If anybody would be an anti-Semitic person, I would never want to have anything to do with them. And after I got used to the idea and everybody knows we are Jewish, it's not a problem anymore. And our kids, too, they have mixture of non-Jewish friends and Jewish friends. Now, my son, Robert, in Nashville, he married a Catholic girl. So, it's not a matter that it has to be Jewish or not, but it has to be the same type of people.

AD: Have you had experiences where you've spoken to groups who wouldn't have expected that a Holocaust survivor lives in the state?

AK: Well, the teachers prepare the kids, most of them. They had Holocaust pictures on the wall. And they hear once in a while stories where people don't want to believe. And that's the only reason I'm doing it.

And then, you know, I was very affected by Yugoslavia's problems, too, with this Kosovo deal. Because it was so similar to what we have gone through.[2] I had very mixed feelings toward the end, when the bombs kept on falling and maybe innocent people were killed. That bothered me, but at the same time, I thought to myself, if anybody would have bombed the railroad tracks, when the train was going to Auschwitz, it could have maybe stopped something. And nobody did anything. Therefore, because I feel that way so strongly, I was saying that they did the right thing. Although it's a very complicated situation, and it's never going to be peace in that part of the world.

Sylvia Green

Oscar Haber

Oscar Haber

ROBERT HOLCZER

ABOVE AND RIGHT: ABRAM JAKUBOWICZ

ANN KLEIN

JUSTINE LERNER

JUSTINE LERNER

ALEXANDER ROSENBERG

ALEXANDER ROSENBERG

JOHN ROSENBERG

JOHN ROSENBERG

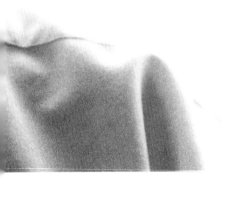

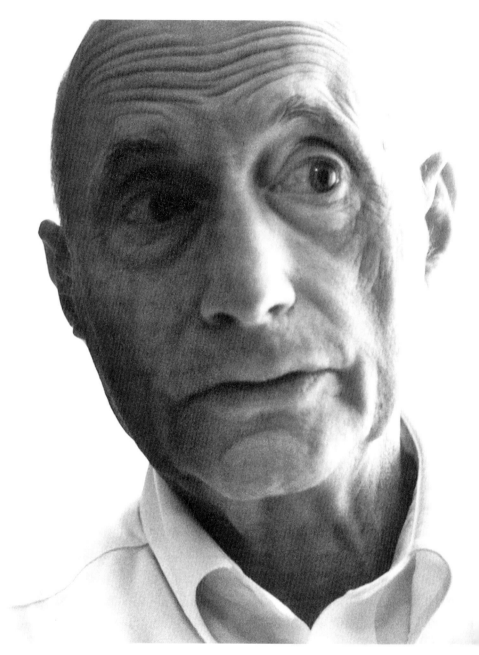

John Rosenberg

Paul Schlisser

PAUL SCHLISSER

Justine Lerner

Justine Lerner was born in Białystok, Poland, in 1923, one of eight children in a close-knit family. Justine was the only member of her family who survived the Holocaust. This interview took place on May 5, 1999, in Justine's home in Louisville. She had moved to Kentucky only two years before, to be near her son, after she'd been brutally attacked by a robber in her Brooklyn apartment. Justine had always rejected being interviewed, but now that she was growing older, she felt that it was time to record her story.

JL: My father, may he rest in peace, was a medic in the First World War and he always says that the Germans may put you to work, but they will never harm you in any way. And like anything else, you listen to your parents, whatever they told you. In our town, first came in the Russians. And we were with the Russians maybe a year. Then the Russians left and the Germans came in. When the men went to the temple, they burned down the whole temple with the people inside, whoever it was there. A while later, they put us into the ghetto, and this was terrible. The ghetto was terrible.[1]

In the ghetto, I had to go out to get some food, because nobody else could. My brother wouldn't go out, he was afraid. And my father couldn't carry anything, so I used to take off the yellow star that we wore. And I was blonde. I went out through a hole they made [in the fence that surrounded the ghetto]. I went to the Poles, the ones that used to do business with my mother. I used to buy from them potatoes and bring it in [to the ghetto], the same way like I came out. And I did it quite often for the family, they should have what to eat.

AD: So, of the children that were left with your parents, you were the main caregiver?

JL: Right. Caregiver. [Two of my sisters] were married already and they had babies, so they couldn't go with us when we were hiding. Because if the kids start crying, the SS will hear.

AD: When did you go into hiding? How did that come about?

JL: Because you heard rumors that they're going to take people away from the ghetto. And they're going to ship them to Auschwitz. So everybody went in, either to a basement or they built something underneath, and that's the way they're hiding. You took some water with you or some bread. We heard them walking upstairs, Germans with the boots, and we were underneath. And from nowheres they found out. They knocked on the door. They took us out from there.

People remained after they took us away, of course.[2] And you couldn't take nothing with you, because you had to carry it. Just like a pillow case, that's where you put your belongings. I was not with my mother. My mom went with the [sisters] that had the babies. I was with my father, my oldest sister and her two older children, and my younger brother and my older brother. So we were separated.

They put us on the trains. Crowded. There was no room to go to the bathroom. You should excuse me, a lot of people made on themselves. Cattle have a better look than we had. It was just unbearable. And my oldest brother jumped the train. He didn't want to come into Auschwitz, and they were standing there and shooting. So I don't know if he got shot or he got killed afterwards. My father to the last minute still had good ideas, that they're not going to hurt us, they're going to put us to work. But it was not so. The minute we arrived to Auschwitz, we saw people standing and digging ditches. And he said, "What did I tell you children? They're more civilized than anything else. They're not going to kill."

As soon as the train stopped, it became like a terrible wind. And they separated us, the women this way and the men that way. Didn't see my father anymore. Didn't see my sister, she was next to me, but she wouldn't part with her children, so you pulled her out on this side. So, I ran out from my side and I went to be with my sister. And the SS, they had canes. They took the cane and put around my neck and pulled me back to that line. So, I ran again over to my sister. I wanted to be with her. So he took me out for the second time, and he hit me with the cane over the head and that was the end of it. I never saw them afterwards.

When you come into Auschwitz, you had to get undressed, and of course, I started to cry very much. An SS woman comes over and she says to me, "Why are you crying?" I said, "Because I want to go to my sister." She said, "You'll never see her again." And since that point, I never cried again. Because first they cut your hair, and then they tattooed, and my hand got swollen like this. And lonesome, you have nobody. The following day when they took us to work, we saw the smoke coming out of the chimney and I put two and two together and I knew exactly what was going on, that [my family was] not around anymore.

In the morning, they used to take you to work by groups. They counted off thirty, forty, sixty, whatever they needed, and we marched. Mostly young people, they never chose elderly, because they only needed you to work. And the elderly, of course, didn't have no strength, so they gassed them right away. But the younger ones, as long as they needed you, they used you, and then after that they killed you. We followed them and whatever they said to do, that's what you had to do that day. A lot of times they brought back a lot of girls, dead ones, because they didn't like the way they looked, or for no reason at all. And they brought them back on two pieces of wood, actually. Because each and every one they took out from the gate, to bring the same amount back, even if dead.

Every day, two people had to go to get coffee in the morning. And sure enough I went, and from nowhere a girl came along and she stopped the pot to get some coffee. An SS woman saw her through the window. She came running out with the dog, and she poured the boiling coffee on my leg. And the skin came off right away. There was nobody to complain, because nobody would listen to you. They would gas you. So, they had like a little blanket to cover yourself. And I ripped up a piece and I made a bandage. It used to get stuck during the night, and in the morning I used to take it off and I went to work like that.

After three weeks, I couldn't go on no more. So, I went to work and we were digging ditches, and they moved away from there and I threw myself into the ditches and I figured I'll let me lay there. It's like a grave. Let me remain there. But somehow they walked away and I crept out and I went on revier. The revier meant, like a hospital. I went in there and they asked me who did it. I said, "I burned myself." I was not allowed to say that the SS woman did it to me. And they accepted me. You didn't get no help or medication or anything like that, but at least you had the rest. They used to count everyone [outdoors] in the morning. And this took an hour if it rained or snowed, whatever, they didn't care, because they were dressed. So I said to myself, at least I don't have to go through this. And that's the way I remained for two, three weeks.

The SS came in and they said, "Everybody come down from the bed." I touched my next door girl and the other side and they were dead. They came from Greece and they couldn't take the climate. At that point it was not warm in Auschwitz. And they just fell like flies. I said to myself, "I don't stand a chance by going down," because you had to take off whatever you wore and parade through them naked. And if they like the way you looked, they put you one way, and if they didn't, they gassed you.[3] So, I said, "I'm not going to give them satisfaction. I'm not going down." And I remained like that on the bed. And the doctor touched one, two, and here I was laying in the middle. And he didn't touch me. And I remained like that, so this actually saved my life.

The woman that took care [of] me, she was a Polish woman—not took care, but she spoke to me, let's put it this way—was a very nice person. She used to come in the morning, she was wearing a white coat. And she was clean and she had a short haircut. I said to her, "What do you do with the water after you finish washing yourself?" She says, "Why? Do you want to drink it?" I said, "No, who drinks dirty water? I want to wash myself. I want to look good like you do." So every morning, she brought me a small basin with water with the soap and the dirt and everything when she washed herself. And I used to wash myself around. And I felt so good, like a million dollars. So I said to myself, "How could I help the woman?" I said, "Okay, I'm going to help her to clean. Before she gets here, I'm going to do it and when she comes she won't have so much work." But when I went down, I fainted from laying so long on the bed.

So I got up, and somebody helped me to go back on the bed. When she came in that day, I told her what happened. She says, "If you want to live, you must get off that bed." I said, "Sure, I want to live." So I climbed down again from the bed and I was able to stand for a minute. This was really a big accomplishment. But every day I tried, until I got stronger.

She thought it was very clever of me to do a thing like that. She used to give me an extra piece of bread. And she said that pretty soon they were going to ask who wants to become a nurse. She said to me, "I would advise you to volunteer for that." So I volunteered, and I was transferred from this into a better place. I didn't get as a nurse, but when the new arrivals came on, when they took off their clothes, the personal things you had to leave there too, everything. You had to go through to look for diamonds, or for money people used to sew in their clothes. And that was my job.

AD: This is the Kanada commando?[4]

JL: Yeah, that's right. And this helped me, too, not to get outside with my leg. Of course, it healed by now, but it left me a terrible scar. It grew like wild flesh on it, but I was happy that I could walk. When I came out of there, when people saw me that knew me, they didn't believe that I'm alive, because months I was not with them.

That's where I met Halina Lichtenstein. We became very good friends, like sisters. We were sleeping together and eating together. She lives in England now. Between the two of us, we had two slices of bread, so we were rich. So one slice we used to save it up for the night meal, and for the morning we took along the other one to work. We never finished both slices of bread. Everybody used to be envious. How could we do it? I says, "We're not vultures. We thought we're going to live maybe till tomorrow, so we'll have the bread for tomorrow." A lot of people didn't do that. And I never cut my bread. I always gave her, she should do it. Because thinking, God forbid, maybe I'm taking a bigger slice for myself. That's the way I was raised.

AD: Do you think it helped you to survive, to have that little bit of humanity and kindness in your life? Did that help you to have hope for your future?

JL: I don't know. I never changed as far as helping people. All my life I suffered for that. After the war, too. My mother was that way.

AD: Did you get any news from the outside world?

JL: You didn't have to get news. First of all, they were evacuating us from Auschwitz, because the Russians came close and the Germans did not want to fall into the Russian hands. They put us back on open buses. I remember like now, it was snowing. And we didn't know where they were taking us, but we got to Ravensbrück. Ravensbrück was another camp, but it was not as bad as Auschwitz. They didn't have the gassing chambers. It was just a concentration camp, and there I got a job in the kitchen. And I was dishing out food and everybody came over, "Jospele, Jospele,⁵ give me some food." So I always did that. In that respect I was lucky, I always got good jobs. And then from Ravensbrück they transferred us to Switau [probably Svítkov, Czechoslovakia]. That's where we were liberated.

AD: Did you have the sense that the war was coming close to an end?

JL: Only because you were talking among yourselves. I mean, here and there somebody passed by and they heard a radio. Otherwise we were not allowed to have any news. But you heard the guns, I mean you had to be deaf not to hear it, because it was nearby. Of course, we did not know when we were going to be liberated. Because at one point like we used to hear "roooh, roooh" all night long, and then all of a sudden it got quiet. So we figured it out, geniuses, that they [the Allied forces] pushed them [the Germans] back. We knew that the end is near, but we didn't know how near it was.

AD: Did you have any information at all when you were in Auschwitz about what had happened to your family?

JL: No, no. When the third transport came, the people from Białystok said that they saw my mother coming into Auschwitz. But I did not see her. When we arrived in Auschwitz, I never saw them again. Always hoping, always searching, always looking, but of course, nothing. We lived in Paris for a year, after the war of course. And I was always going on the trains, looking. From the back, look like my sister, from the back look like my brother. Always thinking, looking into their eyes, but of course, it was not them. But I always thought, yes, yes, I'm going to find somebody.

AD: You described before you arrived in Auschwitz what a close-knit family you were. You were dependent on your parents to tell you what was going on, and to give you a sense of what the future might be. And you talked about how your father always believed that things would turn out all right. It must have been a terrible shock to arrive and be suddenly separated from everyone you knew, and yet somehow you survived that. Can you say something about how you adjusted to that extreme change?

JL: I always felt that this was my mother's and my father's last wish, that somebody has to remain from the family and carry on. And I was the one to survive and that's what I have to do. I have to build back what we lost. That's the way I lived after the war. Of course, it's just a made-up story, but this helped me a lot in my life. Like I'm not doing it, but somebody else tells me to do it.

AD: You said you were looking out for other people. Do you think people were looking out for you, too, as a result?

JL: I always believed that they would. I had very dear friends and that's what helped me in actual life, because family we didn't have. And we were like sisters and brothers. When you first came to the United States and prior to that, we were looking for one another and when we found each other it was like you found somebody from the family. And don't forget, it's over fifty years and the ones that are alive are still very, very close.

AD: Did you have any sense of faith during the war years?

JL: I would say that I had. I always believed that somebody above carries on with you. Whatever happens in your life, somebody's there to help you. Yeah, faith means a big thing to me.

AD: And that wasn't destroyed by what you saw at Auschwitz?

JL: I wouldn't say that I became more pious, you know, but I would say I'm on the same level like I was. A lot of people made fun out of me, too. I always believed. I always kept a kosher home. After the war, up till today, I wouldn't mix certain foods, like we are not allowed to have cheese and meat. I was brought up that way. And that's the way I tried to keep it. Now I have my different town. It's very hard to get certain foods. So I used to have separate dishes all my life. Now, to be honest, I don't do that. But I still will not eat the meat and the dairy together. Goes against me.

AD: People in the camps made fun of you for having faith?

JL: No. After the war. Not fun exactly. "Oh, stop being stupid," or things like that. They had no religion in them at all. I couldn't do that. I like to go to the temple when a holiday came along or anything that came up. I felt that's my place. Even my husband was not a believer, and he came out from a very pious family. But he saw what's happening, he lost it completely.

AD: Do you remember the day of liberation?

JL: Oh, sure. I remember like now. Everything that happened in my life, I'm always in the bathroom. Any excitement. And all of a sudden you hear screaming. "The Americans are here! The Americans are here!" You heard them coming with motorcycles up the hill, up and down, a lot of them. They all came to a certain spot, and they stopped. They announced that they are the Americans and they came to liberate us. And we shouldn't be afraid. Of course, they had the business of picking up the Germans, too, that watched us. And I ran out from the bathroom with my pants down. It was like a miracle, like you see it in the movies. Unbelievable, that we are free.

They said to us we shouldn't eat no meat, because our stomachs are not used to it, because a lot of people fell and they died from it. And we should be very careful. If possible, we should mostly eat rice and drink water. Among them was a chaplain, and he said to everybody, "Whoever is Jewish should come forward." We were still hesitating, because we didn't trust anybody already. And a few minutes later we stepped out, all of us. He said not to be afraid, they'll try to help us in every way, and that we shouldn't go back to Poland, because the Russians are there already. And that they'll help us, we should go to Paris and from there the organizations will take over.

AD: What was your physical condition like at that time?

JL: The impact was driving you, but underneath you were not healthy, because when I came to Paris—this was months later—I used to fall, had no strength in my legs. But at that point, I was strong like a bull, you know, that drive to survive. And after a while, when you find out that you have nobody, you get disappointed and it's harder to take. I started to get very depressed and didn't want to go on. There was no use in life already. [In Paris, we lived in] a hotel for the misplaced people. We slept two in a room, and downstairs was a kitchen. And we used to be able to come down and eat. Now, I don't remember how long I was there, but I just couldn't go down with a dish again and eat. I cried so much, it was more tears in the dish than it was food.

Then my friend Halina said to me, "You know, I'm sure that the mother's wish was somebody should survive. And you are the one that survived, and if you don't want to go on, open up the window and throw yourself out and get it over with. But don't make everybody miserable and yourself." And this few words put so much sense into my mind. I took a turn around and I said, "She's right, I've got to go on. I've got to do it for them." And that's the way I live all my life. That they would want me to be that way.

AD: Did you feel a lot of anger after the war ended, at the Germans? Or at the world?

JL: Anger was not the word for it. Disgraced. Anger, I knew I can do nothing, but how could people live like that? To do that, one to another? This was hard to understand. And not to have anybody. To be alone in the whole world. But you got to build, you got to start from scratch and be productive and do what your parents wanted you to do.

One night, I was sitting in my room, and all of a sudden I heard screaming on the corridor. And I said, "Oh my God, the Germans came back?" You didn't know. You were like a lamb. Finally I opened up the door. And there was my husband, at that time I didn't know him yet, kissing my two friends, who were sisters. And they were crying and they introduced me to him. "This is a *landsman*," this means from the same town. He came looking for people that survived. He heard that there was people there, and he was still in the Army. So they introduced me to him, and I said, "Good night, nice knowing you," and I left. He used to come to them every single day. He used to bring them soap, a piece of chocolate, and sardines. And if they had too much, they gave it to me. A short time later, they left. They went to Paraguay, they had family there. My husband came around a few times, but I didn't pay no attention to him. And then he was discharged from the Army and he went back to the States.

At one point practically everybody found their family already and they were leaving. All of my friends left [Paris] before me. I had an uncle in the United States. And of course, me, I didn't find my family, didn't find my uncle. I said to myself, either he's very rich—he doesn't want to identify himself—or he died, one of the two. A lot of times people came, helping you, asking you questions. "Where are you from? What was your family name?" Reporters. "How many in your family?" You know. All kinds of questions till you get tired of answering. And nothing came out of it. Towards the end, I didn't want to talk about it, because it brings too much hurt in you.

When my husband came back, he asked me, did I find my uncle. And I said, "No." So my husband said to me, "Give me all the particulars that you knew about your uncle." So I gave my husband all the particulars. He went back to the States. And later, I get a letter, my uncle. And he sent me twenty dollars, he put it into the envelope. He wants very, very much I should come to the United States.

By that time, my husband came again, once more. He joined the Merchant Marines and he went back and forth. And he wanted to marry me. I said to myself, "Okay." It was over a year. I couldn't find anybody. And we decided to get married. But in order to go together to the United States, we had to get married in Paris. So in 1947, we had a beautiful wedding in Paris, invited all my friends. And then we came to the States.

AD: Was your husband the first man that you had ever dated, or had ever been involved with romantically?

JL: Yes.

AD: You had lost so much of your childhood and of your teenage years, when young women are normally learning about each other and having fun. Was that difficult for you, to become involved with someone after what you had just been through?

JL: Well, I was not like today the girls, they go and they sleep with their men. We didn't do these things. Had to wait to get married in order to be near each other. But you have to trust somebody in order to be honest with somebody. We had a broken childhood, actually. I didn't put on lipstick until my wedding day.

AD: What about your hopes and dreams for yourself after the war? You got over your depression and you made the decision that you were going to go on living your life. Did you want to continue your education? Or to have children?

JL: Of course, I wanted to go have a child. I just wanted to help my husband and build a home. And I used to go to school at night. I was helping my husband. He was [in] real estate. And I used to take the complaints in the house. We were working like hand to hand, to make something out of yourself. And then we wanted to have a baby, so it took me almost seven years until I had my son. This was a big thing, because all my friends had children already. But thank God, he was born, and I was very proud of him. He was the whole life to me and to my husband, both of us. We only saw that he should have a better life than we did. He should go to college and he should be somebody. That was my main thing.

AD: What were your expectations of the United States?

JL: Before I came, dreaming, just tall buildings, how different would it be? How would people accept me? My husband had a father, that we lived together on Newport Street in Brooklyn. And he was very, very nice to me. I adored that man. He wanted to give us everything, whatever he had. He wanted to give us his room. There were two bedrooms. I says, "Pa, how could I take your bedroom? It's yours."

I went down in the morning to get breakfast on the same block, a grocery. And from the beginning when I went into the store everybody wanted to see if I have horns. How do I speak. I didn't have to wait on lines, but it didn't last long. Because after a while they heard that I'm the same like they are, so they let me go to wait in line. I used to shop, and bring home the food, and make three meals a day, and it was just like my mother did, the same thing.

AD: When you said people wanted to see whether you had horns, were you talking about people who were—

JL: American, they were born here. They were Jewish, too.

AD: They just had stereotypes about Holocaust survivors?

JL: I wouldn't say that. But I made up that joke. They wanted to see if I have horns, how do I talk, how do I move myself different than they are. Curiosity, I would say, more than anything else.

AD: Did you talk to people about your experiences during the war?

JL: No, never. I didn't want to. I didn't want to be different than anybody else. The [tattooed] number [on my arm], I couldn't live with it. I had to take it out. And I did and I was very happy. And once I took it out, I'm like everybody else. You don't know what's in my heart, but on the outside I look alike. If I open up my mouth, of course you'll see I'm a foreigner, but I was never ashamed of being a foreigner. But I couldn't live with the number, because this made me different than everybody else. So, when my son started to go to school, I said, that's when I'll take it off. And exactly I did that. If somebody rang the bell and it was in the morning, I could open up the door in a house dress or my nightgown, but I could not, would not let you see my number. Had to take a dish towel from the kitchen or something to put it on top. One time a child caught me and she asked me, "What is that?" And I told her, "Oh, it's my telephone number." Of course, she didn't accept that. She says, "Nobody puts a telephone number," but I said, "I don't remember, so I didn't want to lose it. So, that's why I put it there." But you couldn't catch me the second time already without anything. I used to put on a tape to cover it if I had to go out. It was like a disbelief, a hurt.

AD: Did you talk to your son about your experiences during the Holocaust?

JL: I didn't talk to him directly, let's put it this way. Here and there I had the picture together. Because he always saw me crying. I remember when my son was five or six years old, and he came into the house and I was sitting and crying. It had to be some kind of a holiday, because this was the worst time of my life, not to have family sit at the table, just the three of us. It was very hard for me, because I had a big, warm family, and I was missing it a lot. He said to me, "What's the matter? What happened?" "Nothing happened, Joel. I don't feel good. I'm just crying. Everything is okay." And I wouldn't tell him. He took me around and he said to me, "Ma, when I get bigger I'm going to marry you, don't cry." I never forgot that. But I'm sure that he knows everything, what went on. Here and there he heard it. But I never sat down, like I'm sitting down with you and telling, never.

AD: What made you want to tell your story now?

JL: I'm getting on in age. Kids are learning in school about it. My granddaughter went to Poland for the March of Living.[6] And she tells everybody the story. And I said, "What the heck, let me tell my story, too." I always said they have enough without me, but I guess each and every one brings a different story to it.

AD: Did you have nightmares?

JL: Nightmares I didn't have. In my own mind, all my life, I live with it. Feeling sorry for myself and hating myself. Why did I have to be the one to survive? But there's no answer for me. That's the way God wanted it and that's what it's all about. I never spoke to anybody. I was a strong woman, very strong.

AD: You talked about how it was important for you to not feel different than everybody else. Did you come to feel like you belonged in this country and that you were an American?

JL: Yes. I felt I'm just as good as everybody else.

AD: Did you ever go back and visit Poland?

JL: No, I would never go back there, never in a million years. I went to Israel. We traveled a lot. And we went to South America. We went a lot of places, but I would never go back to Poland. I feel that I have nothing there but misery. I have nothing to go to, even no graves. So what am I going to go see? Never.

AD: You moved to Kentucky after a very horrible event happened to you. You were attacked in your home in Brooklyn, and left for dead.

JL: Yes, I was attacked and left in the house. I was all alone. My husband had passed away, and there was nobody, nobody. This was on a Friday, and I started to prepare for dinner. And I opened up the window. Not thinking that, God forbid, somebody's going to climb in through that and get in. And he hit me in the head, cut my face. He broke my arms, they were hanging, both of them. He did something terrible. And my friend kept calling, and no answer. So, Sunday he came along to the house. "Justine, Justine, where are you?" I yelled out, "Here I am. Save me, help me." And that's when he heard my voice. So, they climbed through the kitchen window, and they found me laying on the floor in my bedroom in a puddle of blood. That's when they called the police. The police called an ambulance, and that's why they put me into a hospital. And they called my son.

AD: How did you recover emotionally, psychologically, after what you had already been through in your life? Were you able to recover your hope and your faith after that?

JL: It's a very funny thing. I still have my beliefs and I cannot change it. I take him for a bad boy. The child was on dope. That's what the mother says. I didn't know him and I wish I would have never known him. I'm not there to fight the case. He only got six and a half years, which is nothing. He left me a cripple for the rest of my life and all the pain that I have with me, but nothing helped. He'll come out, he'll do it again. But I can do nothing about it. Cannot take a gun and go and kill him, because it's against me. I could lay down and die? No. My time wasn't up yet. When my time is going to be up, I'll go. But I have another extension of life, so I have to go and enjoy it. And that's the way I'm doing it. I'm not enjoying it, but I'm alive. Let's put it this way. Like for the holidays, my son belongs to the Reform temple, so I went with him. And the four doctors that used to take care [of] me in the hospital were there and they came over to wish me a happy New Year. They couldn't get over how good you look. I said, "Thank God for the make-up, it covers all the sins." I always have something what to say. He said, "A lot of people's make-up cannot do such a good job like this." But I could always make a joke out of it.

AD: Will you say something about your son?

JL: I have to compliment myself. I was always a good mother, looking out for the child. And I think that's what he repays me back. He's there for me all the time. He cares about me. But I understand very much he has his own life and I don't want to take nothing away from him. But he's a very good boy. I'm thankful to God that I have him. And I have four grandkids.

AD: And they've taken a special interest in your history?

JL: I would say they all do. I know they are very busy. I would like to see them more often. But I understand that not only do they have their life, but I can't demand anything from them, because I'm not going to get it. I should be thankful whatever I got and that's the way I go on. They respect me and I respect them and that's what it is. I'm always appreciative whatever you do, it's good, it's okay. I still know between right and wrong and I'm a happy bird. I'm very happy, all my life, like a stupid . . . I'm a happy-go-lucky.

AD: You came to Kentucky after you were attacked in New York in 1997. What were your first impressions of Louisville?

JL: What was my impression? I mean, I knew I'll never make a friend over here, because that's my age. You make friends when you're young and you hold onto them. When you are an older person, I don't want to hear their problems and they don't want to hear my problems. You talk about sicknesses. Especially if I don't drive, that's a disability already. I have to wait for somebody to take me. And I don't like that. I always used to walk and do my own thing. And solve my own problems. I was a private person. I didn't like anybody to feel sorry for me. But here I have no alternative. I have a woman that helps me. She takes me all over, wherever I have to go. She makes the appointments for me with my doctors and that's it. I do my own cooking. It's a lonely life.

AD: Did you make any connections with the Jewish community, with Holocaust survivors?

JL: I didn't even know that they had [Holocaust survivors] over here. If you have an address, I would like you to leave it and I'll find out more about it. I went to the Jewish Community Center after my husband passed away, and I came down for a holiday over here by myself. I try, but somehow, it's not for me. I don't know them. To get acquainted at this point and to have their lunches, which I don't care for—it brings back too many memories. So, I'd rather stay home. And here they have a pool and maybe I'll join the pool. I'll go over. I'll take a look.

CHAPTER 7

Alexander Rosenberg lives with his wife, Alice, in a handsome house on a quiet cul-de-sac in Louisville. He is an avid gardener of both flowers and vegetables—when I visited in June of 2000, I was treated to a tour of his well-kept garden beds. Our interview was punctuated by the chiming of his wall-clock, which features a different birdsong each hour.

Alexander was born in 1927 in Frankfurt am Main, Germany. In 1933, the family—Alexander, his father, mother, and younger brother—moved to Berlin. By 1937, many German businesses were being purged of Jewish workers, and Alexander's father lost his job as an investment banker. The Rosenbergs moved from Berlin to Amsterdam, Holland. They were part of a tremendous influx of German-Jewish refugees to that country in the years following the Nazis' rise to power.

Holland's Jews did not remain safe for long. In May of 1940, Germany invaded the country. By 1942, all of Amsterdam's Jews were required to wear a yellow star to identify themselves, and were periodically rounded up and deported to Nazi camps.

AD: Your family was not very religious. You basically went to synagogue for high holidays. Was your family assimilated?

AR: Yes, I would say so, with hindsight in particular I would say so. My dad certainly considered himself German first and never expected the violence to get to the level that it did. And certainly [believed it] would not affect him since he was a veteran of World War I. Had volunteered for the Army in the first place and was wounded, I believe, two or three times, and had the Iron Cross [a German military decoration]. So that I would say they considered themselves primarily German, and assimilated is the right word.

AD: Can you describe what happened when you were living in Amsterdam in 1942, and your family was caught in a round-up and deported to Westerbork?

AR: As they always did, [the police] came in the middle of the night and you had five minutes to get dressed. Your bags were always packed because you knew it could happen. And you were hauled off in a truck along with other people, taken to the railroad station. Put on a train, not knowing where to. And then I went to Westerbork, which was the transit camp that the Germans had established; it's in the eastern part of Holland, near Zwolle. And we were held there for about six months.

AD: Did you know anything about Westerbork before you arrived?

AR: No, never heard of Westerbork. And of course, you know, it's maybe a two-hour train ride at most.

AD: Did you have any idea at the time of what had started to happen to Jews?

AR: No, no. They always said we'd be relocating in a work camp or whatever. Or vague promises of exchanging for money, that relatives, particularly in America, could buy you and so forth. But no, nobody had any inkling of what lay ahead in terms of the violence.

AD: Did you form bonds in the camp with people outside of your family?

AR: I don't think anybody formed any bonds at all. It became a matter of trying to survive, and a fellow that was in the bunk next to you may not wake up in the morning. Nobody really tried to get attached to anybody else. Well, there really wasn't much time either.

AD: Do you remember the day that you were deported from Westerbork to Bergen-Belsen?

AR: No, nothing in particular. I guess in the afternoon the empty train was pushed into the compound. It was passenger cars. Then they posted names, they called them out and you had to be there an hour or so later.

Got on the train, nobody knew where it was going to go. Supposedly it was just a relocation, and they always promised you something better. Of course it never was. But initially you didn't know. That, I'm sure, explains why there was no really massive resistance. If you knew you were going to go to the gas chamber, you may as well try and fight it. So you get shot on the spot. I think that's why there's the general docility of the deportees.

I had never heard of Belsen before. As a matter of fact, we were some of the earliest ones in there. When we got there, of course, it was a very large facility. Part of it was a Russian POW camp. But obviously designed for officers, because they had little cabins and gravel walks between them and that sort of thing. And then there were two sections [for] the non-POW prisoners. One was for criminals and the second section was for the Jews. And as they started to fill up the Jewish section, there were a number of trainfulls of Jews from Holland, a lot of Hungarians, French women. They were the wives of officers who were POWs from the French Army. And then in '44, after the invasion of Italy, a lot of Libyan Jews [arrived] that [German general Erwin] Rommel had shipped off to Italy, and they had been held in camps in Italy, apparently under Red Cross supervision. They all had British uniforms and heavy British woolen coats and the like. They came with humongous quantities of food. And we had the opportunity to steal some of it. We actually buried it between the tracks so we could bring it back slowly.[1]

AD: Was stealing food in order to survive something that the newer prisoners wouldn't have known how to do, that you had eventually learned?

AR: Well, you didn't steal from each other, generally. Even though it was a matter of survival. Bergen-Belsen was inside a military training camp, similar to Fort Knox. They must have had a bad storm some years prior to establishing the camp. A lot of trees had fallen over in storms. And they had cut the trees and hauled them off, but there were the roots, you know, standing up.

And for a number of months I worked in the woods digging up those tree stumps. Once a week they came out with the horse-drawn wagons and we had to load those tree stumps that we had dug up on it and they were hauled in. There was another detail inside the camp that was chopping them up into firewood. There were blueberries growing in the woods and of course we ate as much as we could, but also we all had a bag that was tied to your belt inside your pants. So you could pick berries and bring them in for the family to eat. So there was that, and then, of course, if we could we stole the food from the guards. They would get their food and most of the time if they didn't finish it, it just sat there. And if we got a chance, we would try and get those cans and eat it. But apparently one day we ate them before they had eaten, and so we got a pretty good whipping for that. It was probably worth it. It was good food.

AD: Was there a gradual sense of deepening horror and insecurity, or was there a moment when you realized what was happening?

AR: In a way the tragedy was that it was a gradual tightening of the noose, so to speak. I remember the first two days in Belsen, there was so much food we couldn't eat it. There was no nutrition, but a liter of soup, even if it was only a liter of warm water with nothing in it. You're not used to drinking a liter of volume, a quart. And then the amount of food that you got kept getting less and less. Initially, the guards kept changing constantly, and surprisingly they kept getting more and more vicious rather than less so. The last group, which maybe was there for a year, year and a half, were World War I veterans who were too old or too feeble or had been wounded. They were not suitable for frontline service in the German Army. You would think that they would be not so hateful. And they weren't maybe the first week, but they very quickly got to be pretty vicious. I'm not sure whether they were told to, or it was a natural progression as the sensitivities wore off.

AD: Do you feel that, in the long term, having been in Belsen early on was an advantage? You did mention that it was an advantage as far as food. But I wondered if your resistance was stronger, and if you knew the system better?

AR: Well, *system,* there was really no system. But yeah, I think so, because the people who came very late—particularly if they did not come from another camp but straight from home so to speak—were plunged from a normal diet to two hundred, three hundred, whatever it was, calories a day. And I think that even though they may have had physically more reserves than we did, they died faster than those of us whose reserves were spent. But we may have been a little bit more cautious. And also we were so disease-ridden and I don't know whether our immune systems had strengthened. Those are medical issues that I don't know about. People who were plunged into this diarrhea, flea, lice, you know all the vermin. They could not tolerate it as much as those of us who were exposed to it more slowly.

AD: To what extent did you have contact with the other members of your family while you were in Belsen?

AR: We saw them almost every day. My dad and my brother and I were in the same barrack. At night the men and the women were separated, but during the day they could mingle freely. We all were in work details. My mother worked in the infirmary. So, she stayed inside the camp. My brother was working outside the camp, I think. I think my dad worked the whole time on the shoe disassembly detail. I was on it for a little while before they shipped me to work details outside. There was an area where they had set up a huge circus tent. That's where they had the shoes. Apparently, the Germans had collected shoes for recycling or for donations or whatever the reason they gave to collect them. There were also a lot of military boots in there, since many of them had bullet holes in them, or shrapnel holes, apparently from either wounded or dead soldiers. One of the big, quote, "industries" was separating the upper leather from the soles and heels and then separating the leather from the rubber heels and/or soles. The leather soles, I guess, was what they couldn't reuse. And so they were stacked up in a humongous pile that was on the main drag and kept getting higher and higher. You had a wheelbarrow for hauling those, and then you had to stack them so the whole thing wouldn't just fall over. And they emptied that tent of all the shoes, and they started to bring in women, and they established a separate women's camp. You could talk to them usually across the fence as long as you didn't get too close to the fence.

AD: Was there a uniformity of cruelty among the guards, or were any of them kind at all to you?

AR: There was one sergeant, rumor had it later on that he was a spy for the British, who seemed to be more . . . I wouldn't want to call him humane, but had a better sense of humor. And some individual guards were exceedingly cruel and would use any excuse to either kick you or club you with a rifle or shoot at you. Some of them would turn their back and just did their job. But they constantly changed. You never knew. You never spoke to any of them. Some of them would drop a cigarette butt and walk away. Others would drop the cigarette butt and wait for you to try to pick it up and then step on your fingers.

AD: What about friendships in Belsen? Was it still pretty much each one for his own?

AR: Yeah, you didn't have time for friendships. You tried to sleep as long as you could in the mornings. You had a few minutes to wash your face and get dressed and stand at roll call. And then you went to wherever your work assignment was, and then when you came back at night, there could have been another roll call before or after and you may have got something to eat and you went straight to bed. There was never any time to talk to anybody, unless somebody you worked with, [if] the guard had a back turned, you could talk to each other. But most of the time you couldn't. They wouldn't let you.

AD: Did you have any way to keep track of time?

AR: Yeah, you knew pretty much what day of the week it was, what time of day it was, I'm not sure. I don't think anybody had watches. Because at noon time they would bring the food out to where you were working. We may get five or ten minutes to eat and that was it. And sunrise and sunset, but other than that whether it was ten of eleven or ten of twelve, nobody cared whether you knew it or not.

Alexander and his mother, father, and brother were shipped out of Belsen again in April of 1945, along with twenty-five hundred other prisoners. They were marched to a railhead and taken on what Alexander called a "ridiculous safari": crammed onto a train, they traveled around Germany for two weeks, during which time the prisoners' German guards aimed to dodge encounters with Allied forces. On April 23, 1945, the Russian Army overtook them in the German town of Tribitz, where Alexander remained for about six weeks.

While his father, mother, and brother survived the war, many members of Alexander's extended family were killed in Auschwitz.

AD: What kind of condition were you in at the time of liberation?

AR: Barely alive, if you can even count that. We had to be very careful. Many people died because they ate things that they couldn't digest. Their digestive system was so severely weakened or disturbed that a glass of milk would kill you. You just couldn't tolerate that sort of thing. You had to be very careful that you ate only a little bit and a little bit. And of course a little bit was more than what we had had for a long time. We heard that nearby was a Army food depot, and we went there. I got cans or an open bucket of condensed milk, you know, had a lot of sugar in it. And we just couldn't eat it, not for a while. Because we couldn't digest it, it was that rich.

AD: How much did you weigh?

AR: Well, when I got back to Amsterdam, I weighed seventy-eight pounds. So I don't know how much I weighed then, maybe fifty or sixty, strictly skin over bones.

AD: That moment of encountering the Cossack unit, were you aware that this is it, it's over? And was that a particularly emotionally charged—

AR: Yes, yes. Absolutely joyous. Now you had an opportunity, you might live. Might actually see 1946. All of the people that were still alive from that train, there were about a thousand of them, were evacuated by the Americans and taken to Leipzig, where they had a DP [Displaced Persons] camp. And the Russians let the trucks come in and get them.

Essentially it was a military barracks that was used. We could come and go as we pleased. We were not prisoners. Matter of fact, [we were] very grateful about many things. They sprayed us from head to toe with DDT. Think how environmentally unacceptable that is today. And I'm still alive in spite of it. But it got rid of the fleas, and in particular the lice, which was so important. And I don't remember [if] it was with my brother or some other boys, we would get on the trolley and the conductor [was] trying to collect money from us and we were pretty nasty. So they left us pretty much alone. And then we weren't there all that long. We wouldn't go onto the beds because they were absolutely starched, bleached, perfectly white sheets. And here we were, in spite of getting regular baths, pretty filthy. We only had one set of clothes and shoes. I had a woman's Army blouse, I remember it, because it buttoned the wrong way. They insisted we get in the beds and don't worry about getting them dirty. And then they brought us bread that was as white as the sheets were. Couldn't believe that.

AD: Do you recall how you felt at the time? Angry, or happy, or any hopes?

AR: Hopeful is probably the best. I don't think anger set in until later. At that point you're just trying to revive, was probably the closest word to describe it. You're still fairly weak. You're beginning to get a little better.

You can eat a little bit more. Beginning to feel a little better all the time. You're really not thinking about the future, what you want to do, or what you have to do, or what you're going to do. You're still preoccupied with eating, primarily.

AD: What about when you returned to Amsterdam, adjusting to daily life again?

AR: Well, initially of course, I think we were all spread out. I stayed with one family who was a friend of my parents. My brother stayed with a friend of his. And my parents stayed with somebody, I don't even remember who it was. So we were in different locations. And this was like the summer of '45. There really wasn't much going on. Trying to see about getting back into school. My high school class had graduated. I think we may have actually been back in Amsterdam when the graduation was, but of course they wouldn't give me my diploma. Hadn't been there in four years. And so my mother was making arrangements to try to get [me] back into school in the fall.

The Dutch did things fairly reasonably. The person that was living in our house had gotten there in good faith. They did not know that was the residence of deported Jews. And so what they did, if the person had something in good faith, so you don't just transfer the victim from one person to another, they could stay there. So my parents found an apartment where we lived. And then school started pretty soon. I was allowed into the senior class on the condition that if I didn't measure up, that the school would have the right not to let me take the comprehensive exams at the end of the year. And I do remember having to go to a couple of teachers after classes for additional instruction. It's kind of tough to pick up solid geometry if you haven't had trigonometry.

AD: Was it easy for you to focus on studies after what you had been through?

AR: I never thought of it in those terms, but I suppose so, because that's the only thing we did, was to go to school. You spent every night doing homework, and we went to school on Saturdays half a day. And so maybe we were allowed to go and play for ten minutes before dinner. Or if we happened to get done by eight o'clock—the homework—we could play for a half hour before going to bed. But it was all-consuming, essentially, except maybe for the weekends.

AD: Was there a point when you started really reflecting on what had happened to you?

AR: No, not really. It really would have been pointless anyway. The Dutch had been exceedingly helpful, and trying to shield people. The population as a whole, with minor exceptions, had always been very supportive. And now you're back after the war and you're no longer wearing the star, you're no longer distinguishable from the rest of the population. And so there was no need for anybody to either bend over backwards or kick you in the shins.

As a matter of fact, I really haven't dwelled on it much all my life. I have a cousin who was a professional Holocaust survivor and I always detested that. It was one of those things that happened, nothing you can do about it. I'm not ashamed of it certainly. I'm not proud of it. I mean, nothing you can do about it. I suppose, like most unpleasant things, you try and put them out of your mind.

AD: Was there a point when you felt compelled to talk about your experiences to anyone?

AR: No, never did. I've never been much for psychologists. And I suppose I don't remember a lot of things because they're probably suppressed memory, and why bring it up? What purpose does it serve? A friend of mine keeps after me to try and write a book. And I say, "Absolutely not. There's not enough to fill a page."

AD: Do you feel that there's any benefit to be derived from identifying yourself as a Holocaust survivor? [*Rosenberg bursts out laughing*] . . . It's a strange way of putting the question, isn't it?

AR: No, I tell you reason I am laughing is I suppose if you look for sympathy it would be. But no, I don't. Occasionally if I get pushed I will mention it. I normally don't as a matter of conversation.

We were in Spain, on the trip up to Granada to see the Alhambra. And there was a couple in that group that we were with who were Germans, and they had invited a friend of theirs from Germany to come down and join us. And on the way back we were sitting at a table and this man came wandering in by himself. I said to him in German, "How are you doing?" He complained, "Not very well." He didn't speak English, and so unless his friends were around . . . blah, blah, blah. And then on a stop on the way back, we were standing in line together and he said, "How come you speak German so well?" And I was debating what to say. I just said, "I was in a concentration camp." And I totally devastated that man. That evening he sought me out in the bar and came to apologize. I said, "Hey, it's not your fault, you were too young." This man was in his fifties, he may have been a child at the time. So I'm always very careful because there's no need to upset people that have no responsibility. I'm not looking for an advantage. So no, I rarely volunteer the information.

AD: You're doing this interview today. You did one other interview. What has made you agree to do those?

AR: Well, it's the neo-Nazism that says it never happened. And I think there needs to be as much evidence as possible to show that it really did happen. And that those many of us who survived are perfectly normal people, or what passes for normal. At least I think so. And don't all go around looking, "Hey, you owe me a favor because I survived." But it's not a bias-free society.

I've been wanting to go and visit my grandparents' grave. I just couldn't bring myself to the thought of going to Germany. One, because it's Germany; and two, that I wasn't sure whether I could control my temper if somebody were to say something to me that would set me off. And so we decided on a trial, and that was we went to Switzerland for a week with day trips out of Lucerne. And the first trip was to the Black Forest. You get out of it for lunch and you get back on the bus. The bus was the safe haven. And it went all right. I didn't feel particularly bad or tense. But on that boat trip, after Cologne, it got to me suddenly, and I had to get out of there. And during dinner, I got up, went up on top of the boat, on the top deck, to make sure we passed that border back into Holland. Because I just got obsessed all of a sudden, panicky. And haven't been back since.

AD: What about your children? Do you feel like it's important to leave them some kind of knowledge about your life and your experiences?

AR: Well, they know about it, of course. I think they all have copies of the tape of the interview.[2] It's really my father's cousin that was much more informative than mine. He remembers names and dates and the name of the commander of the camp and all that kind of stuff that I have no idea about and don't really care. And yeah, my kids know, but they also have no relation to it. My youngest daughter, when I said something to her about the Vietnam War, says, "But Dad, I was only six then." You know, so it's all ancient history. They're not really interested.

AD: You mentioned someone you know who's a professional Holocaust survivor. Can you say more about what bothers you about that, or what you think the danger of that is?

AR: Oh, I don't think there's danger in it, it may bore people to death, but you can do that with other things, too. That was the singular defining incident of his life. And everything is being related to that. That may have been the most important event in my life, even though I don't think so. I think there are much more important things. I mean, it's part of my history. I was fortunate that I survived it, and I moved on. I don't particularly dwell on it. Or try and say, "Now wait a minute, I married that woman because I didn't see that woman . . . " or—you know, and relate it to the Holocaust. It has nothing to do with it.

AD: Have you had the experience of people assuming that because you are a Holocaust survivor, that was the defining event of your life, and therefore not seeing you clearly?

AR: No, because I doubt whether anybody that would know me would find out that I am a Holocaust survivor until they really have known me for a long time. Because I don't normally bring it up. Not unless something happens to make it pop up for some reason or another, inadvertently, but no, I wouldn't think so. They just see the lack of hair. [*Laughing*]

AD: Is being Jewish important to you?

AR: Yeah, definitely. I am the only Jew in my family. [*Laughing*] And I am proud of it.

AD: What does that mean to you, to be the only Jew in your family?

AR: Oh, I am saying it jokingly and seriously. My wife is Episcopalian. Our children were baptized in the Episcopalian church, but are not particularly religious. My youngest daughter was married in the Catholic church and apparently they are now going to church regularly, which is fine. I have no problem with it one way or the other. Our oldest daughter was married for the first time in the Episcopal cathedral in Lexington, which as you may know is so Orthodox that the mass was in Latin. That marriage didn't last, and her current husband is a Baptist. I'm not sure that they are going to church, but their son goes to Bible school. And the other one doesn't have any children and, as far as I know, they were married by a minister whom they knew. So that's why I'm saying that.

AD: Can you say what it means to you to be Jewish?

AR: No, not really. No more so than what it means being a chemist or of German extraction or married or grandfather or anything else. You better not say anything anti-Semitic or I'll blow your head off. [*Laughing*] But other than that, no.

AD: It doesn't necessarily mean keeping certain traditions or going to synagogue?

AR: Not really, no, no. Keep certain traditions, but I . . . [I'm a] bit of a pragmatist, and I'm not all that tradition-bound. I think the dietary laws make good sense from a health perspective, but I don't particularly find the need to avoid eating shrimp.

AD: When you say it's important to you to be Jewish, is it as a religion?

AR: Well it's really more ethnic than a religion. You can't help whatever your racial or ethnic background is. I'm not hiding it and I'm not flaunting it. So, I don't care whether somebody knows or doesn't know. It's not that I don't care personally, what I mean is I'm not concerned about it.

AD: Let's pick up the time line again. We left off in Amsterdam just after the war. You're going back to school, you're working hard at being a student. You were talking about being hopeful at the time. Do you recall what you were hopeful for, what you really wanted for the rest of your life?

AR: Well, initially to graduate from high school, sweating like everybody else to pass the exams. But I did [pass]. I wanted to become a chemist or a chemical engineer. And after I graduated from high school I went to the Technical Institute in Delft for one year to study chemical engineering.

Then, much to my dismay, my parents decided to come to the United States, and I didn't want to go. Well, for one thing, you had to leave your friends, just getting into the swing of things, having done my freshman year in college. But they didn't give me a choice. A lot of my mother's family and some of my dad's family had been over here for years, so we came over here Memorial Day, '47.

AD: What were your notions about the U.S. at that time?

AR: Well, the only notions you have are the cowboys, and the skyscrapers of New York. And since it was Memorial Day when we got here, the night before, traveling along the south shore of Long Island, you saw the fireworks. Of course, you didn't know what was going on. Memorial Day didn't mean anything to us. Then it was hot, one of these early hot spells. My mother's brothers came and met us at the boat, and took us over to my mother's sister's apartment.

My mother's brothers had gotten an apartment for us, in Queens, in New York City. And so we lived there. I guess, but I'm not sure, we stayed with my aunt for a while until our furniture arrived, because I'm not sure it was on the same boat. It came later.

AD: Do you remember first impressions of New York?

AR: Hot, hot and dirty. Of course the high rise, and the frantic activity, cars going everywhere.

AD: How was your English?

AR: Non-existent or very poor. Well, I had high school English. But didn't have much choice, had to learn in a hurry, because I got a job within a week as a lab technician at Mount Sinai Hospital. Paid the glorious wage of one hundred dollars a month. And we had to work half-day Saturdays. And then we took turns taking calls on the weekends. That paid an extra six dollars. And the girls all were more interested in going to the beach, so I took all of their calls, because I needed the six dollars more than I needed a suntan.

And then I got a ticket. Two weeks in this country and I got a ticket. That was Saturday morning, going to work, I was going down the subway and a cop stopped me. I didn't understand enough of what he was saying. And so I pulled my passport out and I opened it on the immigration stamp. I did understand what identification was. And so he proceeded to write, and gave me my passport back, and tore this thing out and told me it was a ticket. Well, the only meaning of the word "ticket" I knew was admission to a theater. Didn't want to, don't have time to go. Tried to explain . . . finally made me take it, he told me I didn't have to go myself, I could give it to somebody else. When I got to work I tried to tell the fellow I work with, I asked him if he wanted the ticket. He said what for? [*Laughing*] I told him I didn't know, but a cop had given it to me.

And [in 1952,] when I became a citizen, you have to list violations. It's on my records. I have no idea what it was that I did. You know, hopscotch down the steps into the subway, who knows. The reason you had to be so careful . . . prior to let's say the fifties and sixties, anti-Semitism was an acceptable feeling in this country. And the State Department was so strongly anti-Semitic, they saw it as their function to keep as many Jews out as they could, not to try and rescue as many and let them in.

Alexander shared an apartment with his parents and brother, working by day at Mount Sinai Hospital and attending school by night at the City College of New York.

AD: So, you came in '47, and became a citizen in '52. Those first years that you came to the U.S., were you aware of having to be very cautious as a Jew?

AR: Well, in New York there really was very little that you could or couldn't do as such. But being ignorant as to the American way, I asked a girl in one of my classes at City College for a date and she turned me down flat. She was Italian and I was Jewish and it just didn't go. I didn't know that. I applied for admission to Columbia and RPI [Rensselaer Polytechnic Institute], in Albany, Schenectady. And I was turned down. In one instance, the Dutch quota was filled. You know, all kinds of barriers existed that you ran into either unwittingly or stupidly, whichever, for me mostly unwittingly. Natives would have known better and would have avoided the embarrassment, or whatever you want to call it.

AD: You hadn't been happy to come to this country. Did you end up feeling at home here?

AR: Oh yeah, very quickly, certainly. And I don't want you to think that I was paranoid about these barriers that you ran into. It was just ignorance, you learn from it. One of my uncles took me aside and gave me the facts of life. That there are some things that Jews can't do in this country. Whether you like them or not, you have to abide by them. You're not supposed to drive more than sixty-five miles an hour. And then New York being such a big place you can avoid unpleasantries. There's no need to go looking for them.

AD: Did it strike you as hypocritical? This so-called Home of the Free, discriminating against—

AR: No, frankly, I really never thought about it. I guess it really wasn't very important. They were minor inconveniences. It wasn't any big deal.

AD: So, what happened next? You're going to school at night and you're working in the day.

AR: Trying to get better jobs. Getting paid more. And then the Korean War started. I was classified 1-A [available for military service] to begin with before I ever took the physical. And then trying to get a student deferment. I had a very nasty draft board that made all kinds of unpleasant remarks when I went for a hearing for a student deferment, about "What's the matter, don't you want to shoot some Chinks?" I graduated in January of '51, and went on to graduate school, and they just gave me fits all the way through. Half the time I was deferred, half the time I wasn't, which was a real distraction while in school. But I made it through all right. Didn't even think about it, I went to work for Shell Oil Company and that was deferrable employment because of the oil industry. Of course the war was pretty well over by that time anyway, '54.

AD: Would you have felt willing to go and fight in the Korean War if you hadn't been a student, or what were your feelings behind that?

AR: Not very happy about it. I wasn't even a citizen. Wasted enough time in my life already without having to serve a few more years in the Army. I mean, I wasn't going to refuse. But I wasn't going to volunteer either.

Alexander obtained his Ph.D. in analytical chemistry from Duke University. While there, he met his future wife, Alice, who lived in an apartment downstairs from Alexander's.

AD: When you met your wife, did she have any idea of what your history had been during the war? Did you talk about that during your courtship at all?

AR: I don't think so. You'd have to ask her, but I don't think so. That never became an issue. I had back problems thirty-some years ago. I asked the surgeon, "Was there any indication what the cause was?" And he said, without knowing what my background was, "Yeah, severe malnutrition during your growing years."

AD: Does she ask you at all about it now, or in recent years?

AR: No, no. She knows. Probably my mother told her a number of things, and she's seen the videos also. All the kids have seen them. They're aware of it, but it's just *a* piece of history, not *the*. A lot of difference there.

AD: What happened after you got married? Did you move?

AR: Yeah, a bit hectic few days. I had my Ph.D. orals on Thursday and a final in a class on Monday. We got married on Tuesday and we left after the wedding and went around the coast of Houston, where I had to report for work at Shell a little less than two weeks later. I was a research chemist. I stayed there for five years. I didn't like what I was doing—it just got to be a bore—and started looking for another job, and got a job with GE in Cincinnati and was there for almost ten years and then got transferred down here.

AD: As far as your profession, what was your real interest?

AR: Problem-solving using chemistry as a tool to solve a lot of technical problems. That was probably my forte. I was pretty good at it, at the time. And the assignment in Cincinnati was pretty interesting. I had a good time. It was nerve-racking, because it was [AEC], the Atomic Energy Commission was the primary contractor. And so it was at the whims of the government. And two years after I was up there we went overnight from three thousand to three hundred employees. Fortunately, I was one of the three hundred that they kept. I finally decided this is getting too much, these ups and downs, and mostly downs. And there was another one coming, so I decided to look around the company [GE] for other possible opportunities, and they happened to have an opening down here, so I applied for it and got it, in the appliance business here as an analytical chemist. And then a year later or two years later, I was made manager of analytical chemistry and processes.

AD: Did you have any preconceived notions about living in Kentucky?

AR: Well . . . funny, because we talked about it yesterday. While we were still living in Ohio, the Riverfront Stadium was the big issue. They started construction. And they said when they got done with that they were going to build the biggest zoo in the world. They were going to put a fence around Kentucky. So, that answers that question, right? No, not really, didn't know much about it. I was commuting for about two months. And so got acquainted a little bit with the area while I was still living up there. And there wasn't that much difference. People are people everywhere. And a pretty nice group of people here that I worked with and worked for. Matter of fact, I'm still fairly good friends with one of my former bosses. And I'm particularly happy about that.

AD: When did you move to Louisville?

AR: '68, a little over thirty-two years ago.

AD: And no involvement with a synagogue here?

AR: No, not particularly.

AD: You mentioned earlier about how you don't really have contact with other Holocaust survivors in the area. And you're not sure you want to.

AR: Not on that basis. I mean, I'm not saying that I say, "You're a Holocaust survivor, move aside, I don't want a part of it." What I'm saying is, if I happen to meet somebody who also is, I have no problem with that.

AD: Looking back over your years here after the war in the United States, were you mainly focusing on your work and your family, or did you have other passions?

AR: Oh yeah, I have a number of hobbies. For one thing, I like to cook and obviously like to eat. And gardening, although my garden right now doesn't show that. And I always like to travel, but of course, with a family and work that isn't always possible. So we made up for it since I retired. And I enjoy history, learning about it, learned more about it since I retired, I guess. And then, too, when we travel, I don't go for these Caribbean cruises, you know, "Show me, feed me, entertain me." I like cruises because they are a lazy man's way of traveling—you only pack and unpack once—but there has to be a reason for it. And sometimes they are real eye-openers. A couple of years [ago] we went on an Eastern Mediterranean and Black Sea cruise and we were in Constanţa, Romania, which is the major port of Romania on the Black Sea. Well, never even thought that the Romans as well as the Greeks, both came up the west coast of the Black Sea, east coast of the Balkan Peninsula. And that they had gone that far north into what is now Odessa and to the Crimea. I'm sure it's of no importance right now, but in terms of historical event, just didn't think about that or heard about it.

AD: What about Holocaust-era history? Have you taken an interest in finding out what happened on a broader scale?

AR: Oh yes, yes, definitely. There are a number of [educational television] programs that deal with the Holocaust or deal with certain aspects of the Holocaust. And the Holocaust in the broadest sense, in terms of the enslaving of particularly the Slavs, the Eastern Europeans, and the genocide of them, not necessarily just the Jews. And of course, I went to the Holocaust Museum, but I couldn't make it past the *St. Louis,*[3] because I remember that one vividly. Another black mark in our history.

AD: It was too painful to be going through and reminded?

AR: Yeah, painful, and the thing is that the *St. Louis* had roughly nine hundred passengers and I don't think two dozen survived. It's incredible, the things that the U.S. government could have done, should have done, and never did do. It's that kind of malfeasance that really upset me, particularly in that context.

AD: I'm interested in something you said in your last interview, which was a piece of advice that you gave to other Holocaust survivors: that many have met with very good fortune in their postwar lives, and that they ought to do what they can to give something back to the community. And so on the one hand you have that compulsion, and on the other hand, you have this knowledge of the shortcomings of the U.S. government and the ways that it has not served, in the instance you just brought up, Holocaust survivors. How do you reconcile those two?

AR: Well, those are, in my opinion, two totally separate issues. Maybe they are related, and that is by giving back to the community, by helping people that are in need of help. Maybe because the government should, and isn't, you're overcoming the shortcomings of our government. Even though I don't take that into consideration. There are two ways that one can give back: one is financially, and that's the easy way out that most of us take, is to make contributions to a variety of charitable organizations. But then the more important one is to give of your time and help people. In Louisville there is an incredible shortage of volunteers. And all of us retirees who have spare time, and we should have spare time, should donate some of that time to some of these organizations. Whether it's Dare to Care to sort out cans of food, or work at the Wayside Christian Mission as an example, any of these shelters, and dish out food for people in need.

It's amazing—I don't do that much, I'm not trying to pat myself on the back, but one of the people that used to work for me professionally now actually works for me in a volunteer [capacity]. One of his volunteer activities got the GE volunteer award of the year, he and his wife, jointly, this past year. Between the two of them they put in three thousand hours a year—that's a hell of a lot of hours. That's almost a full-time job. If we could get half the people to do half that or for that matter, ten percent of the people to do ten percent of that, it would be a lot of help. And that's what I mean by that.

I don't know whether this gets perpetuated or not, but I certainly would urge, not just Holocaust survivors, but all retirees to think about [giving] something back to the community. There's such a terrible need. And here in Louisville, we are blessed with a number of things. We have here three groups that make recordings for the blind. There isn't another city in this country that does that. We have three public radio stations. Even New York only has one. There are a lot of things that are good things—matter of fact, I don't brag about Louisville, keep down the population influx. [*Laughing*] Selfish.

AD: You're pretty much of a Louisville patriot.

AR: We have it very good here in Kentucky, and particularly in Louisville, and of course, Lexington. Louisville has grown up a lot in the last fifteen, twenty years. I used to get all my bread from Chicago, now there's a grocery store over on Taylorsville Road that carries it and I can go get it there. We used to go to Cincinnati to get a three-month supply of cold cuts, now I can buy almost all of it here. And so on and so forth. We're blessed here with, within two miles or three, excellent bakeries and different bakeries. If you want a certain thing, you get it here. How many communities can you say that? In twenty minutes I'm at the airport.

AD: You feel welcome here, comfortable here, as a Jew?

AR: Oh yes, absolutely. That is not an issue at all in this community. The Ku Klux Klan exists here, but you can ignore that. I have never had anybody make a disparaging remark to me or denied me something because I'm Jewish.

CHAPTER 8

This interview, which spanned three days in 1999 and 2000, was conducted in John Rosenberg's Prestonsburg office. By then, John had lived and worked in the Eastern Kentucky town for thirty years. As the director of the Appalachian Research and Defense Fund—also known as AppalReD—John oversaw the operations of eleven offices around Kentucky. AppalReD is a public interest law firm that focuses on systemic issues of poverty in Appalachia.

John retired from AppalReD in 2001, but remains highly active in his community. He spearheaded, for example, the establishment of the Eastern Kentucky Science Center in Prestonsburg, which opened to the public in 2004. He has received many prestigious awards and accolades, both locally and nationally, for his service to community through law.

John was born in Magdeburg, Germany, in 1931.

JR: There was a very heavy religious influence in my father's family. And my dad was very knowledgeable in Jewish law. He knew the five books of Moses by heart. If you go into the synagogue, the five books of Moses are in the scroll and you could start my father anywhere and he could give you the rest of the passage. He was a teacher for Jewish schools. When he got his degree, he went to Idar-Oberstein to be a school teacher. And he met my mother, who was a student. And she was eighteen, I guess, quite young, when they were married. And then [he] brought her to Magdeburg in this little garden apartment, this very pretty young woman. I don't know if you realize that people who are born in very early October are often New Year's Eve babies. They had a big party. Here I am.

AD: Did you have much of a religious education?

JR: Well, as much as you can get from six to eight. Because Kristallnacht[1] was November '38, so I was just seven years old. We lived in Magdeburg, in the house that was adjacent to the synagogue, a big courtyard out front. When the Storm Troopers[2] came to the house and rousted us out that night and brought us into the courtyard, Mother asked somebody whether they're going to kill us, and he said they didn't know. Then they dynamited the temple, and they brought all the religious scrolls and all the books out into the courtyard and burned them. That's what I can remember very vividly, just seeing all that stuff burn up. And then two or three in the morning, they said, "Go back into your house." Things were pretty well upside-down, they just smashed a lot of stuff. And we went back to bed.

Then the next morning, early on, the Nazis came and arrested my father and his brother. My father was in the concentration camp Buchenwald about eleven days. They arrested hundreds, maybe thousands of Jewish men. My mother took me to Frankfurt, [to stay with] different people every night for several days during that interim. [But] apparently the political establishment [in Magdeburg] was not sympathetic to Hitler. And so, with their help, they were able to get my father out. And he was ordered to get out of the country within thirty days. When my father and his brother were released from concentration camp, I can remember them coming to this apartment [Aunt Mary's apartment in Frankfurt]. They were totally bald. They'd had their heads shaved. My father, at that time, had a lot of hair. So it was dramatic to see them, even as a very young child. My father's sister had a little boy named Bubi, who was my age. I remember we were eight years old, and my cousin and I were playing under the table and seeing the knees of all these adults sitting around. Almost everybody, this family and this cousin, were [later] gassed.

AD: You described being taken out of your house in the middle of the night by the Storm Troopers and then watching them burn all the Torah scrolls. Was that the first time that you had realized the danger of the situation?

JR: I want to believe that I remember some of the signs that said *No Jews*

Allowed which popped up on stores. But as a six- or seven-year-old, you just learn what the rules are. So I don't know that I ever was afraid. And I don't think my parents ever gave me any reason to be afraid. We lived a very normal life.

[We] made [our] way to Rotterdam, Holland, where we were in this sort of an internment camp. We ended up being there for a year. I remember the sign on the wall said, in five languages, *Don't spit on the floor.* And we came over to the United States on the boat in February 1940. That was just before the war broke out with Holland. In fact, we were either on the last boat or the next to last boat. I remember when we were on the boat, *The Wizard of Oz* was playing. Was the first American technicolor movie, sound, Judy Garland.

AD: Do you remember how you felt at the time?

JR: No. I mean, I think you're in wonderment. All of sudden you take a boat trip and there's the Statue of Liberty and then you come up with your family. [Mother's] sisters came to the boat and we moved in with them initially. Just squeezing into an apartment. And there was very little work in New York. Most of the jobs were cleaning, or people were doing stuff at home. My mother and her sisters would sit around sewing the bottoms and tops of bedroom slippers together, piecework, to make money. My father, after a very short time, heard that there were jobs in the South. He went to Spartanburg, South Carolina, and started sweeping floors in a textile mill so he could take care of his family. He pretty quickly became a shift manager and he saved his money and got a small apartment, and about six months later we moved to Spartanburg.

Then, unfortunately, after a few months he fell off a ladder. In this apartment where we lived, we had just two or three rooms. My mother did the laundry on a potbellied stove. So, she had relied on him to always pick up this big vat of clothes and laundry and put it on. We had this little wood-burning stove and burned corn cobs and, I suppose, coal. And she'd boil the clothes and wash them the old-fashioned way. When he broke his foot, he couldn't do that. As a result, he went downtown and we had the first Bendix automatic washer. This little immigrant family in Spartanburg, South Carolina, had one of the very first automatic washing machines in 1941. Neighbors would come in to look at it and see the clothes spinning round and round and round.

There was no rabbi in Spartanburg. The Jewish community learned right away about my father's vast knowledge of Jewish culture and religion and that he could actually officiate at a service. And so he began officiating in Spartanburg and started writing sermons in English. And did the whole thing. There was a military base in Spartanburg, Camp Croft. And so the Jewish soldiers, who would sometimes come to the synagogue and see Daddy, would [also] come to our little poor apartment on weekends. I've always thought it's very remarkable. I mean, they didn't stay in New York, where people spoke German. But they came South and here's my dad, writing sermons and officiating when he's not in his fairly menial job at the factory.

Then somehow the congregation in Gastonia, North Carolina, which was about seventy-five miles away, also had no rabbi. And so my dad started commuting between Spartanburg and Gastonia and officiating at services in Gastonia. After a couple of years, Daddy started moving up a little bit and became a shift manager and a foreman. And learned the textile knitting business, totally something he'd never done in his life. And became very good at it.

We lived in Spartanburg about three years [and then moved to Gastonia]. I was like in the fourth, fifth, and sixth grade. And I was kind of a novelty, immigrant son. People would ask questions about how it was on the boat. So, the classrooms would start scheduling me around as a speaker to other schools, because they had this little ten-year-old who could talk about life in Germany and coming over on a boat and being Jewish. And I was still speaking broken English.

AD: Was your lack of socialization a problem at all, or did you feel confident enough that it didn't affect you?

JR: Oh, I think it went very well. In junior high school I developed a lot more confidence. By the time I was in the eighth grade I was president of the class. In high school I was president of the class in my sophomore and my senior years. I became pretty Americanized. I was very involved in Scouting, which was a great help, and in some other civic stuff. And I worked after school. When I was twelve, I had my first newspaper route. As some people would say, we were poor and didn't know it. But those early years, when you think about it, we had such an enormous adjustment to make.

AD: I was going to ask you about that. I've heard other people talk about arriving in New York, and there was a lot of encouragement for Jews who were immigrating to go to various other parts of the country. So many people just didn't want to do that, and they stayed in New York even though there was no economic opportunity at all. Your parents seem to have been very open-minded and aware of opportunities, and that probably shaped your life a lot, too.

JR: It did, I'm sure, shape my life, from the time we went South. But you know, my parents have a strong work ethic. And so they were not opposed to seeing me have a paper route at a very young age. And that's a very liberating experience. I remember getting up at five in the morning, and going out to get the paper, and then going by the coffee store and putting that nickel down on the lunch counter and saying, "I'd like a cup of coffee." I mean, I was probably not much higher than the stool. I was always doing some kind of work.

AD: Was there ever a conflict between your Jewish identity and your social life? When you were a Boy Scout, for instance, did people expect you to be participating in things as a Christian?

JR: No, it was very interesting. All the Scout troops were sponsored by churches. But when I got to Scout camp as a counselor one summer, one of my jobs was to arrange the [church] services. And so, I found myself in the position of being sort-of the associate minister to these folks, and I learned many of the hymns. And as we grew up, I went to church a few times. But I think it was just a healthy respect. I think people in the church were respectful of the Jewish community and religion. Now, many other Jewish men might have said, "Why are you being a minister in this largely Protestant camp, and sort-of embracing their way of having a service?" But I didn't have any problem with that. My parents didn't have any problem with it.

AD: Do you think your parents taught you Judaism in a way that allowed you to think of that as not being a contradiction?

JR: I think my parents were very tolerant of other religions. Now, my father had this very strong Jewish background. When my father came South and started working in the factory, [he] realized that it was not going to make sense to be kosher and that maybe bacon and eggs were good together. And they basically adapted to living in a Protestant society.

I don't know that we were ever conscious of anti-Semitism. It was never a problem. My parents were not in the country club set, so they didn't have to worry about whether they could get into the country club. We had many more friends who were not Jewish than the ones who were, probably because of the economics of the situation. Those people [the Jewish communities in Spartanburg and Gastonia] were well off, and they were friends in the synagogue and were always very nice, but they would travel and do things that my parents didn't do, because we couldn't afford it, and because they weren't interested in it.

In retrospect, after I worked in the Civil Rights Division and after I was in the service, I always felt a little sad that the Jewish community [in Gastonia] was not a little more assertive about desegregation. But I think the store owners were all afraid to lose their business.

AD: You think that if they weren't afraid to lose their business, they would have been inclined to push for desegregation?

JR: Judaism is founded on the theory of justice. Churches were segregated, too. It was a segregated life. Although you grow up with it, you don't pay attention to it. I think it's always hard to look back and say, but I think if they had felt they could have done more, they might have done more.

The service was the first major arena where there was desegregation in this country, the military. And, you know, we brought an airplane back from England one year by way of Iceland and Greenland. Came back to New York. The radar operator on my plane—I was the navigator—was a fellow named Abe Jenkins, who was from South Carolina, who was black. And he and I got on the train in New York together to come home. When we got to Washington he got up all of a sudden and said, "I'll see you when we get back." I said, "Where are you going?" He said, "I'm going to the back of the train, where the blacks are." I said, "What?" And he said, "Yeah, I need to go there, otherwise we're going to have some trouble."

It was an incident that changed my life, really. I was really outraged and aggravated and thought eventually maybe I can help to do something about that. It's more easily said than done, but when you think about the history of the persecution that the Jews have had, and the Holocaust and all of the things that they've gone through, you would have hoped that Jews would have been more sympathetic to the situation that blacks faced every day. And not quite as much of a willing participant.

AD: Was the time that you were in the Air Force the first time that you had close personal contact with black people and formed friendships?

JR: I think so. I went to Duke on a scholarship which terminated. I didn't have any trouble, I just worked my way through Duke. But Duke had a quota on Jewish students even in those years. And it was before the years that Duke had any black athletes to speak of. And when I came out of Duke, I went into the ROTC. I was president of the senior class and had been working and it seemed like a good thing to do.

AD: Was being Jewish important to you from a young age?

JR: Oh, sure. It's always been important to me, and is important to me today. And you know, it's had a profound effect on my life. Not that I think about it every day, but it's a very attractive religion. It's very simple. Its principles make a lot of sense to me, if one is going to believe in a higher being. People are aware that I am Jewish, and I spend some time talking about Judaism, sometimes in schools, sometimes to civic groups, that sort of thing. I'm sure that all of this Holocaust history has contributed a great deal to what I've been doing in my later life.

AD: Did you have a strong sense of allegiance to the United States?

JR: I always had a very strong feeling about allegiance to America or patriotism. That goes back to my parents' coming here. I think we were so grateful to be here that generally everything seemed like it was very positive to be in this country. I was the first person of my generation to go to college. My parents were very proud of that. This country was very supportive of Israel. So, in our eyes, it might be a stretch to say the country could do no wrong, but pretty close to it. So I don't think I was very politically astute. I didn't have any problem about joining the ROTC [Reserve Officers' Training Corps, a college-based military program]. I thought it was a good thing to do, as far as trying to serve the country. You'd get tuition, be able to contribute a little bit. And I think there was a commitment to two years afterwards.

And then the two-year commitment, I first thought I would like to fly. And I went to flight school for a short period of time and that didn't really work out, so I ended up going to navigation training, which I liked. And I became a navigator, and that had a three-year commitment attached to it, which I served out in England. It was during the Korean War, but I was very far from Korea.

While I was in England, at one point towards the end of my tour, we were on alert for the Suez Canal crisis [of 1956–1957, also known as the Tripartite Aggression]. Nobody knew whose side we were on. And I said, "I think this is not a good way to spend your life, when you don't know which side you're on, and then they tell you which side you're on, whether you like it or not." I think if it were a little clearer than that, I might have stayed in the military just because of the very close associations I had with the people in the service. We were just very, very good friends. But if we had come in on the other side against Israel, I would have been in a terrible predicament.

And then [years later] after I married a Quaker, I left my tennis shoes at the Pentagon Athletic Club and never went back to get them. I wouldn't at all call myself a pacifist. Philosophically, if you take a strong pacifist position [as the Quakers do], you are in a sense ready to die when someone points a weapon at someone you love and is ready to pull a trigger. You feel that there is never any justification for violent action. And I don't think I'm in that place. I think there probably are situations where you may find yourself willing to react violently or to take up arms against somebody else. Like a war. And you use a war to end a war. I think it's the last resort, and not one that I would promote, but I don't think I could easily stand by. Of course, I was in the Air Force voluntarily, no one drafted me.

I came out of the service in '57, then I went to work for the Rohm and Haas Company in Philadelphia as a technical representative for a year and a half. I traveled Pennsylvania, New York, and northeastern states, basically selling chemicals, but doing technical sales work, which involves having some knowledge of chemistry, developing some product. But I worked at the Rohm and Haas during 1958 and took the law school test. So I entered law school [at the University of North Carolina] in 1959.

One of my classmates was an African American named Julius Chambers, who became a very prominent civil rights lawyer. And we were good friends. And the Freedom Rides were happening and we were all conscious of what was going on. I think law school made you aware that things would have to change in the South. If you liked your hometown and you liked being a southerner and you saw the good things that the South had to offer, this racial situation had to change. It might have to be forced to make those changes. But I began to think about using the law to help do that.

AD: Why did you choose law school in particular?

JR: You know, I wish I could say I wanted to go to law school so I could go to work for the Civil Rights Division of the Department of Justice. But I don't think that was quite the way it was. I wanted to go to law school because it seemed like it would be a good skill to have. But I remember the first couple of months in school I wondered, what am I doing here? I was not making any money anymore. But by my last year, when we were doing seminars and more research and writing, I enjoyed being there. And started to see that it would be very challenging to be involved in the civil rights struggle through using the law.

In 1962, when I graduated, I thought that I would really want to be in the [Civil Rights] Division [of the Department of Justice] if I could get there. I felt that what the government was doing [in pursuing civil rights legislation] was right, and that it would be a great opportunity to be a part of that as a southerner. You feel like you're helping to improve the place that you live in from a position where you could do some good.

I was with the Antitrust Division maybe a month or two and then I went to work for the Civil Rights Division. And I was very, very pleased to be able to go there. The Civil Rights Division was almost impossible to get into, because they only had about eight lawyers that were doing civil rights work. One of them was John Doar,[3] and he was Assistant Attorney General and you couldn't get a job there unless he saw you and he decided he was going to hire you. And he was in the South most of the time.

AD: How did you manage to get an interview with him?

JR: I mean, you had to keep coming down. The Division was a very small and a little bit of an elite group of people. It was so small because Congress didn't appropriate a lot of money yet. Most of the work the Division was involved in involved voting rights at the time. There was no legislation, until 1964, where anything could be done about public accommodations or employment. All of those were yet to come.

I [got the job, and] was assigned to LeFlore County, Mississippi. I spent a lot of time in Greenwood. Met all of the leaders in the community. There were a lot of voting marches in 1963, and there were a lot of arrests. I went into the jail and interviewed a lot of the people who had been arrested. And then we filed a suit to get them out of jail. That was also the period of time when there was more action by SNCC [the Student Nonviolent Coordinating Committee] and CORE [the Congress of Racial Equality]. There was a lot of civil rights activity all summer long [in Greenwood]. The SNCC headquarters was there, and Stokely Carmichael, and Bob Moses, who's now up in Boston, I understand. I spent some time with Medgar Evers,[4] not much. He wasn't in LeFlore County, but I had actually been to his house not too long before he was killed.

And you know, in 1964 you had the killing of the three civil rights workers.[5] They were holding voting rights meetings in Neshoba County, Mississippi. They called it Freedom Summer. Students from all over the country were there.

AD: Were you ever personally threatened, or did you feel threatened, being there?

JR: I never felt really in danger. After the Neshoba killings, we started always driving together—in Neshoba County, at least—in pairs, being together with another person who was working. Before that we were generally by ourselves. I never carried a weapon. But I never really was in fear, at least I don't recall. We all knew that we were in such a different situation from the people who we were working with. I mean the blacks, who were so vulnerable, who had to display such courage just to go register to vote. You just couldn't help but be impressed by these folks. Many of them were just hard-working people, who wanted to just have the same right as everyone else. It seems so very simple.

Mistreatment of blacks in the South by police officers was seen as something that the government was not doing much about. The discrimination and segregation was very blatant.

[Mississippi] governor [Ross R.] Barnett and [Alabama governor George] Wallace just defied the government, said we're not going to let blacks in these universities. And that was the way the voting thing was all over the South at the time. Blacks couldn't vote. If they went up to try and register they'd lose their jobs or their lives. And there were very few resources that were being devoted to doing anything about it, until the Kennedy administration.

We were lawyers who spent a lot of time in the community, but we would go back to Washington. Blacks wanted more protections. They wanted federal marshals when they went to register. And they wanted more lawyers, and Congress wasn't going to do that. There was still the question of what the states do and what the federal government does and the evolving law. And I think oftentimes those of us who were there in our coats and ties and with our federal ID badges—some of the more activist people thought we were just sort of window dressing. And you know, it was not the same as direct action.

[But] I think the Division had a very prominent role that isn't always recognized. We demonstrated that using the court system was extremely slow, and that we could win one little case at a time, but that was doing some good. That was helping. And it also gave blacks some confidence to win. But for the broader picture to change, we also helped write the Voting Rights Act of 1965. The Voting Rights Act really changed everything. [Because of it, across] the South there were black sheriffs in these counties that had more blacks than whites, or [in] heavy black counties. I think it was really probably the most important legislation in many ways passed anywhere. Because it really gave blacks the right to vote and changed the political process.

AD: You mentioned earlier that you were proud of being a southerner. You were aware of the things that were good, and were motivated to be there to change some of the things that were not as good. I have the idea that many northerners, and maybe particularly Jews who lived in the North, felt that the South was backwards and anti-Semitic and controlled by the Klan. What was it that you saw about living in the South that was so positive, that made yourself identify as a southerner and motivated you in this whole endeavor?

JR: I think it's the same, to some extent, [as] what you see in small towns, or rural areas. In a simplistic way, you get the idea that people accept you for who you are. People do have an interest in where they live, and in the sense of place where they are. I think that's maybe true of smaller communities across the board. I'm sure it's true in New Hampshire and Vermont and in smaller places up North, but it was true of the South. When I was in the Civil Rights Division, being a southerner was helpful in many ways, especially in dealing with white officials. I mean, I'm not proud of the Confederacy, but it's part of its [the South's] history. We were strangers in this country, in Spartanburg and in Gastonia, and it became our home. It's the same way I feel about being here in Prestonsburg in some ways. Been here almost thirty years and it's become home. And I think the people here share that same kind of feeling about their place and their community. Appalachia, it's different than North Carolina, but it's the same sort of environment.

AD: Do you think that your awareness of persecution of the Jews during World War II influenced your interest in working for civil rights for African Americans?

JR: Oh, I'm sure it did. I'm sure that what we went through as a family and as Jews had a lot to do with my wanting to participate in the civil rights movement. I mean, it is essentially the same thing. The mistreatment of blacks, maybe it isn't genocide, but there were certainly the lynching periods when many blacks were killed. Not in the scale that was true in the Holocaust. But I think it's the same thing that helped to motivate me to work [in the Civil Rights Division] and work in legal services, where you're essentially trying to do something similar to that on an individual basis.[6] To provide those opportunities so that people are at least even in the courts and that they can find lawyers to advocate their positions. And I've said many times, I think one of the things that this country ought to be proud of is the fact that it does fund programs like ours, and provide lawyers to low-income people. And even makes it possible to sue the government if necessary, biting the hand that feeds you, if you have to. But I think it all has to do with human rights, giving everyone the same opportunity, whether they are young or old, or white or black, or whoever.

AD: How did you meet your wife, Jean?

JR: I met Jean in the Civil Rights Division of the Department of Justice. I was the Deputy of the Southeastern Section. And there were a couple of situations where we began to suspect that John Doar was deliberately sending her to cases that I was working on, since people knew that we had sort-of started dating.

My classmate from law school, Julius Chambers, was practicing in Charlotte [and] had become a very well-known lawyer. Eventually, in later years, [he] argued the Charlotte desegregation case in the Supreme Court. But he had started a law firm and was involved in a lot of civil rights activities, and there had been an attempt to bomb his house. He hadn't gotten hurt; it didn't do a lot of damage. We had started an FBI investigation and it looked like it was clearly to do with the Klan. And so John [Doar] asked me to go up there and look into that. My friend Nick Flannery went with me to Charlotte and we started doing some investigation. We went out to eat, and I asked him to hold my place in line. And I called Jean at her house. I said, "Don't you think we should get married, since we've been together all this time and seem to get along pretty well?"

AD: Was that premeditated, that phone call? It sounds like you were waiting in line for food and all of a sudden you just felt like, "I gotta go propose marriage."

JR: I suppose [I] knew that I was pretty much in love with her and that we ought to do that. Why I did it at that particular moment, who knows? Maybe it was the first free moment. We were working on this Klan case and I just had a desire to do it. So, then I was able to tell Nick when I got back in line, "There's a wedding in the offing." We got married in February 1967.

When we came back from our honeymoon, John Doar called [and] asked me to come down and work on the Mississippi case [the "Mississippi Burning" trial] if I felt like my honeymoon was over. And I said to Jean that I just thought I was ready to go back to work to try and finish this case.

Besides investigating, I spent about a month putting together a notebook on the background of the jurors. My one major responsibility was to firm up the identification of these three civil rights workers who were killed. And that was done through their dental records. We went back and found who their dentists were and the dentists' charts and compared them, in the event that that was in dispute. And then there was clothing that had been retrieved from the workers, and the whole issue of proving that they were who we claimed they were, that they had been the murdered workers.

AD: You strike me as a person with a lot of energy and a lot of drive to go on, but did you ever just feel depressed and have trouble getting out of the bed in the morning? I mean, studying the dental records of these people who had been brutally murdered for working on a good cause. And then you've done other work since then that's had to have been very depressing.

JR: Oh, I think it always has an impact on you. You never forget the smell of those clothes. We had the clothing put away in boxes behind the door. But the stench of the clothing was so strong that it was always there. And for some reason that always stuck with me more than the dental records. Well, you feel very badly for the families, you feel not very forgiving for the people who did this. Sam Bowers,[7] the mastermind of this one, also was behind the firebombing of another African American, Vernon Dahmer, who was a voting rights leader in Hattiesburg, Mississippi. These people were just pretty evil. If anything, you're probably driven. I don't know that I ever felt depressed. At the time this was a pretty highly motivated group of lawyers, who worked in the Civil Rights Division. And we worked extraordinary long hours. Of course, there were some folks who got divorces over that hard work. I think that lawyers get depressed when they lose cases. And we lost many cases in the early stages in the lower courts, voting rights cases and others, because the judges themselves were segregationists and were appointed and came out of that society. So we had to appeal their decisions before and they were reversed and all of that took time. And that's what happened, we overprepared and we generally won, eventually we would win. And then gradually the law started to change.

In 1970, when the Nixon Administration had taken the reins of the Justice Department, the government began to retreat on school desegregation, and John and Jean decided to leave the Civil Rights Division. They bought a used Peugeot for $800, packed up themselves and their new baby, Michael, and set off on a summer-long camping trip. After they returned to D.C., they learned of an effort to establish an organization that would work with issues around poverty in the central Appalachian area: out-of-state mineral interests, black lung disease, environmental damages related to coal mining, deep mining, and surface mining. So John, Jean, and the baby piled back into the Peugeot and headed to Eastern Kentucky to learn more.

JR: So, we came down here to Prestonsburg on an August or a September evening, and pitched our tent out there near Auxier. Jean wanted me to go out and make sure there weren't any bears or foxes. There wasn't anybody there but us. But we met the people who were here and everybody seemed very friendly.

I had already gotten some names of people—Harry Caudill, who wrote *Night Comes to the Cumberlands,* was on the AppalReD board in West Virginia.[8] He wanted this thing to be more of a regional program because so many of the issues were common to central Appalachia, and the state lines really didn't mean anything. The strip mining problems in Kentucky and West Virginia were the same. Unregulated strip mining, landowners having their land torn up without their consent, and that sort of thing. So, I went down and talked to Harry Caudill. [I also talked to] a woman on Mud Creek, Eula Hall was her name, she is a good friend, who founded the Mud Creek Clinic here in our area.[9] They were having a lot of problems around health issues. Hospitals weren't taking people who couldn't pay.

And I went over into Blackey, Kentucky. There was a fellow named Joe Begley, who was running a country store, who was a very strong anti-strip mining advocate.[10] And his wife, Gaynell Begley, was a wonderful person. We talked a lot about their history and the problems that he saw, and that people were getting run over by strip miners. Kentucky's courts allowed strip mining without landowner approval. Because these out-of-state mineral owners had come here in the late 1890s and bought out all the minerals.

The deeds they signed were known as "broad form deeds" because they were so broad in their language. They literally gave the owner of the minerals the right to take the minerals and all steps reasonably nec-essary to build roads and railroads and tram roads. Whatever might be necessary that's incidental to taking out the coal. The Kentucky courts held that those deeds were so broad that they gave the mineral owner the paramount right to the surface owner, as long as the mineral owner didn't arbitrarily misuse that right. So Joe had one of those old deeds and told me that at the time when they executed the deeds, no one could have envisioned these current methods of mining and the huge, mechanized equipment that was in use seventy-five years later. So Joe [and I] talked for a long time, [and he] was pointing out also how poor people couldn't get lawyers to challenge those deeds. There were many situations where he thought it would be just a wonderful thing if we could have lawyers available to represent poor people. Because he saw these situations com-ing up so often.

And so we went on to Florida to visit my mom and dad, and while on the way we decided that this would be an interesting opportunity, to come to Eastern Kentucky. It would be a worthwhile way to practice law. There was a lot of useful and perhaps important work to do on behalf of low-income clients. And also to help start this legal services program, which had sort-of a small beginning in mountain people's rights. So, we decided to come, and we came. And moved to Prestonsburg.

It wasn't an easy beginning. The local Bar was quite hostile. I went to them on one occasion and told them I wanted to set up a system to refer clients to lawyers, if the clients weren't eligible for our services, if they made too much money. So, he appointed a committee to look into it. The president said he thought that was a good suggestion. Well, the committee met and their resolution was to suggest that we leave town, that we not practice law here without their permission. I think they were threatened, and thought we were going to compete with lawyers for clients that would be able to pay. And then many lawyers who were employed by coal companies were not particularly sympathetic to the notion that lawyers might start to challenge some of these practices and give people representation in the courts. So, we were not the most popular people in town when we started. I had difficulty renting an office. Finally found an office in the place where Jean and I ended up living for a long time on the other side of town. And we got started.

AD: When you and Jean first came to Prestonsburg, were you planning on settling here, staying for the long haul?

JR: I doubt it. We probably thought we might be here two or three years. It was a real big transition for Jean, because she had never lived in a rural area or a town the size of Gastonia, which was 25,000 or 30,000. She was from Philadelphia and had lived in Washington. When I looked for a house, she wanted a sidewalk that she could roll the baby carriage on and be near a shopping area. Well, I found a house in town that was kind of in a residential area.

AD: Did any of the difficulty make you feel like, "Okay, if things don't turn around soon, we're out of here?"

JR: No, I don't think I had thought about being out of here. I really didn't have any friends or that much of a support system, especially since I was also sort-of fighting with the other lawyers who had been here. And

Jean was a new mother and was just trying to get to know a few people who might share values, because the wives of the private practitioners were really garden club–types or people who were pretty much interested in money and materialism. But she then gradually started teaching child-birth classes. That was a big avocation of hers, and got her to have an interest outside of being at home. So those early years, our feeling wasn't much of lonesomeness. It was, "They're not going to run me out of town. We're going to set this up. We're going to get started. There's a lot of work that needs to be done."

It was also a difficult time because at the national level President Nixon had an Office of Economic Opportunity director who was opposed to legal services. And he wanted to de-fund those programs. So I had only been here about a year when all of that began in 1973, and it looked like we might lose our money. But fortunately we managed to weather those storms, and we were able to reach an accommodation with legal services. In 1973 we sort-of severed our ties to West Virginia by establishing a separate corporation here. And we added "of Kentucky" at the end of our name. Between 1975 and 1978 we expanded from the single office here in Prestonsburg to the ten offices that we opened and still have. And we went from probably three hundred thousand to about two million dollars a year in our budget. We had eleven offices by 1980, including a research office in Lexington, which we still have.

We represented a lot of people in everyday problems with family law, consumer rights, housing problems. And we did some of the larger challenges with regard to the coal mines. We found out that the agencies that governed all of these programs were not very responsive at times. The state's Mine Safety and Health Administration did not do a good job in protecting the rights of coal miners. Miners were fired because they complained about unsafe conditions. And so we were able to start representing them to get their jobs back and to get damages for them. And then in the environmental area we represented numbers of people who were challenging surface mining permits because they posed dangers to their homes and their property.

We kept after this broad form deed, we challenged it in the courts unsuccessfully. And we eventually wrote legislation that corrected the problem. We drafted a statute that said that if the kinds of mining methods were not described in the deed, it would be assumed that it referred only to methods that were in existence at the time the deed was executed. And in Eastern Kentucky or in most places that would mean deep mining only.

So that amendment was on the ballot in 1988, along with the lottery. And the lottery barely passed. It passed by, I think, fifty-one or -two percent of the vote. Ninety-two percent of people voted for the broad form deed amendment, which showed people knew what they were doing.

But the coal industry decided they wanted to challenge that constitutional amendment as violating the federal constitution. We ended up arguing the constitutionality of the amendment in the Supreme Court. So it took a lot of years, but you cannot today surface mine anybody's land without their consent.

The development of the David community was another really major part of what we did. David is about nine miles from Prestonsburg, and in the 1930s, especially, it was a booming coal town. When the mine closed in the '40s, it kind of went downhill. The town of David was purchased by a small group of businessmen here in Prestonsburg, and people paid rent to them. A group of Catholic priests from St. Vincent's Mission came to David in the late '60s and '70s and started teaching Bible school and some literacy training. And apparently they were approached by the businessmen to see if the Mission was interested in buying the town. They saw the water system going downhill. The homes were in pretty bad shape. So Father Matthew one day came to see me and told us about the offer to buy the town. They weren't interested in doing it, but they wondered whether the community might be able to buy it in some way. So, I asked a law student to do some research and we got a little help from the National Economic Development Law Center. And we put together a Kentucky corporation, and started having some community meetings in David. [Eventually,] we were able to purchase the town. It's a very nice, attractive town now. [Our] kids both went to a day care center at David. Our daughter, Annie, went to the David School, which didn't have many girls at the time and they were able to take her. She did really well there and thought the David School was a wonderful place because of the one-on-one.

AD: Can you reflect on your work here in Prestonsburg, and what it turns out that you've devoted your life to? I mean, you had the opportunity of becoming a chemical salesman and you decided that wasn't what you wanted to do. You've gone more and more in the direction of service.

JR: I think what I'm doing over the last thirty years has been in many ways [the] most fulfilling [work that I have done]. Working with the Civil Rights Division was a great opportunity to learn to practice law and to do something very worthwhile. The big difference is that in the Civil Rights Division, we didn't live in those communities and that we came and went. I have great admiration for the people who stayed there and their courage and how difficult their lives were. The life we've had for the last thirty years in Prestonsburg has been here. Legal services offices are in the communities where our clients are, and so you are a part of that community. You get to know your clients. And you get to live with the problems from day to day. Not to say that all of us are poor, but especially when your children get into the schools, you begin to feel that you have much more of a stake in trying to do something about that community. You find other parents who really want the best thing for their children, even though it may be what we're doing in court is not always popular.

There have been times that Jean might have wondered whether we wouldn't be better off going for a better educational system for our kids. Michael was academically very gifted and sort of ahead of the pack. One of the teachers asked him one day to explain Hanukkah, the Jewish holiday, and some kids teased him while he was doing that. It hurt him because he was doing it at their request. But we were fortunate that we had some teachers who saw how bright he was and that he was able to do quite well. And we had a principal who was very interested in providing good education for mountain kids, and who encouraged Jean to help start a gifted and talented program in the school. There wasn't a single swing on the yard when we first came there. And so we put together a little committee and gradually got a coal company to do some grading and developed a wonderful playground with the PTA on the school grounds. I think as people realize that what you want is the same thing they want, then you begin to feel that people are on your side, even if the few lawyers aren't, and that we have a lot of support in this community.

We represent about seven thousand clients a year, and for each of those clients the case we help them on is the most important thing in the world, whether you've got to talk about an abused spouse, or someone who's about to be evicted from an apartment, or someone who we're helping with social security benefits or something small, or whether we're involved in some major issue involving the broad form deed or safety discrimination, the cases that tend to get the headlines. Or working on trying to help make black lung regulations more liberal, [to get them to the point] where more than 5 percent of the claims are approved. Or something like David. Each of those are a real, positive contribution to helping people lead better lives and making the society a more just one.

AD: You mentioned that there is some racism in the area. Did you experience any anti-Semitism?

JR: I don't think so, because many people in this area really have had no experience with Jews at all, or Quakers for that matter. In the more recent years, I've been to church groups and talked about Judaism. I've never been conscious of anti-Semitism here in any major way. I know that people who are strong Christians do feel that if you're not saved, you're going to Hell. And so they have a real concern about us, whom they may like and they don't want us to go to Hell. We've been to many funerals where they preach about salvation and that you're doomed if you're not saved. And they're looking at you. [*Laughs*] But they mean well.

AD: What is your and Jean's practice as far as faith, religion? You go to synagogue once a month? You go to a Quaker meeting once a month?

JR: Yeah. We sort of maintain the Jewish tradition, especially when everybody is together. And we go to Williamson, West Virginia, for the Jewish services. They are on Sunday night. A rabbi comes down from Huntington, so he has a Friday night service on a Sunday night. The Quakers meet monthly in somebody's home. And of course you can have a Quaker meeting whether you have three people or three thousand, because they are silent meetings for worship. And I always go. I'm a very big fan of Quakerism. It is a very tolerant religion, built on faith, and the light that shines on everyone. I don't know that there's a great enormous amount of difference [between it and Judaism], except that it's built on the teachings of Jesus, essentially. But they don't dwell on salvation and the other parts of it. I think they really dwell on living your life out and serving others, and the principles of humanity that I share and that I feel good about. So I think it's been pretty easy for [Jean and I] to adapt to each other.

We had Passover seders at our house; Jean did the cooking and became fairly well-versed in what's involved. [She] did some reading and, embarrassingly, probably knows more about some of those traditions now than I do. But that's the way the kids were raised.

AD: You mentioned that when you go to speak at various places within the community, people are partially interested in hearing you speak because of your Holocaust-related experiences. You've done so much important work—why do you think it is that people want to hear about that particular aspect of your life?

JR: When we first came we were involved with the Presbyterian church a good bit because they were involved in local social projects. People by word of mouth realized that I wasn't born in this country and that I did have this experience. But I guess in more recent years, as I spoke more about the Holocaust and about being Jewish, there's been a bit more of an awareness about the Holocaust. I think partly because of the [United States] Holocaust Memorial [Museum], and there's been more publicity generally about the importance of this whole era and trying to make people remember it and not let it be forgotten.

[When I speak publicly about the Holocaust,] I talk about the contrast between a society that we have in this country, where we have a government and a nation which is governed by the rule of law, and what happened in fascist Germany, where the legal system was basically put aside for a dictatorship. And how grateful we need to be, and how students and their teachers and all of us ought to reflect on the system we have in this country, which would not, hopefully, permit anything like that to happen. That the checks and balances in the legislative, executive, and judicial systems would keep that from happening. That free speech is important, that all of the guarantees we have under the Constitution and under the Bill of Rights are very meaningful, and that it's important to talk about them.

AD: You mentioned how much, in the beginning, you idealized this country and the principles on which it was founded, and that you really had high expectations of it. Did your perspective change over time? During the Vietnam War, for example?

JR: Well, I think there are lots of times when you wish different political decisions were made. I'm not disillusioned. I still feel very strongly that this is the best country, in many, many ways, in the world. There are a lot of imperfections with it, and some of the issues that we have to resolve are very difficult issues. In this area, the economy being as poor as it is, we've lost a lot of jobs. I think we do have a legal system that really is the basis for the freedom that we have. And a lot of those freedoms are at times tenuous. I mean, I wish we had greater funding for legal services at the state and federal level. There are lots of places where we can improve, being as rich as this country is. We seem not to regard the problems poor people have as seriously as we ought to.

AD: In your work, you have devoted yourself to people who you don't share a lot in common with, as far as your background and tradition. Because those people were disadvantaged in various ways, you felt the need to work with them. Yet your own tradition as a Jew and as a refugee from Nazi Germany has been an important part of your identity. I wonder whether that's been a difficult balance for you. I think many Holocaust survivors have felt the need to be among people who really understand what they've been through, and who experienced something similar to what they experienced.

JR: Well, I don't know. I've appreciated being in Eastern Kentucky very much, in terms of learning about this culture and its history. The crafts and the independence of people who are here and their ancestors. I've always admired people who have lived in a rugged way and appreciated the environment. I've always liked being in smaller towns. Just the trusting nature of people who are in smaller communities. I've been here almost thirty years and it's become home.

I feel very lucky. If you think back on the fact that my father was in a concentration camp, [and] if you think back on all the experiences that I've had, I've been a pretty fortunate person to be where we are today and to have so many different connections. You kind of look around you and you say, "Well, you've had a little opportunity to do something that made a difference over time." I mean, it's not over yet. It's not an epitaph. You can come back in thirty years, and maybe when I hit a hundred, I'll reflect on the last forty.

AD: Okay, I'll see you in thirty years.

CHAPTER 9

Paul Schlisser

Paul Schlisser lives in a subdivision near Fort Knox, outside of Louisville. When I visited in June of 2000, Paul's patriotism was in evidence throughout his home, from the flagpole in his front yard to the photographs of himself in uniform on the walls. Paul is a man of perfect posture and authoritative voice—"My voice carries, I can assure you of that," he said as I set up my recording equipment—and would seem the stereotypical U.S. Army master sergeant, were it not for his small stature and Hungarian accent.

Paul was born in Álmosd, Hungary, in 1935, the youngest of four children. His father was a leather merchant and his mother a seamstress. His family moved to the Hungarian city of Debrecen in 1940—a more central location for his father's business.

AD: Did you notice any anti-Semitism before the Germans occupied Hungary in 1944?

PS: Oh yes, it started in actually about '43. By then you already had to sew on the yellow stars and all that stuff. And the Christian friends all of a sudden disappeared. They didn't know you anymore. Even if they wanted to, probably their parents told them, "Stay away from them, don't play with them."

It started in '43, but it really didn't get serious until '44. And that I remember vividly. We went down to my mother's parents [in Álmosd].

I remember it was Passover night or the night thereafter, the policeman from the village came in. He said that all Jews must go back to where they lived. And so in the middle of the night we had to get a buggy and horses and catch a train back to Debrecen. From there they told us that we have to move into the ghetto. And so they set aside about two or three square blocks, which they put wooden gates up on each end of the street, blocked it off. And then windows that were looking outside from the ghetto, they bricked them in, so basically you had an enclosed area of so many houses. A couple of streets, basically, is what it amounted to. And they herded everybody in there.

AD: Do you remember being herded in there?

PS: Well, basically they told us you have so much time to gather whatever you could carry, belongings, and move in there. So, we moved in. And they allocated, for each family, a room or whatever. And from there they took the men to work. They would come and take them off in the morning with shovels and stuff, and then come back at night. My dad wasn't there, because he was already taken to labor battalions for the Hungarian Army, which was fighting the Russians. Back in '43 he was already gone.

So, we were moved into the ghetto, just my mother and us four children. And my mother kept on sewing. That's basically what we were supported on. But we weren't there that long, because once they got everybody together, they started cleaning out that place. Load people up and they went to Auschwitz.

The only reason I'm sitting here talking to you right now is because the fact that my father was American. He was born in New York City and he never accepted Hungarian citizenship. Consequently, we were protected by the [politically neutral] Swiss Embassy. So they put us in a separate house from the rest of the ghetto. There were some other families there who were considered foreign nationals. They were protected by the Hungarian police, not by the Germans. Once the whole ghetto got emptied, we were taken on train to Budapest, and they put us there in what they called a protective house. Basically it was a prison. So, that's where they kept us till December 1944.

AD: Do you remember what you were feeling during that time? Being this young boy, being afraid?

PS: The house that we were in was close to the central train station, and they got bombed a lot, so we always had to go down to the shelter. I don't remember being afraid, to be perfectly honest with you. Sounds crazy, but if I was, I do not remember it as such. I guess at that age, you really do not comprehend what was going on.

AD: Were you close with your brothers and sisters?

PS: I think so. We always did everything together. Back in Debrecen, we used to have matinee operettas, you know. I was just a tiny little thing. But we used to always save our money and go on Sundays to the matinee. There was a place they called Nagy Erdö, which is basically a little forest area, and they had a big pond there and rowboats. And I remember my brother taking me there for a rowboat ride. I mean, we were close family. Even today, every year we try to see each other. Once a year we get together somewhere, if it's at all possible. Matter of fact, I just came back. I visited my sister in Israel. My sister from Sweden was sick, so she couldn't join us. But that's the first year that all three of us weren't together. So, next year we are going to Sweden. Whether she is sick or not, we'll be there.

AD: Did all of your brothers and sisters survive the war?

PS: My two sisters did and my brother did, but he got killed in Israel during one of the altercations over there between the Arabs and them. He fought during the Independence War.

AD: Do you remember anything else about your time in the protected house?

PS: Well, basically there was a lot of families there. I remember one guy taught me how to play chess. They had all different nationalities, whoever were at war with the Nazis. I think that all of them were Jews. I know there were a lot of little kids and we played. The quarters were very tight. My father joined us back in Budapest at the protective house. They brought him back from whatever work battalion he was in. I guess the Swiss Embassy intervened. I think for the whole family, we only had one big room. And we had a window that opened up on the courtyard. But it was enclosed. The Hungarian police sitting in each hallway, armed.

AD: Did they treat you decently, or were they cruel?

PS: Yes, as far as I know the Hungarian police treated us decently. Okay? The rough time was with the Hungarian Nazis during the ghetto. And there they hit you with the butt of the rifle, whatever, if they didn't like your looks, or whatever turned them on. But at the protective house, they did treat us decently. There was no rough stuff.

December of '44, I guess the Russian[s] were getting too close, and then they just moved everybody out in the street. Said, "Everybody out, pick up whatever you can carry." Well, that day is when all hell broke loose. They lined us up in the street. This was in December, cold, snow on the ground. There was no trains from Budapest, so they marched us. We walked about four days, maybe a hundred and twenty miles, to a rail head. And we were cold, snow and young children. And they called it a death march, because whoever couldn't keep up they just shot him. Dropped him whenever he couldn't go no more and killed him. Either you went or you died, as simple as that.

AD: Did you have any of your belongings with you, were you having to carry—

PS: Initially we had belongings with us, but as we walked we got rid of most of the stuff we couldn't carry. Just the most important necessities is what you kept. Everything else got thrown to the side of the road. And, you know, just kept on trucking.

AD: Did you have any food with you? Or were you given any?

PS: Well, each evening they usually had some big barns I guess they took over from some farms. They herded us in there. I wouldn't think it was more than maybe four or five hundred people, all from that protective house. Usually they fed us some kind of a hot soup and some black bread. And that was basically all the food we got.

AD: Was it the Germans who were evacuating and leading the march?

PS: Yes, there was Germans, and some Hungarian Nazis were working with them, but basically the German SS was in charge. So once we got to the rail head, there they separated the women and the children [from] the men and they loaded us on separate cattle cars. They packed us full in these cars. We barely could breathe, and one little bucket in a corner for everybody to use as a toilet. They closed the doors, and off we went. My father was taken separately, all the men were taken to different camps. So they took us to Ravensbrück, that's where our first concentration camp was.

AD: Do you remember starting to feel afraid during that time about what was going to happen to you and your family?

PS: I'm not saying I wasn't, but I never, ever can remember that I was afraid. I don't even know what I was feeling. I guess I was just trying to survive. In the cattle car, if you don't watch it you will be trampled to death.

Matter of fact, my sister tells me—and I could not verify it for you, because I'm not remembering—but once we were in Ravensbrück, they had *appell,* basically like reveille in the morning in the Army. Everybody had to fall out of the barracks and line up and had roll call. And that whole camp was basically women. There were a few children, but not too many. My mother had a real terrible headache and she asked for some medication, and the German whipped her with a riding crop. He slapped her, and I went and kicked him in the shin. And my sister said everybody got deathly still. They were afraid that he was going to kill me or something. But he just turned around and he slapped me and I went flying, but he didn't do nothing else to me.

From when we arrived at the camp, everybody got taken all the clothes and everything away from them. And my mother had sewed gold coins and stuff into each one of our overcoats, just in case we could use it. Maybe the whole family could have been saved. My dad got hold of the farmer one of the nights when we stopped overnight on the way to the rail head from Budapest, and talked to the farmer. He had sewed in his overcoat a big diamond ring, and he told the farmer he was going to give him the diamond ring if he hides the kids and him and my mom. He agreed, so it must have been a pretty good diamond ring. But my mom wouldn't go. She said that he might kill us himself for the rest of the stuff.

Anyway, they took all the clothes away, and they gave us those striped, pajama-type stuff. They cut everybody's hair—women, children—and they gave us a shower, and assigned us to barracks. When we went out, after the reveille in the morning, they took us out to the field to pick cattle beets. And we ate cattle beets to keep us from starving.

AD: Did they give you anything else to eat?

PS: Basically once a day they gave you a slice of black bread and soup made from cattle beets. Hot liquid, but it was wintertime, was cold. That's basically what you got, and while you worked out there, if you could sneak away some beets, then you chewed on that while you worked. And that was it.

AD: Did you have to work long hours?

PS: Well, they marched us from the camp out to the field. I don't know how long it took to get us out there. It wasn't too far from the fields. Mainly I think the difficulty was walking in the snow and ice. But we went out to the fields and you pulled them beets, you know? They had a cart that you threw it on. Afternoon they walk you back to the camp.

AD: Did you work with your mother and your sisters?

PS: Yeah. I didn't every day go out with them. But most of the time they just took everybody out. So we stayed there for a couple of months, and then one day they hollered everybody out from the barracks and they lined us up again. And at the time my sister Miriam was very sick, and they had her in the dispensary over there. So started marching us toward the rail head, and I remember Mama hollering, "Miriam, Miriam!" She didn't want to leave her.

They loaded us back up again and my sister stayed behind. From there they took us to Bergen-Belsen. We arrived and they took us in where the crematorium was, and maybe because I was just a little child, but there was a mountain, nothing but dead corpses piled on top of each other. And the smell, and everything else—

And stayed over there overnight. The next day, they took us and put us in the barracks. There was no beds or anything. They had some straw. And give you a sack to fill up with straw. That was your bed. So, basically you laid on concrete in the winter. No food. My mother died there.

Then in May '45, we got liberated.[1] The British troops actually liberated Bergen-Belsen. And then the Red Cross took us to hospital, and the Swedish Red Cross took us from there to Sweden. I stayed about a year in hospital. They nursed me back to health. Then once I got out of the hospital, I joined my sister in the orphanage.

AD: I'm sorry, did your mother die of typhus? Was she ill?

PS: I don't know what she died from. I have no idea. But a lot of people during that period of time died from typhus. I think she probably more died from starvation than anything else, because what little food we could get hold, she would feed the kids, me and my sister. I don't know if she ate any, and so we were susceptible to any disease that was rampaging around in the place there. There was no cleaning, you didn't wash.

AD: So it was you and your sister, Ilona, who were liberated.

PS: Yeah, me and Ilona was liberated from Bergen-Belsen. The only thing I remember, somebody said that they'd seen some white flags on the guard towers. What is the white flags? Germans put white flags on the towers. Didn't mean nothing to me. And then somebody I heard holler something about, "the Germans are leaving." I guess they try to hide. You know? The camp guards all were booking. And then the next thing you know, the [British] military was coming through the camps. I guess picking up whoever was still living.

Then they put up big old hospital tents. That's where they brought the children. And I guess they started feeding us slowly, slowly, because we had hardly any stomach left. That's what killed a lot of people, is they gave them too much food too soon. Wasn't much left of me by that time. But from there the Red Cross came and picked up all the children without any family and everything and took us to the hospital in Malmö, Sweden. Had those white buses with red crosses on them.

AD: How did the Swedish people treat you?

PS: Oh, they treated us very well. They cared for us. When we went to the orphanage, I think it was run by a Jewish agency. It was kind of tough. I would be ten [years old] in November. Started putting us back to school. One teacher was teaching me in German. One teacher was teaching me in Polish. So, it was pretty hard to learn anything, because of all the language. Nobody was teaching me anything in Hungarian, which was the only language I really knew. But I was able to speak pretty good Polish by the time I was done there, and German, too.

Anyway, they disbanded the orphanage. By that time my sister was fifteen, and they told her she has to find a job and go to work. And they took me to a DP [Displaced Persons] camp. I mean, it wasn't a camp, it was a house in a place called Tabo, in Sweden. And basically I was on my own. They enrolled me in a Swedish school, so now I had to learn Swedish. Now, I had gone to one grade in Hungary, and had what little schooling I got there at the orphanage. And from there they started me off according to my age, which was sixth grade or something like that. Obviously, it wasn't easy. But the children there were fairly friendly.

And a Jewish family came, and they introduced me to them. They were going to be my guardians. They lived in Stockholm, so we moved to Stockholm. They enrolled me in school over there. They treated me nice, as a matter of fact they wanted to adopt me, but by that time I found my brother and my other sister, Miriam, in Israel, through the Red Cross and through the Jewish Agency. So I said, "No, I don't want to be adopted. I'm going to Israel." So that's what I did.

I found my father also. He went back to Hungary looking for us. He wrote and said, "Do not come back to Hungary. I'm going back to the United States. When I get there I want you to join me there. In the meantime, stay where you are." But I didn't want to stay there, so I signed up to go to Israel. And my sister decided she wanted to stay in Sweden.

AD: What made you decide you wanted to go to Israel, rather than staying in Sweden as your father had suggested?

PS: Well, because I [had] been always close to my older brother, and my older brother and sister was in Israel, so I said, "Well, I'll just go there and wait until Father gets to the United States, instead of here." So in May '49, I went to Israel. The Swedish family wanted me to stay, and they were going to adopt me and everything. I didn't want to. They were nice people, they treated me fine. As a matter of fact, my thirteen birthday, my Bar Mitzvah, they did that at the big temple in Stockholm. But religion is not my thing. After what I've seen, nobody can convince me that faith is worth anything. I said, "There's nobody up there watching anything if this can happen here." That's me, anyway.

AD: Did the Jewish family in Stockholm ask you anything about your experiences?

PS: No, no. They never did. And I never talked about it. As a matter of fact, you're probably only about the second or third person I ever talked [to] about it at all. I'm not going to constantly dig it up. I just can't live like that. I want to put it behind me, not in front of me.

AD: What made you agree to talk to me?

PS: Well, I really don't know. I think probably the main thing that motivated me on that is I read about people saying it never happened, it's somebody's fantasies. And I'm here to tell you that it did happen. People are trying to change history. And if you don't learn no lesson from what happened, it can happen again. That was my biggest motivation of joining the U.S. Army, is I felt that the Russians weren't that much better than the Nazis were. They had the gulags, they had the camps. May not have been prosecuting Jews per se, but they were prosecuting human beings.

Probably the only force in the world during this period of time that could prevent something like that happening is the U.S. armed forces. And so that was my main reasoning for joining the service. I served in the Israeli Army. I fought in the Sinai Desert in '56. And so I've been through the wringer.

AD: Looking back on those days just after the war when you were a young boy in Sweden, did you understand why you and your family and others had been singled out for this horrible persecution?

PS: Yeah, I understood that it was based on my religion. I'm not educated very well. But I read a lot, and my understanding [is] that the foundation for this disaster has been laid a long, long time. I don't blame any particular faith, but basically they were teaching in churches that the Jews killed Jesus, and this and that, and always had limitation on what Jews can do. They always kept them outside of the mainstream society. So they were always kept like strangers or foreigners. And then the church teaching basically demonized them. So, I don't think it was too hard for somebody like Hitler to come along and demagogue the issue to the point where people didn't care. Because it's supposed to be that most of them were Christians, supposed to love thy brother and turn the other cheek. But that wasn't what actually happened. I've seen them take a little baby and smash his head against the wall. Kill him. And what human being would do something like that? And then they go to church to pray? I mean, you look back at most of the wars in this world today, most of the time, most of it is based on religion. So every place you look at, to me anyway, the biggest disaster in this world is religion.

AD: How does that translate to your feelings about protecting Israel? You fought and risked your life fighting for Israel.

PS: Well, that's something different, because if there was an Israel before the Second World War, the Holocaust probably never would have happened. Because I'm not looking at it as religion, okay? I look at it as a homeland for a people. I'm Jewish, and the Old Testament to me is the history of my people, and as such every people need a homeland. And that's what motivated me. But I always consider myself American. Even before the war, my dad always told me that he was American, so I considered myself American. He was born in Brooklyn, New York, in 1906. And he told me that one of these days we're going to go back to the United States. So, it was very natural for me that in '59 I came and joined him.

AD: Going back first to May of 1949, and your journey from Sweden to Israel: who paid for your travel?

PS: As far as I know, it was [a] Jewish agency. I didn't have the money to pay for it, so they gave me the ticket and I went. By that time it wasn't illegal anymore. The British were gone. They took us with a boat to Haifa, and we arrived and my brother was waiting on me. We were glad to see each other and hugged and all that good stuff. He said that he's going to take me to the village where he lives. The name of it was Kefar Warburg, it was a moshav. Moshav means that everybody owns his own land, got his own farm. The milk processing and the major equipment is jointly owned, but each one got his own land and his own farm that he works. I worked half a day and went to school half a day. So again, I had to learn a new language to go to school. We went to school in the morning and worked in the afternoon on the farm. He had about fourteen milking cows, so you had to grow feed for them. And he grew vegetables, tomatoes, and cucumbers and that kind of stuff. I worked out on the farm, plowed, picked tomatoes, picked this and picked that and weeded and milked cows. All the things you do on a farm.

AD: I have read and heard that Holocaust survivors, in some cases, were discriminated against in Israel, looked down upon by people who had come before the war started. Did you experience anything like that?

PS: No, I personally didn't. In the village where I was at, there was no down-look. You pulled your share. I've never been a whiner anyway. I worked and I went to school. Pulled guard duty at night with everybody else. Went with the youth and learned how to use a weapon, and at night when the Arabs came and stole cows, we chased after them. I personally did not feel that I was in any way looked down at. But could have been better treatment? Sure, it could have been better treatment for everybody involved. But, you know, you're talking about a country just been formed, poor, wasn't a whole lot of anything there. And everybody did the best they could with what they had. Sure, I would have liked to have gone to school full-time and had a degree in something, at least had a trade of some kind. But I didn't expect that, it was just the way things worked out.

AD: When did you start serving in the Army?

PS: I joined the Israeli Army in '52. I was seventeen. I wasn't old enough and I volunteered, so my brother had to sign my paper so I could join. I just wanted to do my couple of years in the service. Before that I already worked on tractors, down with the Bedouins in the Negev. I plowed their fields for them. I was about fifteen years old. Had a .45 on my hip, tractor, and my two Bedouins who guarded me. And I was plowing fields for Sheikh Suleiman, who was the head of their tribe. I was the only Jew there. I wasn't afraid.

In the Israeli Army I was in the engineers. The Army engineers built the first paved road down to Elat. After I was already out of the Army I worked for a construction company, building the oil pipelines back up from the Red Sea toward Ashqelon. That was before I left for the United States. Also I helped build the phosphate pools down in the Dead Sea. We built big pools filled up with water, and then the sun would evaporate the water and leave the salt. You made a lot of different products out of that, potassium and iodine, and they make all kinds of chemicals. I done all kinds of stuff in my life, as far as work. I dug ditches. I built walls from Jerusalem stone. You know, I been supporting myself since I was fourteen years old. What needed to be done, I did.

The reason it took me until '59 to get to the United States was because there was no visas. The only reason by '59 I finally got one is because in '56 they increased the number of visas for the Hungarian refugees, because of the Hungarian revolt—remember that?—against the Russians. It wasn't that I didn't want to come earlier.

AD: What do you remember about the '56 war?

PS: It's war. People get killed. You get shot at. I was with the combat engineers there [in Egypt]. To breach the roads we had to blow up roadblocks and stuff in Rafah. I was up in the northern section: Rafah, Al'Arīsh, Qantara, all the way out to the Suez Canal. So basically we breached the road and opened it for the armor to get through, and we went through. And the Egyptians didn't want to fight. We found tanks, they were still operational, the engine running, just left them. They just jumped out and ran out barefoot into the desert. We lost some people, sure we did.

I did my job, whatever I was supposed to have done. Eisenhower forced the Israelis to withdraw from the Sinai. And since I was in the engineers, I stayed behind. We plowed up all the roads coming back from

Sinai. We blew up the train tracks, and all the bridges, anything to slow the Egyptian Army from coming back in. And so we were the last ones out of Sinai.

AD: How did you come to the U.S.?

PS: I flew, one of the Super Constellation, four-engine prop jobs. Flew from Tel Aviv to France. Then we flew on to Idlewild, now it's [John F.] Kennedy [International Airport, in New York City]. In those days it was almost new. And my dad waited for me there. He worked in a store in Newark as a salesman and he got remarried. They lived in Newark in an apartment.

I have never had [a] problem finding work. I worked for a chemical company, Ephart Fiber and Rubber Company. We were making erasers in a factory. Worked for them, and then father said we're going to move down to Florida. I said, okay. We moved down to Miami Beach. He worked as a waiter and I worked as a busboy at the Sterling Hotel, down on the beach.

In 1960 I got a letter saying, "Greetings from your neighbors, you just have been drafted." So, I was just barely a year in the United States and I got drafted in the U.S. Army.

AD: How did you feel about being drafted?

PS: Well, I really didn't have no bad feeling about it. I felt that if I wanted to become a citizen of the United States it's my obligation to serve my country. The only problem I really had was language. I wasn't speaking English that well yet. I had a good friend, went to basic training together, his name was James B. Smith, J. B. And he basically took me under his wings and he was teaching me English. He was tall, skinny guy, and I was short, stocky. Like Mutt and Jeff. And you didn't have to look far—if you seen one of us there, the other one was somewhere nearby. We both were straight-leg infantry and they sent us to Germany. So that's the only part that was kind of rough on me, you know. I got over it anyway.

AD: Do you think that they would have considered your case if you had objected and asked to be posted somewhere else?

PS: They might have, I never tried. I've never, ever used my personal experience to try to get special consideration or anything else. They sent me, I went, and that's basically it.

AD: Did you have to mingle at all with Germans?

PS: Well, I didn't have to. Basically the U.S. got its own bases. There's some Germans who work there on post, but you know, you don't have to mingle with the German population. You got PX, you got snack bar, you got movies, you got a club. You got everything on post that you would need. So for a long time I didn't go downtown. After a while I said, "Well, go downtown and look around." You can't lock yourself away. You can't blame a whole nation for what happened, it just doesn't make sense. God knows I don't love them. But I have no particular hate for the Germans.

AD: Did people in the Army know that you were Jewish?

PS: Oh yeah. Matter of fact, I used to get Saturday mornings off, while they stood full field inspection. I had to lay my stuff out, but I didn't stand by my bed while the inspection was going on. Friday night and Saturday morning I went to chapel for services.

AD: So you did have some faith at that point?

PS: Well, I never denied my Jewish identity. Everybody that knows me knows that I'm Jewish. And I believe in God, don't get me wrong, even to this day. I just do not believe that God really gives a hoot about any particular individual. In my view He don't care for anybody. He created and it's up to you to do the best you can. He couldn't care less about anything at all.

AD: But would you actually pray when you went to services on Saturday morning?

PS: No, not really. I don't think I ever prayed since before the war. Well, I did when my father died. And me and my step-brother, we usually meet once a year. We go down to Florida because both my father and his mother is buried in cemetery there. And so yes, I say [a] prayer for the dead at his grave. That I do, not because I believe, but to honor him.

AD: Did you experience any anti-Semitism at all in the U.S. Army?

PS: Yes, well, there were always some who hated everybody. They didn't bother me personally, but I heard them talking. Once they knew I was Jewish they did not tell jokes in front of me. I don't know whether out of respect for me, or they knew if they did then me and him going to go to Fist City. And if he was a buddy of mine, then fine. "I got a Jewish joke for you." I says, "That's okay, let's hear it." But that was friendly banter, not out of malicious, hurtful type of thing. I honestly can't say that I was in any way discriminated or treated unfairly or differently because I'm Jewish while I was in the service.

But we had a lot of racial problems when I first got into the service in the sixties. As a matter of fact, we had a race riot and we had racial fights. First time I ever seen blacks was when I got to the United States. I wasn't raised with any kind of prejudice against anybody. So, I would take an individual for himself. But when I got in, in 1960, you had a Brown Boot Army. Basically, our company had a room that was empty. There wasn't a stitch of furniture, anything. If you had any problem with anybody, you and him just went into the room and settled your business with your fists. That's the way things were done. We had a platoon sergeant, his name was Cooper. He was half Indian and half Irish. He was about 6'4" and weighed about two hundred thirty. You messed up and he'd take you into the room there and put you through the woodshed. So he had a very well-behaved platoon. Everybody worked together.

You can't legislate away prejudice. What you can do with the Army is, you force civility. Regardless of whether you like him or not, while you are in the unit and while you are in the Army, you treat him the way you expect to be treated. Later on when I became a platoon sergeant, that was my guiding principle. I say, "I don't care if you like him or not. That's neither here nor there. You two work together, perform the job, be civil to each other. Once you get to know each other, maybe you like him." That's all you can expect.

Just like now, all this silly thing about the gays and all that stuff. I don't hate gays. Bible says that's wrong, but I would want to know if anybody in my unit was gay that I had to fight with. He might have to give me mouth-to-mouth resuscitation. Or I had to go to the shower with him, if I know he is gay I would be uncomfortable. In the service you live so close together, you know? And you got AIDS, you don't want to have to deal with somebody out in the battlefield if you get shot if you know he is gay. Those are the issues that people don't think about when they condemn the Armed Forces as prejudiced. There's a lot more to it than that.

AD: Were you surprised by the racism that you found in this country that is founded on principles of equality?

PS: Yeah, I was surprised. When I worked for Ephart Fiber and Rubber Company, I noticed that when you sit down to eat, you would see all the whites congregating. All the blacks would go sit over there. There was no interaction between the races. That kind of struck me funny. And a fellow worker who was black, he sat down to eat lunch. I just got my lunch and sat down beside him. He kind of looked at me a little funny. I didn't realize there was anything wrong with it.

AD: Did you keep on sitting with him after that?

PS: Sure, yeah, every day, usually, we'd sit down and have lunch and talk. He was asking me about Israel and I was telling him about Israel. And he would tell me about what they were doing in Newark, his neighborhood. Yeah, we became friends.

AD: Where were you posted in Germany?

PS: My first tour I was Bamberg. I was with the 1st Battle Group, 15th Infantry. And I served two years in the straight-leg infantry. I got out and went back to Miami and looked around and decided I was going to go into heating and air conditioning. So I went to school and then I had to work. And I said, "Well, this ain't going to get it." No time for myself or anything else. Went to school, from school you went to work and next morning got up, went to school, went to work. You had no time for yourself, nothing. So I said, "Well, I'm going to go back into the Army, this time voluntarily. I'll make the Army a career." Because I liked the service, its purpose. And during that time I realized the Russians were no better than the Germans were. So, I re-enlisted, and lo and behold, they went and sent me back to Germany. We were sent to Kaiserslautern and spent three years there.

Then I came back, went to the 18th Airborne Corps in Bragg, North Carolina. And from Bragg, there was a little altercation in the Dominican Republic, and we were in there for support. Came back from there, and in 1966, I was sent to Vietnam. I was there in the Central Highlands for a year. And say, well, I'm just going to go back to the States and get shipped back here again, so I might as well extend. So, I extended, got promoted, and was sent to the Korean Tiger Division, along Highway One. From '66 through '68, I was in Vietnam. I came back from Vietnam, and was assigned to Fort Knox, and I became an instructor in the Armor School.

AD: Were you in a combat unit while you were in 'Nam?

PS: I was actually in the Signal outfit [responsible for the Army's systems of communication]. The first time I was there I was in a place called Binh Dinh Mountain. There was no road in or out. All our supplies had to come by air. So we're sitting on a seven-thousand-foot mountain, and jungle all the way around us. Charlie was down there. We lived in bunkers. We got attacked by mortars, and that kind of stuff. We didn't have no direct confrontation.

Then from there I moved to a place called Phu Ti Valley,[2] which is not far from Nha Trang, and there we were with the Korean Tiger Division. That is an infantry division, who were actually doing the combat. We were supporting them, and when they went out for a sweep and destroy mission, we went out to provide them communication. So, we got shot at, but we weren't involved in direct, face-to-face, grunt job. The Koreans did that. But I was running Highway One between Ban Me Thuot, and every morning before you even got on there, you had to wait for them to clear all the mines out of there. So you never knew from one minute to the next when you're going to get on a mine. And then the Vietnamese had this nice little trick, they would have little hot-pot, motorcycle-type taxi cabs. You would come around with your truck and they would pull out in front of you to slow you down, like in a curve. When you slowed down, they would ambush you and start shooting at you from the side. So what [do] you define [as] "combat"? No, I wasn't in the infantry unit. But in our base camp, we got attacked. We killed nine guys there. One of them was our base barber. He was a Viet Cong. So you never knew who was your friend, who was your enemy.

It was a weird kind of a war. There was no front line, like in Korea or Second World War. We had to lock down our gas caps on our trucks. What they would do if you didn't have the locks on them, they would take a hand grenade, put a rubber band around it, pull the pin, drop it inside your gas tank. Then the gas would eat away the rubber band, pop the thing, and blow you to smithereens. Children would hawk on the side of the road. They would try to sell you Coke. Well, if you're stupid enough and you bought that Coke, a lot of them had ground glass in it. If you drank that stuff it tore your guts up inside with shreds, slivers of glass. So it was a different kind of war. It wasn't the type of war where you could say who was a combat guy and who wasn't.

AD: You had by then already fought in a war and been through a war as a victim. The war you fought in Israel, you felt passionate about the cause. How did you feel about the cause in Vietnam?

PS: I was all for the war. And I still believe we did the right thing, actually. Except you can't fight a war when the people are not with you. To me that was the thing, because we were justified in what we were doing. The reporters and everything, they all twisted everything to suit their views. If not for us, the communists probably would have gobbled up all of Southeast Asia. If we wouldn't have opposed them, heck, probably over two-thirds of the world today would have been all in the communist top.

I know a lot of people opposed it. And I got called a baby killer when I came back on leave from 'Nam. Everybody said, "Change clothes. Get in civilian clothes, don't go out in the airport in the clothes." I said, "I fought for this country in these clothes, it was my uniform. I'll be doggone if I'm going to change clothes." And I went to Seattle to the airport and there were Hare Krishna and all them other ones. And, "Baby killer!" I went and punched him in the mouth and knocked him down. A cop was standing there looking, he just smiled, he didn't say nothing. And I just kept walking. Don't call me no baby killer. I never killed no baby.

Now, I agree we should never have fought the way we did. We should have gone in with the purpose of winning and we should have won. The way you did that is you gone into North Vietnam and kicked their butt and got it over with. Instead of just, you know, "Well, you can't get into Cambodia, you can't bomb this, you can't do that." You can't fight no war that a-way and win. Crazy.

AD: You had to really believe in this country in order to do the kinds of service that you've done. Is that something that you came to this country with, or is it something that developed?

PS: No, I came with it to this country. Right after the war in Sweden, some of the children in the orphanage were for the Russians, the communists, Left inclination. We always had big argument, even as a little boy then, and I was always defending the United States, because with my dad being born here, I felt as an American. Even though I had never been here. Anyway, I felt a kinship, and I always believed that the United States basically represents the human freedom. And I still do, you know. I have no problem with somebody like Joan Baez and all the other ones who opposed the war. That's why we fought. I mean, they have the right to speak their view. I might not agree with it, but I respect it. I cannot accept somebody like Jane Fonda, who went to North Vietnam with North Vietnamese troops and there was prisoners of war in the Hanoi Hilton. Any show that she is in, that is not on my TV.

Every election, I always vote. I believe in participating. As a matter of fact, I'm just reading a book about the history of democracy in the United States, from back before the colonies, how the democracy developed.

AD: When and how did you meet your wife?

PS: That's a good question. I was stationed here in Fort Knox in the beginning of '69. And I had a friend, Larry, and he was from Bristol, Tennessee. He would always ask me to go home with him. And I said, "Nah, I don't want to go. What do I go over there for? I didn't lose anything there." So, months later his car broke down. He was married and his wife was back in Bristol. And he had no way to get home. So, I said, "You know what? All these months you've been asking me to go with you home, so I'll take you home this weekend." So he stopped on the way home, telling his wife that he's bringing me, says, "Why don't you get him a date while he's there?" That sort of guy. So we got there late in the afternoon. That evening went out to the VFW Club to dance and drink. Anyway, Helen was there. That was April, and I think two weeks later was the Kentucky Derby. Ray's wife was going to come up here, so Helen said, "Well, I'll come with you." So, one thing led to another.

AD: When did you get married?

PS: In July of '69, so I think about three months after we met.

AD: What kind of ceremony did you have?

PS: Just a civil. She wanted a church wedding. Her pastor wouldn't marry us because I was Jewish and she was Presbyterian, whatever. I didn't want any kind of religious ceremony, anyway.

AD: You said a little earlier how you haven't talked much about your history during the war. Did you talk with your wife at all about it during those early days?

PS: No. I told her I was in concentration [camp] and stuff, but I never mentioned anything about it, no. I think the first time she ever heard it was when Professor Dickstein was here from the Shoah Foundation for the interview.[3] I just don't talk about it, period. My sister been twice in the nuthouse, the one in Sweden. She lives in the past all the time. I don't want to be like that. When I talk about the stuff, for a week after that I got nightmares every night. I didn't tell you all kind of stuff that I could have told you, but I don't want to, because I don't want to dig it up. On the march to Budapest, I seen [an] old man with a beard, looked like my grandfather, get shot right in front of me. He couldn't walk, just shot him like nothing. And I can't deal with it. I can't live like that, with the nightmare constantly on my mind. I just put it behind me. I closed it down as tight as I can close it down and that's it.

AD: You mentioned earlier that you're not very connected with the Jewish community here in Louisville?

PS: No, I'm not. Because most of my friends are from the Army and none of them are Jewish. And with my views and my way of thinking, I probably wouldn't fit very well in with the Jewish community, to be perfectly honest with you. There is no connection between me and my view of things and most of the Jewish Community Center. They're mostly Americans, who were born here and raised here. So, we have really nothing in common. I've never been in business, never plan on being in business. I couldn't sell you a glass of water if you were dying of thirst. I'd give you a glass of water, but I wouldn't sell it to you. I'm just a different type of person. I go off to my own little drum. I'm involved with the veterans of this state. I volunteer for Kentucky Center for Veteran's Affairs as a counselor. I'm also vice–state legislative representative for [the] Non-Commissioned Officers Association. So, that keeps me busy. I'm an official briefer for my association out at Fort Knox. I go out to the units and give them classes on VA benefits and that kind of stuff. I do volunteer work under the Retirement Service Office on post at Fort Knox. And every time I have a Second World War veteran, I can help them, it makes me feel good. Even though I wasn't liberated by American troops, I know that he had a hand in liberating me. So I'm glad when I can help one of them. So, that's what I do. I try to help veterans as much as I can.

AD: When did you retire?

PS: I retired medically in '83. I was E-8, master sergeant. I graduated from Sergeant Major Academy. I was going to make E-9, but I got sick and I got medically retired before I actually got promoted. I had two heart attacks and I had my colon removed. I was exposed to Agent Orange. They sprayed that stuff down on me. That didn't stop me. I just keep on trucking. I'm a tough dude. I've got diabetes. Nobody in my family has diabetes, never had. Now it comes out, there's a study that shows that guys exposed to Agent Orange have twice or three times as high a chance of getting diabetes as the normal population. So, I don't know if that's what caused it or something else, but anyway. So, I got heart disease. I got colon gone. Taking about twenty-some pills a day.

AD: You have one child?

PS: One son, he's adopted. He was my wife's child. He was just a young boy, and his name is Anthony Keith Schlisser. I don't have any children of my own. Anyway, not that I know of.

AD: Did your son ever ask you about your past?

PS: Yes. We talked about it. With him I talked about it, not in particular details, just in general terms, so that he'll understand where I'm coming from. And what my views are and why I got my views the way I got them and all that. Yeah, we are pretty close, him and me. We understand each other. We are good friends.

AD: Did your family understand and respect your decision to marry—

PS: Marry my wife, Helen? I never asked anybody. I never told them I'm marrying. I never ask permission. I married. Yeah, they accepted her. My dad, once he got to know her, he loved her. But I really didn't care because it's my choice. If they didn't like it, tough. I know a lot of people want to be loved and all that good stuff, but me, I just go with what I think is right.

AD: Your wife is Presbyterian?

PS: I think she is. I dare not say that for sure. She's a Christian, anyway. When we go down to her home, she goes to church on Sundays with her brother, who is a deacon in the church and all that. I don't go with them, but she goes. And even when we first got married, she insisted I go with her. So for a couple times I went with her, just out of respect for her and her family. I didn't feel comfortable though. And I told her, I said, "Look, that's your faith, not mine. You want to go, you go. I'll gladly take you there and I'll gladly come and pick you up." And so from now, she goes with her brother and it's fine. Yeah, she believes, she's got faith, which is fine with me. I have no quarrel with anybody who has faith. It's just me and my views. I don't push my views on anybody else.

AD: Was there ever a point where you felt it would be important to you to marry a Jewish woman? Where your Jewish identity was important enough to you that you felt like you had to do whatever you could to carry on the tradition?

PS: That's a tough one. I guess at one time, yes. But . . . I shouldn't say this, but anyway. While I was in the military in Israel, we were on duty in the Jerusalem sector. It wasn't a war, it was after. And to go to our post we had to go through a section of Jerusalem which was the ultra-ultra-Orthodox. And on Sabbath we used to go through there with a vehicle. They used to stone us. Okay? So I looked at this and I said to myself, what's the difference between the Jewish fanatics and the Ayatollah fanatics and all the other fanatics? There's not one iota difference between them. They're all zealots for whatever their faith is. So, I believe in Israel, for no other reason [than that] the Jewish people as a nation have a homeland. But for me, not for religious purposes.

Everybody has a right to live their own life the way they see fit. And that's what I believe in. My neighbor here is a very religious Baptist guy. He's been friend with me now for thirty years, since we've been here. We help each other. Anything I got he's welcome to it. Anything I need, if I needed help, he'd be there. I know he would. That's how good of friends we are. And I respect him. He goes to church on Wednesdays. He goes to church on Sundays. He's a church elder. I respect my brother-in-law, you know. It's their faith, it's fine. He never [tries] to force his stuff on me. That's all I'm saying.

What I say is what I mean. If I tell you I was going to do something, you can put in the bank that I was going to do it. Except if I'm dead or laying there paralyzed where I can't move.

AD: I imagine that's been very helpful to you in your career in the Army.

PS: Yes, yes, it has. And I think I've been doing okay. I mean I have no problems. With my education background and with everything else, I guess the biggest asset I had is my dedication. I never been a good speller. I mean, I'm not stupid, you know. I might not have book learning to the max or get a certificate. But I made up for that by reading a lot and getting my education in the school of hard knocks.

AD: By the time you were a young child you had been through more atrocities than most people have even imagined, and you went on to fight in two wars and you didn't have to do that. What do you think it was that—

PS: Drove me?

AD: Yeah. Because I think so many people would have said, "Okay, I've had my share in the wars of the world."

PS: I really couldn't tell you. Something inside of me drove me, and what it was I really couldn't put it into words. I mean, you got to take each one on its own merit. You can't just lump them all together. The war in Israel was a question of survival for the country. I didn't make the decision to go to war. It was a civilian mobilization of the Army, and you went and did what you were supposed to have done. If anything drove me, I guess [it] was duty to what I believe was right. Now as far as 'Nam, it was the United States government decision to go to the aid of the South Vietnamese. It wasn't mine. Again it was duty. I was in the service, I was a career soldier. Why would you be a career soldier? What, you're going to run when the fighting starts?

Why I volunteered and stayed in the service, that's a different story. That had a lot to do with economy and all this stuff. Plus I had an opportunity to use my God-given talents that I had in the best way, and to advance my own career in the military instead of the civilian life.

AD: How do you feel about Kentucky?

PS: I like Kentucky. I hate cities, people on top of each other. I like feeling the open space. I made my home here, and I feel like I'm a Kentuckian. I used to like to go out fishing and hunting. I like country music. I like Bluegrass. Weird for a Jew, right? I used to square dance. I also like classic. I like operas. I'm just me. I'm not anybody else.

NOTES

Introduction: Listening to Kentucky's Holocaust Survivors

1. Comment recorded in the exhibit's guest book.

2. Interviews with Ernie Marx can be accessed through the United States Holocaust Memorial Museum's oral history archives (RG-50.106*0019) and the Survivors of the Shoah Foundation Visual History Collection at the Vandenburgh Public Library in Evansville, Indiana.

3. Samuel G. Freedman, "Struggling to Squelch an Internet Rumor," *New York Times*, February 27, 2008.

4. Becky Todd, "Teacher's Lesson Says Holocaust May Have Been Faked," *Lexington Herald*, March 30, 1981, A1; "Teacher Told to Follow Text on Holocaust," *Lexington Herald*, April 4, 1981, A7.

5. Author conversations with Warren Featherston, March 4, 2008, and with Loris Points, February 5, 2008. McCord likely voluntarily retired from full-time teaching in 1983, when he turned sixty-five, although the date of McCord's retirement is something of a mystery, as the Fayette County Public Schools office apparently has lost the file that related to the teacher's full-time employment. According to the school system's files, Anthony McCord worked in Fayette schools only, from 1983 through 1992, as a substitute teacher. McCord passed away in 1994.

6. The documentary, *And We Were There*, aired September 10, 1983.

7. Figures on the Jewish population in Kentucky and New York are from Jacob R. Marcus, *To Count a People: American Jewish Population Data, 1585–1984*

(Lanham, Md.: Univ. Press of America, 1990). The estimate on Kentucky's Holocaust survivors comes from the author's research, details of which can be found in the "Note on Methodology." Herman Landau, in *Adath Louisville* (Louisville, Ky.: Herman Landau, 1981), cites reports indicating that about four hundred European Jews immigrated to Louisville between 1948 and 1972, most of whom were probably concentration camp survivors (3, 144–45). Thus it is possible that many more than forty Holocaust survivors still remain in the Louisville area; if so, however, they are there without the knowledge of the Jewish Community Center, which has records on many of Louisville's survivors. It is likely that the majority of these immigrants did not remain in Louisville.

8. This figure is based on William Helmreich's estimate that two-thirds of the approximately 140,000 survivors who emigrated to the United States after World War II settled in the New York area (William B. Helmreich, *Against All Odds: Holocaust Survivors and the Successful Lives They Made in America* [New York: Simon and Schuster, 1992], 59). The 90,000 estimate is almost certainly too high, considering attrition by death in the following years.

9. Survivors in other small towns or Southern cities across the United States have borne a similar burden. See, for example, Dorothy Rabinowitz, *New Lives: Survivors of the Holocaust Living in America* (New York: Knopf, 1977), 124; Anton Gill, *The Journey Back from Hell, An Oral History: Conversations with Concentration Camp Survivors* (New York: William Morrow, 1988), 288–89; and Lawrence N. Powell, *Troubled Memory: Anne Levy, the Holocaust, and David Duke's Louisiana* (Chapel Hill: Univ. of North Carolina Press, 2000), 404–35.

10. Oral history interview with Emilie Szekely, January 18, 2000. Szekely passed away in 2002, before we were able to photograph her for this project.

11. We were unable to reach Goldfarb when we were photographing survivors for this project.

12. Gavi was interviewed for this project in June of 2000. He passed away in December of 2002.

13. The figure for the Jewish population of Louisville is for 1999. See David Singer and Lawrence Grossman, eds., *American Jewish Yearbook 2000,* vol. 100 (Philadelphia: Jewish Publication Society, 2000). The overall Louisville population is for 2000, and comes from the U.S. Bureau of the Census, American FactFinder: http://factfinder.census.gov/. Information on Louisville's Jewish congregations retrieved from the Jewish Community Federation of Louisville's website, www.jewishlouisville.com, on August 9, 2008.

14. Helmreich, *Against All Odds,* 149; Helmreich discusses this subject extensively in chapter 5, pages 148–82. Other examples of published sources include Beth B. Cohen, *Case Closed: Holocaust Survivors in Postwar America*

(New Brunswick, N.J.: Rutgers Univ. Press, 2007), 158; Gill, *The Journey Back from Hell,* 58, 297; Aaron Hass, *The Aftermath: Living with the Holocaust* (New York: Cambridge Univ. Press, 1995), 86–88; and Rabinowitz, *New Lives,* 107, 138–39. Many survivors who settled in large urban areas and who were interviewed for the United States Holocaust Memorial Museum's Post-Holocaust collection underline this point. See, for instance, Nesse Godin (RG-50.549.01*0009), Carla Lessing (RG-50.549.02*0050), and Amalie Salsitz (RG-50.549.02*0054).

15. Melvin and Esther Goldfarb, both originally from Poland, met in the soup kitchen of a Displaced Persons camp in Germany in 1946. Ann and Sandor Klein were childhood sweethearts in Eger, Hungary, yet while Sandor escaped Europe in 1938, Ann endured the horrors of the camps. Oscar and Fryda Haber survived the war together in Poland, living under false Catholic identities.

16. Helmreich, *Against All Odds,* 62.

17. Are this group's experiences in this regard significant, when placed in the context of all of Kentucky's survivors? I believe that they are. I interviewed more than half of the survivors I identified in the state who remained in Nazi-controlled Europe or other occupied countries throughout the duration of the war—thirteen of twenty-three—and it is to these "full-term" Holocaust survivors that the studies on the post-Holocaust lives of survivors cited above refer. Of course, it is possible that there are some survivors in the state whom I was not able to identify, yet it is unlikely that an entire group of survivors would exist without the knowledge of local Jewish communities. Even if the ten "full-term" survivors I did not interview fit the description of survivors who keep to themselves rather than integrating into their communities, it is almost certainly true that the majority of survivors in Kentucky have done just the opposite.

18. Hass, *The Aftermath,* 104. A similar story is recounted in Rabinowitz's *New Lives,* 234.

19. Hass, *The Aftermath,* 123.

20. Alexander J. Groth, *Holocaust Voices: An Attitudinal Survey of Survivors* (Amherst, N.Y.: Humanity Books, 2003), 120–21.

21. See Marshall Sklare and Joseph Greenblum, *Jewish Identity on the Suburban Frontier* (Chicago: Univ. of Chicago Press, 1979), 323–24, in which Jewish residents of a midwestern suburb were surveyed on their perceptions of what it means to be Jewish in America.

22. Citizens' confusion in response to the mandatory/voluntary issue was evident in postings related to the resolution on the website kentuckyvotes.org (accessed on May 31, 2008).

Chapter 1. Sylvia Green

1. Residents of the Kraków ghetto were deported to extermination camps beginning in May of 1942. The ghetto's final liquidation took place on March 14, 1943 (Shmuel Krakowski, "Kraków," *Encyclopedia of the Holocaust*, 831–32).

2. The term "Holocaust survivor" did not exist at the time the article was written; the word "Holocaust" was not commonly associated with the Nazi genocide until the 1960s.

Chapter 2. Oscar Haber

1. Oscar was interviewed by the USC Shoah Foundation Institute for Visual History and Education on September 16, 1996. In interviewing Oscar, I occasionally refer to things he related in that first interview.

2. Many small-town Polish Jews before World War II spoke Polish as a second language, if they spoke it at all. Yiddish was the language of the shtetl, and as such it was all the more difficult for many Polish Jews to conceal their identities after the war began.

Chapter 3. Robert Holczer

1. Budapest is divided into two sections, Buda and Pest, that are separated by the Danube River.

2. For more information on Jerezian and the clinic, see Krisztián Ungváry, *The Siege of Budapest: 100 Days in World War II* (New Haven, Conn.: Yale Univ. Press, 2005), 296–98.

Chapter 4. Abram Jakubowicz

1. Other details of Abe's Holocaust-era experiences are discussed in his interview with the USC Shoah Foundation Institute for Visual History and Education (February 19, 1996).

2. Jewish tradition stipulates that it is forbidden to cook milk and meat together; however, traditions vary as to the required amount of time between consuming each of them. "Kosher" itself is a broader term, meaning "ritually fit."

3. The Gypsy camp was a separate camp for Gypsy families, located in Auschwitz-Birkenau. About twenty-one thousand Gypsies passed through this camp before it was liquidated in 1944, when its remaining inhabitants were killed in the Auschwitz gas chambers.

4. "Kanada," so termed because Canada was a symbol of wealth among the prisoners, was a forced-labor detachment whose task was to gather the belongings of prisoners on incoming transports.

5. Abe weighed about seventy-five or eighty pounds at liberation (USC Shoah Foundation Institute for Visual History and Education interview, February 19, 1996).

6. I. G. Farben (IGF) is a German chemical company that, during World War II, had close ties with the Nazi Party. One of IGF's Buna (synthetic rubber) installations was located in Auschwitz in order to take advantage of Jewish slave labor. Zyklon B gas, used in Auschwitz for the killing of Jews, was a product of Degesch, a firm in which IGF owned a decisive share.

7. There are a number of organizations and support groups for children of Holocaust survivors, often referred to as the "second generation."

Chapter 5. Ann Klein

1. Andy died in 1999, about six months before this interview was conducted.

2. During the 1998–1999 conflict in Kosovo, in what has widely been described as a campaign of ethnic cleansing, hundreds of ethnic Albanians were killed and hundreds of thousands forcibly expelled from their homes by Serbian forces.

Chapter 6. Justine Lerner

1. Białystok was occupied by the Germans on September 15, 1939, but a week later, on September 22, it was handed over to the Soviet Union, which held it for the next twenty-one months. On June 27, 1941, the Germans took Białystok for the second time, and the same day, two thousand Jews were burned alive, shot, or tortured to death. On August 1, 1941, fifty thousand Białystok Jews were confined in a ghetto (Sarah Bender and Teresa Prekerowa, "Białystok," in *Encyclopedia of the Holocaust*, 2 vols., ed. Israel Gutman [New York: Macmillan, 1990], 1:210).

2. The liquidation of the Białystok ghetto took place in August of 1943. Many of the ghetto's Jews were deported to the extermination camp Treblinka, where they were murdered. Those deemed fit for forced labor were sent to Auschwitz and other concentration camps. Justine was probably in the ghetto for longer than she remembers. There were no deportations to Auschwitz from Białystok before November of 1942 (Bender and Prekerowa, "Białystok," in *Encyclopedia of the Holocaust*, 1:212–13).

3. "The regularly repeated orders from camp officials to clean out the hospital by means of selection for the gas chamber created an objective situation where death, for a predetermined number of prisoners, was unavoidable" (Anna Pawełczyńska, *Values and Violence in Auschwitz: A Sociological Analysis* (Berkeley: Univ. of California Press, 1979), 73–74.

4. "Kanada," so termed because Canada was a symbol of wealth among the prisoners, was a forced-labor detachment whose task was to gather the belongings of prisoners on incoming transports.

5. Diminutive of "Jospe," Justine's name at birth.

6. The March of the Living is a program in which Jewish youth travel to Auschwitz-Birkenau and to Israel, to study and commemorate the Holocaust.

Chapter 7. Alexander Rosenberg

1. Bergen-Belsen was established in April of 1943. Transports to the camp from Westerbork began in January of 1944, and continued through September. The transport of Libyan Jews (as well as some other Jews from neutral countries) from the Italian camp Fossoli di Carpi arrived during the first half of 1944 (Shmuel Krakowski, "Bergen-Belsen," in *Encyclopedia of the Holocaust,* 2 vols., ed. Israel Gutman [New York: Macmillan, 1990], 1:185–87; Daniel Carpi, "Italy: Concentration Camps," in *Encyclopedia of the Holocaust,* 2 vols., ed. Israel Gutman [New York: Macmillan, 1990], 1:727–28).

2. Oral history interview with the USC Shoah Foundation Institute for Visual History and Education, June 3, 1996.

3. The *St. Louis* was a German liner that set sail from Hamburg to Cuba on May 13, 1939, with 937 passengers aboard, most of them Jews seeking to escape Nazi Germany. Upon arrival in Havana, however, Cuban authorities did not allow the majority of the passengers to disembark. Despite urgent appeals by the passengers and concerned Americans, the U.S. government did not grant the refugees entry to the United States, and the ship was forced to return to Europe. More than 250 of the ship's passengers later perished in the Holocaust.

Chapter 8. John Rosenberg

1. Kristallnacht ("Night of Broken Glass") refers to the violent anti-Jewish rioting that took place around Germany on November 8–10, 1938. The attacks were ostensibly in response to the assassination of the German official Ernst vom Rath by a seventeen-year-old Polish Jew, Herschel Grynszpan.

2. The SA (Sturmabteilung), or Storm Troopers, was a Nazi organization

that had facilitated Hitler's rise to power. During Kristallnacht, the functionaries of the SA instigated assaults on Jewish businesses and synagogues.

3. John Michael Doar, 1921–, served as First Assistant and then Assistant Attorney General, Civil Rights Division, Department of Justice, from 1960 to 1967.

4. Stokely Carmichael (1941–1998), also known as Kwame Ture, was the civil rights leader who coined the term "black power," which became a rallying cry for African Americans frustrated with the movement's ineffectiveness under the integrationist mandate of such leaders as Rev. Martin Luther King Jr. Bob Moses (1935–), led a campaign to register Mississippi blacks to vote. He later became involved in education reform. Medgar Evers (1925–1963) was Mississippi's first field secretary for the NAACP and was instrumental in the desegregation of Ole Miss. Evers was murdered by Ku Klux Klan member Byron De La Beckwith on June 12, 1963.

5. In 1964 three civil rights workers were murdered by members of the KKK in Neshoba County, Mississippi. The case infamously became known as the "Mississippi Burning" trial, which began in 1967. Chief prosecutor John Doar succeeded in securing convictions for seven of the eighteen defendants; none were imprisoned for more than ten years. By 2005, the investigation had been reopened, and Edgar Ray Killen—who had been acquitted in 1967—was convicted on three counts of manslaughter and sentenced to sixty years in prison.

6. Legal services refers to government-supported legal aid programs, such as AppalReD.

7. Sam Bowers, circa 1925–2006. As a leader of the Mississippi KKK, he authorized the killing of Mickey Schwerner, one of the three civil rights workers murdered in Neshoba County in 1964. Bowers spent six years in jail for his role in the murders. In 1998, he was sentenced to life in prison for the murder of the black activist Vernon Dahmer. He died in the state penitentiary in 2006.

8. Harry M. Caudill, 1922–1990. An attorney, writer, and professor, he authored *Night Comes to the Cumberlands: A Biography of a Depressed Area* in 1963.

9. Eula Hall founded the Mud Creek Clinic in Grethel, Floyd County, Kentucky, in 1973.

10. Joe Begley, 1919–2000. Former proprietor of C. B. Caudill Store and History Center in Blackey, Kentucky.

Chapter 9. Paul Schlisser

1. Bergen-Belsen was actually liberated on April 15, 1945.

2. The Phu Ti Valley was also called Rok Valley.

3. Schlisser was interviewed by Professor Leah Dickstein for the USC Shoah Foundation Institute for Visual History and Education in the 1990s; he is uncertain of the date. Due to technical problems with the interview, I was unable to obtain a copy for review.

SELECTED BIBLIOGRAPHY

Holocaust survivors in America

Cohen, Beth B. *Case Closed: Holocaust Survivors in Postwar America*. New Brunswick, N.J.: Rutgers Univ. Press, 2007.

Dinnerstein, Leonard. *America and the Survivors of the Holocaust*. New York: Columbia Univ. Press, 1982.

Epstein, Helen. *Children of the Holocaust: Conversations with Sons and Daughters of Survivors*. New York: Penguin, 1979.

Flanzbaum, Hilene, ed. *The Americanization of the Holocaust*. Baltimore, Md.: Johns Hopkins Univ. Press, 1999.

Gill, Anton. *The Journey Back from Hell, An Oral History: Conversations with Concentration Camp Survivors*. New York: William Morrow, 1988.

Greenspan, Henry. *On Listening to Holocaust Survivors: Recounting and Life History*. Westport, Conn.: Praeger, 1998.

Groth, Alexander J. *Holocaust Voices: An Attitudinal Survey of Survivors*. Amherst, N.Y.: Humanity Books, 2003.

Hass, Aaron. *The Aftermath: Living with the Holocaust*. New York: Cambridge Univ. Press, 1995.

Helmreich, William B. *Against All Odds: Holocaust Survivors and the Successful Lives They Made in America*. New York: Simon and Schuster, 1992.

Hoffman, Eva. *After Such Knowledge: Memory, History, and the Legacy of the Holocaust*. New York: Public Affairs, 2004.

Langer, Lawrence L. *Holocaust Testimonies: The Ruins of Memory*. New Haven, Conn.: Yale Univ. Press, 1991.

Novick, Peter. *The Holocaust in American Life*. Boston: Houghton Mifflin, 1999.

Powell, Lawrence N. *Troubled Memory: Anne Levy, the Holocaust, and David Duke's Louisiana*. Chapel Hill: Univ. of North Carolina Press, 2000.

Rabinowitz, Dorothy. *New Lives: Survivors of the Holocaust Living in America*. New York: Knopf, 1977.

General Holocaust resources

Gutman, Israel, editor in chief. *The Encyclopedia of the Holocaust*. 2 vols. New York: Macmillan, 1990.

Hilberg, Raul. *The Destruction of the European Jews*, vols. 1–3. New Haven, Conn.: Yale Univ. Press, 2003.

Pawełczyńska, Anna. *Values and Violence in Auschwitz: A Sociological Analysis*. Berkeley: Univ. of California Press, 1979.

Kentucky's Holocaust survivors and Southern/Midwestern Jewish communities

Gavi, Joseph. Oral history interview, June 14, 2000. Kentucky Historical Society and United States Holocaust Memorial Museum. Arwen Donahue, interviewer.

Goldfarb, Melvin. Oral history interview, May 12, 2000. Kentucky Historical Society and United States Holocaust Memorial Museum. Arwen Donahue, interviewer.

———. Oral history interview, February 19, 1996. USC Shoah Foundation Institute for Visual History and Education. Leah Dickstein, interviewer.

Haber, Fryda. Oral history interview, May 17, 2000. Kentucky Historical Society and United States Holocaust Memorial Museum. Arwen Donahue, interviewer.

———. Oral history interview, September 16, 1996. USC Shoah Foundation Institute for Visual History and Education. Leah Dickstein, interviewer.

Jackson, Carlton. *Joseph Gavi, a Young Hero of the Minsk Ghetto*. Paducah, Ky.: Turner, 2000.

Landau, Herman. *Adath Louisville*. Louisville, Ky.: Herman Landau, 1981.

Marx, Ernest L. Oral history interview, July 26, 1995. United States Holocaust Memorial Museum. Gail Schwartz, interviewer.

———. Oral history interview, April 22, 1996. USC Shoah Foundation Institute for Visual History and Education. Interviewer unknown.

Shevitz, Amy Hill. *Jewish Communities on the Ohio River: A History*. Lexington: Univ. Press of Kentucky, 2007.

Singer, David, and Lawrence Grossman, eds. *American Jewish Yearbook 2000,* vol. 100. Philadelphia: Jewish Publication Society, 2000.

Sklare, Marshall, and Joseph Greenblum. *Jewish Identity on the Suburban Frontier.* Chicago: Univ. of Chicago Press, 1979.

Szekely, Emilie. Oral history interviews, December 3, 1999, and January 18, 2000. Kentucky Historical Society and United States Holocaust Memorial Museum. Arwen Donahue, interviewer.

———. Oral history interview, November 13, 1996. USC Shoah Foundation Institute for Visual History and Education. Leah Dickstein, interviewer.

Weissbach, Lee Shai. *The Synagogues of Kentucky.* Lexington: Univ. Press of Kentucky, 1995.

Survivors in this book

Sylvia Green
Oral history interview, date unknown. USC Shoah Foundation Institute for Visual History and Education. Leah Dickstein, interviewer.

Oscar Haber
Oral history interview, September 16, 1996. USC Shoah Foundation Institute for Visual History and Education. Leah Dickstein, interviewer.

Robert Holczer
Ungváry, Krisztián. *The Siege of Budapest: 100 Days in World War II.* New Haven, Conn.: Yale Univ. Press, 2005, 296–97.

Abe Jakubowicz
Oral history interview, February 19, 1996. USC Shoah Foundation Institute for Visual History and Education. David Leibson, interviewer.

Ann Klein
Oral history interview, April 22, 1996. USC Shoah Foundation Institute for Visual History and Education. Leah Dickstein, interviewer.

Oral history interview, January 8, 1982. University of Louisville. Mary K. Tachau, interviewer.

Alexander Rosenberg
Oral history interview, June 3, 1996. USC Shoah Foundation Institute for Visual History and Education. Leah Dickstein, interviewer.

John Rosenberg

Ball, Milner S. *The Word and the Law.* Chicago: Univ. of Chicago Press, 1993, chapter 1.

Doar, John. "The Work of the Civil Rights Division in Enforcing Voting Rights under the Civil Rights Acts of 1957 and 1960." *Florida State University Law Review* 25, no. 1(fall 1997): 1–17.

Rosenberg, John M. "Personal Reflections of a Life in Public Interest Law: From the Civil Rights Division of the Department of Justice to Appalred." *West Virginia Law Review,* vol. 96, no. 2 (winter 1993–1994): 317–31.

Winerip, Michael. "What's a Nice Jewish Lawyer Like John Rosenberg Doing in Appalachia?" *New York Times Magazine,* June 29, 1997, 24–27.

INDEX